ONLINE AUCTIONS

The Internet Guide for Bargain Hunters and Collectors

LUANNE O'LOUGHLIN
MARY MILLHOLLON
edited by **JACLYN EASTON**

CommerceNet Press

McGraw-Hill
New York   San Francisco   Washington, D.C.   Auckland   Bogotá
Caracas   Lisbon   London   Madrid   Mexico City   Milan
Montreal   New Delhi   San Juan   Singapore
Sydney   Tokyo   Toronto

Library of Congress Cataloging-in-Publication Data

O'Loughlin, Luanne.
    Online auctions : the Internet guide for bargain hunters and collectors / Luanne
O'Loughlin, Mary Millhollon, edited by Jaclyn Easton.
        p.   cm.
    Includes index.
    ISBN 0-07-135303-8 (trade pbk.)
    1. Auctions—Computer network resources.   I. Millhollon, Mary.   II. Easton, Jaclyn.
III. Title.

HF5478 .O45   2000
025.06'38117—dc21
                                                                                    99-462038

McGraw-Hill

A Division of The McGraw·Hill Companies

1 2 3 4 5 6 7 8 9 0   DOC/DOC   0 9 8 7 6 5 4 3 2 1 0

ISBN 0-07-135303-8

This book was set in Times Roman by North Market Street Graphics.

Printed and bound by R. R. Donnelley & Sons Company.

McGraw-Hill books are available at special quantity discounts to use as premiums and
sales promotions, or for use in corporate training programs. For more information, please
write to the Director of Special Sales, Professional Publishing, McGraw-Hill, Two Penn
Plaza, New York, NY 10121-2298. Or contact your local bookstore.

  This book is printed on recycled, acid-free paper containing a minimum of
50% recycled, de-inked fiber.

ONLINE AUCTIONS

Also by CommerceNet Press

StrikingItRich.com: Profiles of 23 Incredibly Successful Websites You've Probably Never Heard Of by Jaclyn Easton

Make Your Website Work for You by Jeff Cannon

Opening Digital Markets: Battle Plans and Business Strategies for Internet Commerce by Walid Mougayar

Understanding Digital Signatures: Establishing Trust Over the Internet and Other Networks by Gail Grant

Building Database-Driven Web Catalogs by Sherif Danis and Patrick Gannon

The Search for Digital Excellence by James P. Ware et al.

The CommerceNet Guide to IMarket by Arthur D. Little

Understanding SET: Visa International's Official Guide to Secure Electronic Transactions by Gail Grant

How to Invest in E-Commerce Stocks by Bill Burnham and Piper Jaffray

Buying a Home on the Internet by Robert Irwin

Buying a Car on the Internet by Jeremy Lieb

Buying Travel Services on the Internet by Durant Imboden

The Future of Work by Charles Grantham

CommerceNet is a nonprofit industry consortium for companies promoting and building electronic commerce solutions on the Internet. Launched in April 1994 in Silicon Valley, CA, its membership has grown to more than 500 companies and organizations worldwide. They include the leading banks, telecommunications companies, VANs, ISPs, online services, software and service companies, as well as end-users, who together are transforming the Internet into a global electronic marketplace. For membership information, please contact CommerceNet at Tel: 408-446-1260; Fax: 408-446-1268; URL: http://www.commerce.net. For information regarding CommerceNet Press, contact Loël McPhee at loel@commerce.net.

This book is dedicated to the online auctionites throughout the world who continue to make online auctioning an enjoyable, viable, and profitable experience for all.

CONTENTS

A C K N O W L E D G M E N T S

From Mary Millhollon:

First and foremost, my sincerest regard and appreciation go to Jaclyn Easton for her inspiration and business savvy and to Luanne O'Loughlin for her impressive research habits and go-get-it attitude. If only everyone could work with such pleasant, knowledgeable, and agreeable professionals! I also extend a late-late-late night "thanks for the insanity breaks" to the Bughouse (Ir)regulars—with a special schmooze for the two who helped the most with online auction research: the beautiful Chris Annos, who simply oozes creativity and regularly dredges up unbelievable treasures, and the renowned SnackMaster, Patrick Kaminsky, who is the most astounding collector of all that's bright, shiny, rare, and hidden in garage sales, thrift shops, swap meets, and online auctions (beware mortals, Pat will one day rule the collectibles world!). Finally, my deepest love, gratitude, and admiration to the three incredible guys who continually put up with my wacked-out writer's schedule and keep life moving at lightning speed: Cale (YSTB), Robert, and Matthew Taylor.

From Luanne O'Loughlin:

Many thanks to Jaclyn for the inspiration and to Mary for her creative diligence. It's great to be part of a team known as the Auction Girls. Thanks also go to Kelly, Josalyn, and the George Mason University tag team for their excellence in baby-sitting and proofreading. I'm always grateful to Tom and Carly (and now, Katie, too) for their patience as we fit book writing into our busy family schedule. My email buddies and their cyberhugs continue to keep me glued to the computer and the medium: Thanks especially to Wendy Jane, Jillann, Chet, Sally, Suzanne, Eddie, Taryn (another inspiration!), and Linda B. You've kept me on the lookout for auction bargains and Web shopping deals.

From Jaclyn Easton:

My deepest thanks to Luanne and Mary, the most considerate coauthors on the planet. You redefine the meaning of "dedicated, thorough, and professional." The world needs to know that I acted simply as "guide" and that you two are responsible for nearly every word. Thank you for making me part of your team. Additional thanks to my lead agent, John Mass of the William Morris Agency, with endless personal gratitude to Bob Casady, whose starting bid is "priceless." Finally, a thank-you to my dad, Jac Holzman, for his constant faith and support.

From All the Girls:

Special thanks to our agent, Eric Zohn of the William Morris Agency. It is amazing how you handled the complexities of our arrangements with such panache.

INTRODUCTION

The revelation occurred on Christmas Day, 1999. I was opening a gift from a distant relative, and found the contents extremely thoughtful but completely incongruous with my taste. "No problem," I thought. " I can always put it up for auction on eBay." Then it dawned on me that this option had been barely in the psyche of the country a couple of years before—and now eBay was a Jay Leno punchline.

On December 26 my assumption became a headline, as eBay was seeing extraordinary activity from unhappy gift recipients. eBay and other person-to-person auctions offer us choices we never had before. Why shlep back to the mall for a credit, when you can get cash without leaving the house?

eBay and other online auctions are not new. They dawned in 1995 right along with other Web retailing ventures like Amazon.com. My first experience was at OnSale.com, a business-to-consumer auction. Never before could I have believed that I could buy a laptop for $12. Granted these starting bids always rose, but you could always hope that no one else would discover a particular auction and you could have a bargain shopping story to tell at dinner parties for the rest of your life. While I didn't get the laptop for $12, I did get an IBM Thinkpad for $300. I was nearly as happy.

My Thinkpad megabargain was the beginning of my auction wins. Since that time I have participated in about 50 of them, buying everything from a vintage Atari Super Pong game console to an Oprah Winfrey refrigerator magnet to a Sylvester & Tweety fountain. Some kitschy, some practical . . . all of them a fun experience.

Many people refer to eBay as The World's Biggest Garage Sale. They are right. Ironically, though, it can be the offline garage sales fueling the online ones, with some folks making astounding profits.

My friend Chris was the first one to wake me up to this phenomenon. One day he bought a seven-tape set of Julia Child cooking videos at a garage sale for $5. The set was in mint condition, with all the tapes except one still sealed. Filled with the promise of becoming a gourmet chef, Chris bought the set. For the next two years the tapes gathered dust, until one day Chris self-confessed that he was probably not going to ever watch them. eBay was getting a lot of press at the time, so almost as a lark he decided to put the cooking series up for sale. Seven days later he was $120 richer. The tapes sold for $125.

Chris didn't give up his day job to sell full-time on eBay, but many people have, creating lives for themselves that they never could have imagined, working only a few hours a day. Many business prognosticators comment on how the Web is cutting out the middleman. To a certain degree, they are missing the point. Person-to-person auctions may also be getting rid of the retailer. Instead of one entity selling to many, you've got many selling to many.

It's important to note that most auction buying is also about entertainment. Making a bid, tracking your progress, checking the auctions on which you've bid to see that you are, indeed, still the top bidder, or worse, that you've been outbid and the agonizing process begins as you ponder whether to raise it, are all a part of the entertainment value. It's high drama. In other words, there's no such thing as a boring auction.

It was precisely this action that got my friend and noted celebrity coauthor William Novak online. While he happily bought his family a top-notch Windows-based Pentium in 1999, for his own use he was happy to stick with his DOS-based word processor and fax machine. Virtually a Luddite, he found little appeal in the Internet, though he would occasionally surf online with his son Jesse.

After reading much about eBay, Bill decided to run a search for his favorite collectible: toy kaleidoscopes. What amazed him most was how much care people took to properly display their wares, with multiple scanned photos and lengthy descriptions, all for a product with a starting bid as low as $2. Bill watched the toy kaleidoscope auctions daily for 2 or 3 months before getting involved and eventually buying over 50 of them. William Novak is proof that in the same way that applications like email and instant stock tracking have brought some people online, auctions have been the definitive application for others.

Most likely it's this buzz that has brought you to these pages. You're either new to this world and want some guidance to make sure you get the best deals on what you buy and the most money for what you want to sell, or you've been at it already and feel you could be doing better. No matter what your goal, we address every issue you need to know to become an auction expert.

Meanwhile, you will be thrilled to learn that there's more to the auction craze than just eBay. Because it was the first to market and remains the leader by such an extreme margin that it seems impossible any other company could ever catch up, eBay consistently gets the most attention. But there's a lot more to online auctioning.

The skills you develop from reading this book will help in business as well. While Partridge Family lunch boxes and limited-edition Beanie Babies are all the rage on eBay, business-to-business auctions are developing swiftly as well. You can buy steel remnants at auction at MetalSite.com; construction equipment at ironmall. com; even cotton pickers at FarmBid.com. Whether your business is industrial, service, or even mom-and-pop retailing, you can find what you need, or offer what you have, at sites dedicated to your profession.

In fact, the skills you are about to learn will serve you at times when you least expect them to. Auction opportunities are now available at places like The Sharper Image catalogs Web site or at MountainZone.com, an information site that also lets you bid on high-end sports gear for as little as $5.

Some people claim that auctions are only a passing fad. These are the same "experts" who said the Internet was doomed and would merely be a footnote in history. eBay alone is responsible for over 126 million auctions, growing at a rate of 2.5 million *per day*. Such numbers prove that auctions are not a special interest; they are a bona fide part of our lives, as integral to the Web as email, news, and stock trading.

Best of all, auctions are responsible for some of the most entertaining and profitable moments you can spend online. And the more you know about them, the more fun and the more profitable they will become.

Jaclyn Easton
February, 2000

ONE

ABOUT ONLINE AUCTIONS

1

CHAPTER

GOING ONCE, GOING TWICE . . . GOING STRONGER THAN EVER

"Online auctions may be one of the most valuable innovations wrought by the Internet."

—*The Economist*

SOLD ON ONLINE AUCTIONS

Online auctions. They're trendy and innovative, yet based on a concept that has been around since caves were the hottest homes in the real estate market. Over the past couple of years, millions of Internet-connected earthlings have become enamored with the concept of haggling in the online auction community—a global community in which sellers grant goods to the buyers who show the best hands on the table.

While some folks choose to brush the online auction phenomenon aside as a fad as short-lived as the recent resurgence of velour, most analysts believe that online auctions are here to stay. Take a look at these forecasts:

- Forrester Research, an Internet consulting firm, projects that online auctions aimed at consumers will gross $19 billion annually by the year 2003.

- Similarly, Vernon Keenan, an Internet analyst at Keenan Vision in San Francisco, projects that the value of goods and services sold over the Internet auctions (including business-to-business auctions) will be $129 billion in the year 2002.

- According to MSN Money Central, when the dust settles in the year 2000, 15 percent of all consumer e-commerce spending in 1999 will have been in online auctions.

Granted, these numbers are *forecasts* (and local weather reporters have schooled most people in the inaccurate art of forecasting), but the numbers tossed about in reports by reputable economists and marketing analysts are staggering. Even more staggering are the overwhelming number of success stories you hear from buyers and sellers on person-to-person sites like eBay, Amazon, and Yahoo!, three of the biggest online auction sites around.

THE INSTANT APPEAL

The mere presence of online auctions is far from earth-shattering or cutting-edge news. Online auctions came into existence in 1995 with the emergence of eBay. At the birth of the new century, online auctions can easily claim a space among hot topics in retail, marketing, business, and computing circles everywhere. In addition, they're the topic among bona fide "junkers," hobbyists, collectors, antique dealers, college students, Gen Xers, baby boomers, retirees, kids, charity organizations, and just about anyone else. Why are online auctions so appealing to so many people? Because online auctions carry that rare charisma of genuinely having something to offer everyone.

On online auctions, you can buy items ranging from "shabby chic" desk lamps to yachts, including a vast array of rare and collectible pieces if you dig around a little. In addition to the tangible "lots of stuff" perspective of online auctions, the not-so-tangibles draw participants to the action as well. Characteristics such as dynamic pricing, self-reliance, unintrusiveness, and convenience all fall in the plus column when it comes time to rate online auctions. These not-so-tangibles present benefits to buyers and sellers alike:

- *Dynamic pricing.* Sellers benefit by selling items that otherwise might not have sold or by receiving higher prices than expected for normally fixed-priced items. Buyers benefit because they can choose from an unmatched selection of items and determine how much to spend for a piece. Frequently, buyers get items at or below the buyer's desired purchasing price—that's great! But, if a buyer doesn't receive an item at the desired price, the buyer simply must forgo owning the item or rethink purchasing strategies.

- *Self-reliance.* Online auctions give sellers the ability to reach larger markets, work selected hours, and control overhead costs. Likewise, buyers can shop at any time from the comfort of their own homes or offices.

- *Unintrusiveness.* Sellers and buyers can maintain their privacy. Instead of holding yard sales and estate sales with strangers tramping across their lawn, sellers can turn to online auctions and host the same items without the crowds. Buyers do not have to venture out to other homes or cities in search of rare, collectible, or "perfect gift" items.

- *Convenience.* Sellers and buyers can buy and sell when they choose and determine the price ranges for their transactions.

SOME BENNIES OF ONLINE SHOPPING

Visa reported that last year 65 percent of holiday shoppers believed shopping online makes it easier to find the perfect present for that loved one who is hard to shop for. Furthermore, Visa's survey came up with the following:

- 60 percent of survey respondents have shopped online in their pajamas.
- 84 percent have shopped with their shoes off.
- 36 percent have shopped while eating a meal.

More than two-thirds of survey respondents state that the number-one reason they shop online is convenience. And—online auction sellers take note—45 percent of online shoppers do their online shopping weekdays between 5 P.M. and midnight.

Maybe the most appealing factor of online auctions is that among the millions of inventory items, buyers and sellers run into very few barriers when it comes time to participate. People who have never bought or sold online before can begin doing so with just a couple of bucks in their pocket, a computer, and an Internet connection. (The upcoming chapters show how you, too, can join the action quickly and safely.) Once people discover the ease of online auctions, it's sometimes hard to turn back. So consider yourself forewarned! After you have hung out at online auction sites for a while, you may find that paying a fixed price for an item elsewhere seems almost passé.

THE BUTTER DISH

When one of this book's authors was looking for a simple butter dish at a home store, she became annoyed at the dull selection and high prices of the four butter dishes displayed on the shelf. Needless to say, she left the shop empty-handed. Later, she sat down in front of her computer and, in the name of "research," searched for butter dishes on various online auctions. Within 20 minutes, she found over a dozen unique butter dishes of varying vintage, all for under $10. Needless to say, she's no longer butter dish–challenged.

The newspapers are filled with online auction success stories and tales. For example, the *Washington Post* recently ran a story about a college student in Cookeville, Tennessee. He decided to store all sorts of "silly" information on CD-ROMs and sell them on online auctions to help pay his college expenses. Within five months, the student sold between 500 and 600 CDs at $10 apiece—earning enough money to make him practically debt-free. And, as most people know, debt-free students are a rare breed these days! Similarly, there are reports of astronomically high sale prices for rare items. For example, there's a well-circulated report of a Beanie Baby—Peanut, the Royal Blue Elephant—that sold at an auction for $4200! Additionally, real estate and mortgages are among the online auction participants, as are automobiles, computers, books, livestock, collectibles, housewares, artwork, clothing, consumer electronics, autographs, and so forth. Clearly, online auctioning is steadily and successfully spanning in new directions at increasing velocities.

MEET NANCY NARRETT

Some of the greatest online auction success stories on person-to-person auction sites come from people like Nancy Narrett, based in Ellicott City, Maryland. Nancy has a master's degree in psychotherapy but has put that career on hold while she raises her three children. Nancy started to rent space in antique malls in her area's historic district, to display and sell collectibles and vintage items that she found at yard sales, estate sales, and live auctions. Then she discovered eBay. Nancy found that she could easily buy and sell items for her small antique business online. She knew things were going well when a single sale enabled her to purchase a scanner that she could use to add pictures to future online auction ads!

The newfound convenience afforded by online auctions was astounding—Nancy could stock her inventory from the comfort of her home after the kids went down for the night. Furthermore, she found a new outlet for items she was selling. For example, an orange juice reamer that she had on display in the antique mall hadn't sold after a few weeks, so she put it up for sale on eBay. Within seven days, she sold the reamer for $40!

Nancy now regularly mixes online auction buying and selling with her "Vintage House of Design" sales at the antique malls. When we last spoke, she had just "won" four vintage 1920s formal dresses for a mere $14 and a pair of vintage drapes in perfect condition for $25 on eBay. Nancy's perspective sums up the benefits of person-to-person auctions very nicely: "Online auctions give buyers and sellers a lot of choices and a lot of purchasing power!"

In addition to the growing number of individuals with online auction success stories, you'll find an increasing number of charity auctions online, too. Recently, you could bid on "dinner with Bill Cosby, and buy his 1998 Honda Accord," with all of the proceeds going toward Central High Charity in Philadelphia. Another recent charity auction was offered on the City Auction site, in which Pete Sampras's 1999 U.S. Open tennis racket was auctioned off. All of the proceeds went to the Big Brothers and Big Sisters of America. While charity auctions aren't the majority, they're a nice side benefit of a growing market.

Finally, if you haven't gotten your fill of the good karma emanating from online auctions presented thus far, mull over this next bit of information. As part of her show, Oprah Winfrey enlisted the help of Amazon.com founder and CEO Jeff Bezos to guide her through the online auction experience. If Oprah's looking, you can bet that millions of other people have found their interest piqued as well.

REALITY CHECK

Amidst all the positives of online auctions, there are drawbacks. Namely, the fraud factor. According to the *Washington Post*, "Consumer fear of Internet fraud is perceived as the biggest barrier to success for online commerce sites."

Obviously, the fraud factor is a legitimate concern, but it's not a hidden concern. Many agencies and online auction sites are fighting against online auction fraud, and there are a number of ways you can strive to avoid falling victim to online auction scams.

Signs that online auction fraud is being taken seriously include a couple of recent criminal convictions. One fraudulent seller in Florida was convicted of mail fraud, and another scamster, this one in California, was convicted of grand theft. Further, in the words of eBay CEO Meg Whitman, "If fraud were rampant, we would not have had such big growth." As you will see later in this book, online auction sites frequently provide user feedback forums as an effective means for building reputations and trading safely in online auction communities.

One collector of vintage GI Joe action figures sums it up this way, "The payoff of online auctions is that you're getting things at substantially reduced prices or things that you can't get anywhere else. But, you've got to use common sense."

THE LASTING CHARM

While you can easily imagine how online auctions might hold the short-term excitement of an affair, their appeal can in fact be likened more to the long-term wherewithal of a lasting relationship. That's because online auctions provide a market unparalleled in any other retail arena.

According to Jill Frankle, program manager for International Data Corporation (IDC) (**www.idc.com**) Internet and Strategies research, online auctions are so successful because they overcome the traditional inefficiencies of auctions in the offline world. Those inefficiencies include limited geographic coverage, a lack of variety and selection of products, high transaction costs, and information shortages. "These limitations are actually industry traits that make the market ripe for redefinition by the Internet," Frankle says. "Online auctions have been so successful on the Internet because they are able to create the three critical Cs for success on the Web: community, content, and commerce. . . . The online auction is not a passing fad. It represents a new way for companies to conduct business with an increasingly global customer base."

THE FATE OF FIXED PRICES

No one is claiming that online auctions will strike a death blow to fixed prices. Instead, online auctions expand the market's playing field. Buyers and sellers have another viable venue for swapping goods. The entire world won't turn to bidding and outbidding just because online auctions are a success—after all, it takes work to haggle, which is why fixed prices happened in the first place. In the opinion of Amazon CEO Jeffrey P. Bezos, fixed prices will remain the norm: "Would you want to negotiate the price of *The New York Times* every time you bought it?" Of course not, but for many other products, millions of buyers don't mind a little haggling if it ends in a sweet deal.

Online auctions are a legitimate and growing marketing venue, and you can easily prove this to yourself. Turn to online auctions and you may be able to:

- Find rare pieces of Depression glass at a quarter of antique store prices (and replacement china at a fraction of the cost at retail replacement shops)
- Realize hundreds of dollars in profits on ceramic pieces that you picked up at a local yard sale for pennies (one seller made a $300 profit on a single 50-cent item!)
- Dress your entire family in vintage clothing (if you so desire)
- Increase your small business's revenue with minimal investment and little overhead
- Raise money for charities
- Find that perfect gift (the one which you could've never imagined existed until you stumbled upon it as you browsed through auction ads)
- Bring in extra income without leaving your home or picking up a second job

MOVING ON

Clearly, successes continue to accumulate in the online auction world as more and more buyers and sellers learn the system. And that's the purpose of this book—to expand the community of informed online auction buyers and sellers. The pages of *Online Auctions* succinctly explain how to become a highly successful buyer and seller on various person-to-person online sites. For easy reference, the remainder of this book is divided into two sections—a section for buyers and a section for sellers.

P A R T TWO

GUIDE FOR BUYERS

2

CHAPTER

FINDING THE BEST AUCTIONS FOR YOU

DON'T STAND IN LINE—GO ONLINE

Before you can start your online bidding, you need to find the auctions. Therefore, that's the first step in this section and the main focus of this chapter. So, at this early stage in the game, forget about checking your checking account and credit card balances—we'll talk about bidding in later chapters. For now, let's do some virtual legwork, and look around the online auction market.

TYPECASTING ONLINE AUCTION SITES

The online auction market is fairly new to the Internet, but that doesn't mean there are only a couple of online auctions out there. In fact, the reverse is true. According to *The New York Times,* there were over 1000 online auctions in the second quarter of 1999. To see some hard evidence, check out the Auction Tribune's online auctions list at **www.auctiontribune.com/list_1.htm**, the Internet Auction List at **www.internet-auctionlist.com**, the AuctionInsider's list at **www.auctioninsider.com/every.html**, and auction sites organized by category at the bottom of the AuctionWatch page at **www.auctionwatch.com** (see Figure 2.1). These lists aren't all-inclusive, but they are certainly extensive, and they'll give you a good feel for the number of auction sites making their appearance on the Web. So, check out the lists, but don't feel overwhelmed. Think of it this way—with so many online auctions out there, you won't

FIGURE 2.1

The AuctionWatch site can help you find auction sites and keep you up-to-date on online auction news.

have trouble finding auctions; it's simply a matter of deciding which ones are best for you. And that's exactly what we're going to cover here.

Loosely, online auctions can be classified into five groups: business-to-consumers, consumer-to-consumer, "live" auction houses, specialty, and local. Granted, you will find quite a bit of overlap among the categories, but knowing about the types of online auctions will get you started on the right foot.

Business, Consumer, and "Live" Auctions

As a buyer, you have more flexibility than a seller when it comes to finding auctions. Your goal is to find auction sites that have the goods you want for the best deal, within reasonable security levels. This could mean visiting high-traffic auction sites to find wide selections of items, or digging up legitimate yet not-so-well-known auction sites to find less competition and better bargains. Further, you have the option of visiting *business-to-consumer auctions, consumer-to-consumer auctions,* and *"live" auction houses.* In theory, the differences are easy to spot:

- *Business-to-consumer auctions.* Businesses often auction off over-stocked, unused-but-aging, discontinued, refurbished, returned, and popular items to private parties like you and me. For example, Egg-head.com, the computer store chain that's now exclusively online, offers computer hardware and software auctions at **www.egghead.com**. Universal Studios regularly auctions off star-studded items such as autographed photos, scripts, and wardrobe items (**store.universalstudios. com/usauction**). One of Elvis's vests started at $1450! Other examples include Warehouse Auctions (**myauction.warehouse.com**) and First Auction (**www.firstauction.com**).

- *Consumer-to-consumer auctions.* Individuals auction items to private parties. EBay is currently the most popular consumer-to-consumer auction site on the Web (**www.ebay.com**), with Yahoo! (**auctions.yahoo.com**), Amazon (**auctions.amazon.com**), MSN (**auctions.msn.com**), and Excite (**auctions.excite.com**) also getting in on the action.

- *Auction houses.* Traditional auction houses, such as Christie's, Sothebys, and Butterfield & Butterfield showing their stripes on the Web. You can visit auction house Web sites to order catalogs, review upcoming auctions, and in some cases even place online bids after the bidding action goes live. More recently, some of the big names have enlisted with established online auction sites to expand their services. For example, Amazon is working with Sothebys to create an online auction presence at **sothebys.amazon.com**, and Amazon has links with LiveBid (**amazon.livebid.com**) to enable other auction houses to accept online buyer bids during live auctions. Likewise, eBay and Butterfield & Butterfield (**www.butterfields.com**) have joined forces for future online action. In addition to participating in online auctions, you can visit the auction house sites for auction tips, expert advice, and other auction information.

This book primarily deals with consumer-to-consumer auctions, but, to be a well-informed auctionite, you should be aware that business-to-consumer and live auction house auctions exist as well. Both types of auctions could come into play sometime in your future. In fact, according to a report by Jupiter Communications, by the year 2002 business-to-consumer auctions are predicted to cater to 6.5 million purchasers and move over $3.2 billion worth of merchandise. Many of the topics we discuss pertaining to consumer-to-consumer auctions apply equally to business-to-consumer and live auction house auctions as well.

Now, getting back on track, as far as consumer-to-consumer auction sites are concerned, several high-profile sites seem to get the bulk of attention—and for good reason. These auction sites include (in alphabetical order):

- Amazon (**auctions.amazon.com**)
- Auctions.com (**www.auctions.com**)

- City Auction (**www.cityauction.com**)
- eBay (**www.ebay.com**)
- Excite (**auctions.excite.com**)
- MSN (**auctions.msn.com**)
- Up4Sale (**www.up4sale.com**)
- Yahoo! (**auctions.yahoo.com**)

Now that the types of auctions are cleanly organized, the following fact of online auction life needs to be pointed out: *Business-to-consumer and consumer-to-consumer auctions often move beyond peacefully coexisting on the Net and frequently blend together in a nice grayish area.* In other words, there's quite a bit of overlap when it comes to business and consumer online auctions. For example, many businesses auction items on eBay, but the companies are not primarily in the business of running auctions. For example, a friend of mine successfully bid on a signed copy of Neil Gaiman's book *Smoke and Mirrors* on eBay. Before she bid, she discovered that the seller also owns and runs the Booksmith bookstore in San Francisco. Obviously, the bookstore business encompasses much more than selling books in online auctions, but participating in online auctions gives the bookstore some added business and the ever-desirable "exposure." So, the point is that even if you stick to consumer-to-consumer online auctions, you can't always count on the seller being someone with a computer, an Internet connection, and a scanner set up in a spare room.

With all of this talk of business and consumer auctions and auction houses, continue to keep an open mind and try not to overly limit yourself. Remember, the best auction sites have what you need at good prices. Just because buyers are overbidding on an item on a popular auction site doesn't mean that you can't get a good deal elsewhere.

Specialty Auctions

Specialty auction sites are set up expressly for a particular purpose, commodity, or buyer interest. For example, there are sports memorabilia (even sport-specific memorabilia, like basketball-only and baseball-only) online auction sites, charity auctions, car auctions, collectible glass auctions, and computer-related auctions, to name a few. While these sites usually don't get anywhere near the same number of hits as eBay, Yahoo!, or Amazon, they often receive heavy traffic among select crowds of Internet surfers.

To find a specialty auction, you'll need to veer off the beaten path a little. If you do, you will find a number of specialty auctions, especially stamp, coin, Beenie Baby, and computer-related sites. Some of the available topical auction sites include:

- **au.webcharity.com**   Donated items, with the proceeds going to specified charities

- **auctions.cnet.com** Computer hardware and software
- **auctions.sportingnews.com** Sports-related auctions, with lots of professional team cards, collectibles, and autographs
- **bhauction.com** Beverly Hills Charity Auctions, which donates its proceeds to charities
- **DealDeal.com** Computer hardware and software.
- **mobilia.com** Automobile-related items, including cars, books, car accessories, and parts
- **sportstrade.com** Rare and collectible sports memorabilia
- **www.auctionvine.com** Fine and rare wines
- **www.comicexchange.net** Comic books, cards, figures, and other related items
- **www.justbeads.com** Beads and beaded items
- **www.numismatists.com** Coin and currency collectibles for serious collectors
- **www.philatelists.com** Stamps and postal history collectibles for serious collectors
- **www.winebid.com** Premium aged and fine wines

In addition to checking out specialty auction sites, keep an eye out for another type of auction known as the *special format auction.* Special format auctions, often found on general business and consumer sites, include lightning-round auctions, one-hour auctions, 99-cent auctions (where everything starts at 99 cents), and first-bid-wins auctions. After you are comfortable working within the standard auction environment, you might want to mix it up and try alternate auctioning formats. Finally, if you are looking for expensive or hard-to-mail items (like appliances), you should consider checking out local auction sites.

Local Auctions

Local online auctions are relatively new members in the online auction crowd. The beauty of online communication has always been the appeal of overcoming distance limitations on the Internet, so you might wonder, "Why localize online auctions?" There are a couple of good reasons. First, some items are just too big or unwieldy to ship for a reasonable price. For example, let's say that someone auctions off a gas dryer. Maybe you got the dryer at a screaming deal of $50, but factor in the cost to ship that dryer from Maryland to Arizona, and that cheap dryer just got expensive. A great case-in-point involves a beautiful Mahogany piano bench recently sold on eBay. A couple of months ago, a friend purchased a 1902 mahogany piano at an estate sale. Unfortunately, the piano had lost its bench somewhere in time. A seller on eBay was offering a beautifully restored mahogany piano bench that ultimately sold for $61.00. The $61.00 seemed like a nice price until you read the fine print—the shipping charge for the bench would be $50! Therefore, the $61.00 bench quickly turned into a $111.00 bench, which is a price you could match for a new bench at your local piano store. If the buyer and seller were involved in a local auction, however, the buyer could arrange to pick up the item and save a bundle in shipping charges.

The second reason to use local auctions is also shipping-related. In this case, we're addressing extremely inexpensive items. If you're looking for a cheap item, you might want to check out local auctions first. After all, if you bid on a bag of plastic Mardi Gras necklaces for $2.50, do you really want to spend $3.20 (the standard U.S. Postal Service Priority shipping charge) for shipping? If it's a local auction, you could save yourself a couple of bucks and pick up your purchase the next time you're in the seller's neighborhood. This works especially well if the seller is a local business.

A third benefit of local auctions applies to buyers who are bidding on expensive, one-of-a-kind, or rare pieces. In this case, a local auction enables buyers to view items before bidding. This, of course, is at the seller's discretion, but the possibility exists. Most auction sites include sellers' email addresses, and some auction sellers invite you to visit their establishments to view their items. If you see an expensive, sizeable, or rare item—maybe a painting, jewelry, an antique, an automobile, a house, or livestock—you can email the seller and ask whether it's possible for you to view the item(s). Of course, always use common sense when researching auction items—*never* put yourself in situations that you would normally avoid.

Finally, the fourth benefit of local auctions is that sometimes buyers feel a little more secure knowing that a seller lives nearby. Obviously, a seller's location is no guarantee of his or her reliability, but sometimes a local address does make a difference. For example, let's say the local coffee shop is auctioning off some custom-painted ceramic coffee mugs. You know the shop exists, so there's strong evidence that the seller is legitimate. Of course, this local-so-it's-safer reasoning is based on the negative—it's easier to find and file charges against a local fraud than a fraud living thousands of miles away or in another country altogether. If the only reason you're visiting local online auctions is based on this thinking, we encourage you to seriously reconsider your stance. As you'll see in later chapters, you can successfully use many other not-so-nearby online auctions with a high degree of security, and limiting yourself only to local auctions severely limits your choices.

As the appeal of local auctions grows, you'll see more local online auction sites cropping up. A good place to start your local auction search is to look on your local newspaper's Web site. Look for an auctions link on the paper's home page. Furthermore, some sites, such as City Auction (**www.cityauction.com**), enable you to indicate your local area when you register at the site. Other sites also offer links to local auctions. For example, eBay has a Go Local! link at the bottom of its home page. You can click on this link, and select an area of your choice. You can also check for local online auction sites in your area by using an Internet search engine. Try using the search string *online auctions AND state or city name* to see what pops up. With the growth of local auctions, maybe by this time next year it'll be commonplace to use computers to bid on cars, instead of haggling in person with an overly emotive car salesman.

EVALUATING AUCTION SITES

Basically, there are a couple of key techniques that you can use to uncover the online auction sites that are best for you.

Visit the Site

The most effective way to discover information about an online auction site is to visit the site. *Really* visit it—don't just glance around, register, then commence the bidding. When you first visit an online auction site, take time to peruse the home page, scan the Web site's FAQ (frequently asked questions) page, check out some of the online auction features, and view a few of the active auctions. Figure 2.2 shows eBay's home page. As you can see, an online auction site's home page can provide all sorts of useful information.

To determine whether an online auction is equipped with the most desirable auction site qualities, you'll have to spend some time clicking links, reading Help pages, reviewing FAQ pages, and generally poking around the home page and related links.

Help and FAQ Pages

Help pages (see Figure 2.3) can tell you how to register on the Web site; lead you to question-and-answer pages; and assist you in finding, bidding on, and selling auction items. Most Help pages can be accessed by clicking a Help, FAQ, or Frequently

TIP

Regifting Revised

One surefire way to determine whether an auction site is a potential treasure trove or a waste of time is to click the "Categories" link. Most auction sites' categories pages show how many auction items are up for bid in each category. If you see a lot of zeros (which means that a lot of categories contain no items), you might have a hard time finding what you're looking for.

FIGURE 2.2

The eBay home page serves as a hub for links to eBay resources.

Asked Questions link on a site's home page. Sometimes the Help and FAQ pages may be thinly disguised as How To, Customer Service, or Welcome links.

I know it sounds painful, but spend at least 10 minutes reading a site's Help and FAQ pages. You're bound to discover at least some helpful online auction information as well as site-specific tidbits. For example, you'll be able to determine how to register, whether your bids will remain hidden, whether automatic bidding occurs, how to identify Dutch and reserve auctions, where to find buyer and seller feedback information, and how auctions end. As you work your way through the upcoming chapters, you'll read about numerous desirable and not-so-desirable online auction traits. Armed with this knowledge, you'll be able to quickly make judgment calls as you peruse auction sites' FAQ and Help pages.

After your 10 minutes (or more) are up on the FAQ and Help pages, move on and review the site's buyer registration process and auction services. Many times, the FAQ and Help pages mention some of the site's services, so at this point you should be getting a feel for some of the lingo the site uses for common online auction features. Like most other Web entities, online auction sites frequently take the kinetic approach to language and spawn their own terminology.

F I G U R E 2.3

Yahoo! offers tips and hints to buyers and sellers in its Help pages.

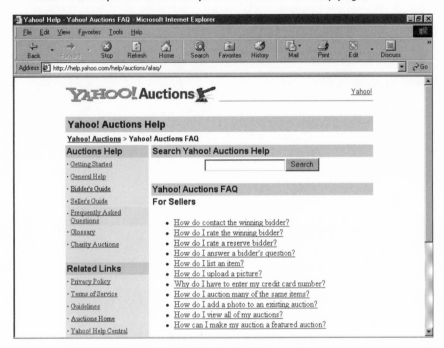

Registration and Services

Every online site we've run across requires you to register before you bid. Registering provides sellers with at least some information about buyers. As a buyer, you should not have to pay any fees to register at an online auction site. To emphasize:

Registration should be free for buyers.

If an online auction site requires you to pay a fee, find out why before you shell out. If the reasons seem the slightest bit flimsy, strongly consider using another site. Aside from advertising revenue, most sites make their money by charging sellers listing fees, percentages of sales, or a combination of the two. A buyer's registration fee is superfluous.

Generally, the process of registering requires you to provide some basic information (name, address, and so forth), supply a user name, and create a password (see Figure 2.4). If more information is required, such as credit card data, make sure the site uses SSL (Secure Sockets Layer) or other data encryption technology to help protect your personal information.

FIGURE 2.4

Up4Sale's registration page is typical of an online auction registration form.

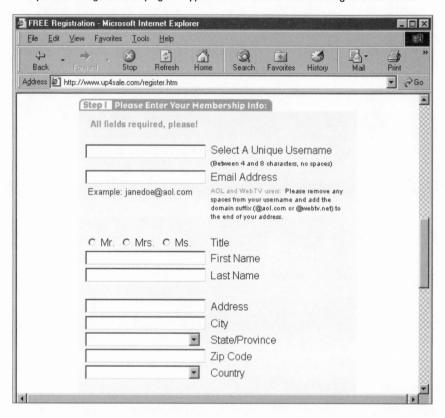

TIP

Viewing site maps (whether the Web site is an auction site or not) always results in helpful information. Instead of trusting in luck or

Aside from free registration, the best sites also offer basic auction services. To read about these services, comb the home page and its links. One key feature to look for is the site's bid and outbid notification policies. Ideally, when you bid on an item, you should receive an email summarizing your bid. In addition, when someone outbids you, you should automatically receive an email message stating that you've been outbid. Finally (hey, just as I was writing this, the computer beeped!), you should be notified when an auction ends. (It looks like the computer beeped because a Dutch auction we were participating in just ended. We were going for some black printer cartridges, and we just got five of them for $25!)

In upcoming chapters, we'll talk about finding auction items, interpreting ads, evaluating sellers, and so forth. Many of these topics present online auction tools and services that will help you to complete these research-related tasks. If a site doesn't support some of the capabilities mentioned in future chapters—such as feedback forums, categorical listings, advanced search tools, secure registration, and so forth—you might need to look for a more comprehensive online auction site. As your knowledge base grows, you'll be able to quickly evaluate and select the auction sites that suit you best.

KEY POINTS

In this chapter we talked about finding auction sites and what to look for when perusing them. Some key thoughts to keep in mind when trolling for auctions include:

- Auction sites can be business-to-consumer, consumer-to-consumer, "live" auction houses, specialty, local, or any combination of the preceding.

- You can quickly evaluate an online auction site by visiting its FAQ and Help pages.

- As a buyer, you should not have to pay a registration fee.

- You need to comb an auction site's home page and links (including the site map link) to determine the site's basic auction services.

- You should read the upcoming chapters to gain information that will help to make selecting online auction sites more intuitive.

following a trail of links to find a page that interests you, consider displaying a Web site's site map. Usually, there's a Site Map link on the home page. On online auction sites, the site map will quickly point you to available auction features and specialty pages—many of which you'd have a hard time finding otherwise. You'll be constantly amazed that site maps can lead you to so many really cool pages and features that are practically impossible to find by simply browsing Web sites.

3

C H A P T E R

FINDING THE ITEMS YOU WANT TO BUY

INVITING TREASURES TO YOUR DESKTOP

After finding auction sites, the natural progression is to start looking for auction items. While searching for treasures, you'll also discover that treasures find you. We'll take a brief look at this phenomenon, and then we'll focus on actions you can initiate to find items that don't find you.

HAVING ITEMS FIND YOU

Most online auction sites make it very easy for you to join the auction action, by bringing items to your virtual doorstep (a.k.a. your monitor). One of the easiest ways for an item to find you is for it to pop up on an online auction's home page.

On most online home pages, amongst other strategically placed links, you'll find links to featured auctions. Check out any major online auction site's home page—Amazon, eBay, Yahoo!—and you'll see at least a few links leading directly to auction item pages. Now, before you get bamboozled into thinking that all featured auctions on auction home pages are no less than truly amazing, keep in mind that most sellers pay an additional fee to list featured items. For example, both eBay and Amazon charge sellers around $100 to list an item as a main-page featured auction and around $15 to list an item as a featured auction within a category listing (we'll talk more about category listings in the next section). Now that you're privy to the added-fee information, it's safe to tell you that featured auctions frequently *are* notable items, which means they're often big-ticket, popular, rare, or expensive. In other words, featured auction items usually have some notable value; otherwise, the sellers wouldn't pay the extra fees. That said, checking out featured items is a fun way to see what's out there.

In addition to featured auction links, online auction sites provide other ways for items to find you. For example, many sites help you to stumble into items by offering links to soon-to-close listings, picture galleries, and seller's other auctions. In addition, as you search for items (as described later in this chapter), your search results will often include items you didn't even think of—this can be likened to getting struck by the can't-help-but-tangent syndrome that's inherent with standard Internet searching. As you can see, the plausibility of items finding you isn't as far-fetched as it might sound at first. You'll quickly discover that this part of auction hunting comes naturally. So, at this point, you're left to your own devices regarding auction items gravitating to your desktop. Now, let's move on and look at ways in which you can actively find items to bid on.

BROWSING SITE CATEGORIES

In this section, we'll take an online-auction-specific look at category lists and discuss how you can use them to find auction items. First, we will clearly define category listings: *An online auction category listing consists of a hierarchy of topical hyperlinks that lead to related groups of auction items. Category listings enable you to display auction items organized by topic.* Most auction home pages usually show at least a portion of the categories available on the site. In addition, online auction home pages usually provide a link to a comprehensive list of the site's categories (if not, visit the site map to see if there's a link to a category page listed there).

Any site worth its salt will provide some way for you to view auction items by categories. Usually, category names are followed by a number in parentheses. These numbers indicate how many items are listed within the category. You can use the number to quickly determine if a categorical search will be worth your time—if it's a lame category with 0 entries, you'll certainly know to look elsewhere!

For categories that contain items, you can click on subcategory links to narrow your search until you find listings that match your criteria. For example, let's say you're looking for collectible Hot Wheels. You could start your search by clicking on a Toys category heading. Then, you might click on a Diecast subcategory within Toys, and, finally, you would click on a Hot Wheels link. At this point, you'd be presented with the entire list of items included in the Hot Wheels subcategory. The list could be a modest list or it could be extremely unwieldy (such as the Hot Wheels list on eBay). Some sites add categorical links to further define a subcategory. For example, in the case of Hot Wheels on eBay, the Hot Wheels subcategory contains two categories: *General* (with 14,000+/− items) and *Redline* (with 2000+/− items). As you can see, even narrowing the category down by clicking on General or Redline leaves you with a sizable list. That's not too unusual when you perform categorical searches, especially on a large site like eBay. (By the way, *Redline* refers to the red lines that appear on tires of some collectible Hot Wheels.)

After you display the contents of a category, seek ways to organize the information for easy viewing. (The category contents page usually shows the category's listings as hyperlinks and includes the category's featured auctions, as mentioned earlier in this chapter.) Among other options, most auction sites enable you to display items that are closing soon, newly listed, or sorted by opening/closing date. Using the site's sort features can help you to narrow your current search, or at least organize the process to help streamline your activities. One effective way to sort a category is to show only items that close today, and then sort them by closing times. That way, you can see if any auctions you're interested in will be closing within the next few hours, and you won't have to search through the entire list in one sitting.

Finally, after you've searched and organized a category's listings, you're ready to browse the auction items' titles. At this point, you could simply click the link that interests you most, but there's a better way. Usually, an auction list includes more than one item that looks interesting, and you've probably exerted at least some effort to display a particular set of auction items. Therefore, you probably don't want to lose track of your list too quickly by clicking on an item. So, here's a big tip:

Open auction item links in a new browser window.

To open a link in a new browser window, right-click on the link and select "Open In New Window" (or a similar option). That way, the selected item's auction page opens in a new window and you won't lose track of your original list, because it remains vis-

TIP

Many online auction home pages include links to charity auctions (auctions that donate their proceeds to charities). Consider making it a habit to follow charity auction links. You never know—a couple of quick clicks could result in a treasure for you and a donation for others.

TIP

When you visit an auction site for the first time, view the category listings to get a feel for the site's level of activity (or inactivity). Furthermore, browsing the category list is a good way to jump-start your thought processes when you're devising your auction wish list.

TIP

Browsing auctions that are about to close is a quick and easy way to find out what's out there without spending hours searching

ible and accessible on your desktop. You might be thinking that you can return to your original list by using your browser's Back button, and, to an extent, the Back button works. But (and we know this from experience) some auction sites drop your Back button capabilities when you click on an auction item link. Therefore, consider using the dual-window approach to help you keep track of your auction items list. In a later chapter, when we talk about bidding, you'll learn how dual windows can also help you to successfully bid on items—so you might as well practice handling multiple windows now. Finally, one more note about browsing auction list item links—try to be patient when viewing auction items accompanied by pictures. If a description includes a picture, it may take a few seconds for the picture to display if you have a slow Internet connection.

Sorting through categorical auction titles might seem tedious, but if you're looking for collectibles or amazing bargains, this is definitely a good way to find them. And here's where we let you in on a secret. If you spend some extra time browsing through categories, you'll often find items that have been listed in unexpected ways—ways that people conducting search engine searches (as discussed in the next section) would be hard-pressed to replicate. This means that there's a high probability that buyers using search tools won't see some items you'll find by browsing a category. For example, let's return to the Hot Wheels example. By reading through the thousands of Hot Wheel listings on eBay, Cale, a friend of ours who collects Hot Wheels, found a link to an auction item with the following heading:

NICE CONDITION!

That was it! The auction item's title carried no reference to Hot Wheels, Hotwheels, or HW. Therefore, anyone using a search tool to look for auction items with the words "Hot Wheels" in the title would not see this ad. Upon further investigation, when Cale opened the auction item's Web page, the description read:

THESE 4 HOTWHEELS ARE IN NICE CONDITION, CHECK OUT THE PICTURE AND SEE FOR YOURSELF!

Obviously the seller wasn't a bona fide Hot Wheels collector, because (1) the seller misspelled Hot Wheels (making it one word instead of two), which means if buyers searched auction item descriptions for the correct, two-word spelling "Hot Wheels," they would not see this ad; and (2) all four Hot Wheels were released in 1968—the first year that Hot Wheels were produced—but this wasn't mentioned anywhere in the ad! With this stroke of luck, Cale ended up winning the Hot Wheels with minimal bidding competition for a mere $20.52, and the cars are easily worth over $100.00.

As you can see, categorical listings are great for finding items and having items find you, if you have the time. But more frequently you'll want to pinpoint your search. In those instances, you'll probably be better off using auction sites' search forms instead of categorical searches.

MAKING THE MOST OF SEARCH FORMS

While browsing category lists is a must (after all, you'll need to have an idea regarding the items available on any particular site), you'll also need to be able to search for specific items. Enter the *search tool*. Using auction sites' search tools will probably seem vaguely familiar. That's because these search tools are similar to other Internet search engines. The difference here, of course, is that the search tools only search for terms and phrases within the current auction site. Further, you can often limit a search to items within a particular auction site category as well. Most auction sites offer two types of search tools: *Basic* and *Advanced.*

Basic Searching

Basic searching generally involves typing a term or search string into a text box, and then clicking the Search button. Almost every auction site that we've visited provides this basic option on the home page. If you can't find a search text box on a home page, look for a Search link (try the toolbar)—there's bound to be some hyperlink leading you to a search tool.

through a category. These listings provide links to auctions that are nearing their final breath. Often, auction bidding picks up dramatically as an auction nears closing, so these links give you an opportunity to get in on some of the closing action. Soon-to-close listings can show auctions ranging from those that will close within seconds to those lasting a few more hours, and most sites show soon-to-close auctions sorted by category headings.

Search tools on auction sites can be manipulated in the same way that Web search engines are manipulated. You can search for a single term, multiple search terms, phrases, and so forth. Most auction sites include an area with search tips that will give you some hints about searching on the particular auction site. Usually, there's a search tips page, but you'll also find searching information on FAQ and Help pages. Further, you can find all kinds of search hints on the Internet—almost all search engine sites (Yahoo!, WebCrawler, AltaVista, and so forth) include searching tips. Keep in mind that some search engine tricks may or may not work on auction search tools, but, for the most part, the common techniques seem to be supported.

Basically, there are two ways to use the standard search tool: (1) start specific, or (2) start broad and narrow it down. If you really know what you want, you can try to make your search as specific as possible (such as Luanne's favorite search string: **Gymboree *item name* (New,NWT,Tag) -like**). By entering specific search strings, you quickly weed out items that don't interest you. To find out some great searching tips, click on the Tips link next to eBay's Find it! button on the eBay home page. Figure 3.1 shows eBay's Search Tips page.

F I G U R E 3.1

Viewing eBay's searching tips.

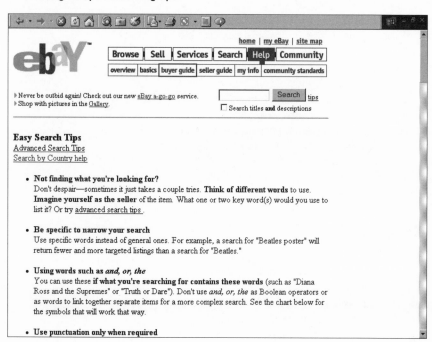

The other alternative is to start broad, and methodically narrow down the options to avoid inadvertently eliminating possible items. One reason to follow this type of search is that sellers don't always list their items in the way you'd expect them to—as illustrated earlier in the Hot Wheels example. Slowly narrowing down the list of options gives you the chance to view auctions you might miss by starting with an overly specific search. Further, you might not always know how to narrow a search until you see the results you receive from a broad search.

Julie, a friend of ours, recently conducted a search that can serve as a prime example of narrowing down options until a particular item is found. In this instance, Julie was looking for some bug clips for a gift. Hair jewelry (yes—that's what it's called) is very popular right now, and jeweled bug clips are especially chic. In this instance, Julie wanted to find some original jeweled bug hair clips as a gift for a friend. Now, when Julie started this search, she had no idea whether sellers would list bug clips as bobby pins, barrettes, hair jewelry, or some other creative name. So, she started with the obvious—*bug*.

She found the auction site's search box, typed

bug

and then clicked "Search." Not surprisingly, the results were so vast they flowed right off her monitor. She quickly saw how she could narrow her search—there were numerous entries for *Bug's Life* and *VW Bug*. So, she turned to the search text box at the top of the page, typed

bug –life –VW

TIP

On most online auction sites, you can easily blend searching by categories with using the search text box. To do this, display the category associated with the item you are looking for; indicate that you want to search for items only within the selected category (if necessary); type your search string in the search text box; and click the Search button.

and then clicked Search. Her search results shrank from about 1,200 returns to approximately 700 items. That still left a lot of entries—more than she wanted to browse through. So, she returned to the search text box again, opted to search descriptions as well as item titles (on eBay, there's a checkbox you can mark to expand your search to include descriptions), and added "+hair" to her search string. At this point, Julie's search string looked like this:

bug –life –VW +hair

That did it! She received about 15 items—a very workable number. Of the 15 entries, about two-thirds turned out to be hair clips or barrettes with bugs on them. The other items ranged from a caveman doll(!) to fishing lures. Eventually, Julie found what she wanted, and she obtained a very nice dragonfly clip for her friend. Of course, any number of paths could have been followed to turn up similar listings, and it's sometimes worthwhile to try different paths to see what you come up with. For example, starting the process with the word *dragonfly* instead of *bug* would have involved a totally different search path.

If you don't immediately find what you are looking for when using the search tool, don't despair. You can use a number of formulas to find items. For instance, you can try various spellings of keywords—you might be surprised at the alternate listings you receive if you change a single letter in your search parameters. To illustrate this to yourself, type "beanie" in an auction site's search box, and click the Search button. View the results. Next, type "beanies" in the search text box, and click the search button. Notice, the second list varies from the first and all you did was add an "s" to the keyword.

In addition to varying keyword spelling, try to be creative when you're searching for items. Think of how sellers might describe an item, or how misspellings might occur (Dr. Martens vs. Doc Martens vs. Doc Martins vs. Docs, or painting vs. picture vs. photograph vs. lithograph). In other words, before you give up or bid on something that's not exactly what you're looking for, run a few creative searches to see what you come up with.

Finally, if your search results turn up an item that's close to what you want, visit the seller's other auctions as described in Chapter 6. You might find what you're looking for, or you might get further ideas regarding how to best search for the item you want to find. And, if you really want to do some serious searching, test out the auction site's advanced searching form, as described next.

Advanced Searching

Advanced searching forms simply add a few more search boxes to the standard search text box. Advanced forms usually provide the option to search titles, descriptions, seller IDs, auction item numbers, price ranges, locations, closing dates, completed auctions, and so forth. Figure 3.2 shows Amazon's Advanced Search page.

Generally, successful use of advanced search forms entails entering data into the appropriate boxes and clicking a search button. Advanced search forms often look complicated when you first view them, but when you take a closer look, they are usually very user-friendly. Keep in mind that when you use advanced search forms, you can pick and choose which criteria you want to use. You don't *have* to fill in all the optional search criteria on advanced search forms—you simply fill in the search parameters that interest you. For example, you can use an advanced search form to paste auction item numbers you saved in a Notepad document into an item number text box. Of course, the more information you provide, the more specific your search results will be.

To open Amazon's search page, click the Advanced Search button in the Amazon auction toolbar.

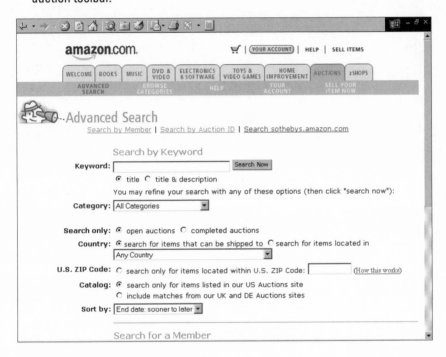

Finally, you might be interested to hear that the Internet offers some automated auction search assistance.

USING AUTOMATED SEARCH SERVICES

A number of Web sites (including online auction sites) offer auction search services. Search assistance comes in a couple of forms. You can use some sites to search multiple auctions at once, and you can use other sites to notify you when auction items you're interested in become available. In the first scenario, you visit an auction search site, use the search tool to look for auction items, and receive a return set that includes links to auction items from a number of online auction sites. In the second scenario, you fill out an online form and describe what types of items you would like to bid on. The search assistant keeps tabs on auction sites for you, and, when it finds auction items that match your criteria, you receive an email message informing you about the auction. Popular search assistants include the following:

- **Auction Watchers (www.auctionwatchers.com).** Enables you to search for computer-related items from Auctionnet, AuctionWorld, DealDeal, ubid, Onsale, Web Auction, and Surplus Auction.

TIP

Just for fun, try an advanced search for all items within the price range of one cent to a dollar. Then, specify to search for all auctions ending today with the word "a" or "the" in the title. Browse through the results and you might be pleasantly surprised with a bargain-basement deal that was overlooked by other buyers.

- **BidFind (www.bidfind.com).** Enables you to search over 325 popular online auctions, and indexes over 200,000 items. To see the list of participating auctions, visit **www.bidfind.com/af/af-list.html**. Auctions that participate in BidFind's service display a BidFind logo.

- **BidStream (www.bidstream.com).** Searches 250+ auction sites with a single click. Visit the BidStream home page to find links to all the auctions that participate in this search service.

- **iTrack (www.itrack.com).** Notifies you when items are up for auction. This service is a newer search assistant on the Web. It tracks auctions on eBay, Amazon.com, Yahoo!, MSN Auctions, Auctions.com, ZDNet, Gold's, Egghead, Haggle, box lot, Onsale, and Xoom. When auctions appear that match your profile, you are sent an email notification.

In addition to the preceding search assistants, look for specific online auction site features that can help you automate your search process and notify you when desired items end up on the auction block. To get a feel for this type of service, check the following popular auction notification tools:

- **Notify Me When . . .** on City Auction (**www.cityauction.com**)

- **Personal Shopper** on eBay (**www.ebay.com**)

- **Cool Notify** on Excite (**auctions.excite.com**)

Between conducting your own searches, performing multiple-site searches, and using notification services, you're bound to eventually find the items you're looking for. After you've located exact items you've been seeking, it's time to determine whether they are worthy of your bid. This is accomplished by interpreting auction item ads, as described in the next chapter.

KEY POINTS

In this chapter, we followed the preceding chapter's cue and moved on from finding auction sites to finding auction items. We discussed:

- The nature of finding auction items as well as having auction items find you.
- How online auction home pages help auction items find their way to your desktop.
- Effective ways to use category listings and categorical searches.
- Basic and advanced search tools.
- How to conduct searches that combine category and search tool features.
- Automated search services, including multiple-auction search engines and auction item notification services.

4 CHAPTER

INTERPRETING AN AUCTION AD

BROWSING BETWEEN THE LINES

In Chapters 2 and 3, you browsed auctions sites and searched for auction items. Now, it's judgment time! This chapter and the one following it show how to interpret online auction ads and sellers. We're going to go beyond simply reading listings and seller information, and enter the realm of honing the practical skill of reading between the lines. Fortunately, most sites enable you to browse without registering. So you can hone your interpretative skills on any online auction site you choose. In this chapter, we'll focus on checking out the ads; in the next chapter, we'll check out the sellers. As you will see, auction sites are generally set up so that ads contain lots of informative tidbits, even if the seller hasn't added much descriptive text. You can find all kinds of information if you know where to look for it.

UNDERSTANDING BASIC SHELF SPACE

Most noteworthy online auctions attempt to create an individualized "look and feel" to their respective sites, but after you get past the color schemes, you'll find that most are set up in about the same way (which makes our discussion fairly straightforward). Basically, online auction listings can be divided into three main areas:

- Header
- Description
- Bidding area

If you look closely enough, each section offers specific information that will ultimately help you to decide whether to submit a bid or click in the other direction. With that said, you can probably guess where we're headed in this chapter. We're going to take a closer look at each auction listing section.

THE HEADER—JUST THE FACTS, PLEASE

The header area of online auction ads contains the vital statistics of auction items. This area can be likened to the sticker price on a new or used car. Like the sticker in the car's window, the header area outlines basic facts, numbers, and general information. You get the facts, but you don't really get a feel for the item just yet. Namely, the header area usually lists the following (see Figure 4.1 for a sample header area):

- *Title.* Displays the title text that appears in search and category lists.
- *Item number.* Identifies the auction item. As you'll see in later chapters, referring to an item number helps buyers and sellers keep track of transactions.

F I G U R E 4.1

The header area in an eBay auction listing.

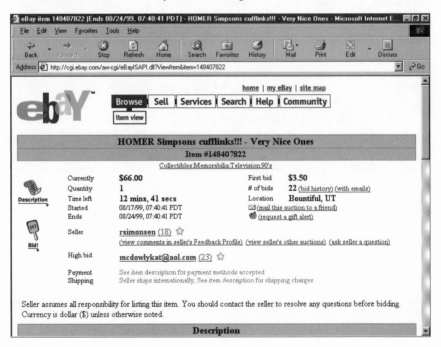

- *Category.* Specifies the auction item's category listing.

- *Current bid amount.* Shows the currently winning bid price.

- *First bid amount.* Shows the amount of the opening bid.

- *Quantity of auction items.* Specifies how many items are being auctioned off. Some auctions offer more than one item, such as four silk plants or three stuffed Pokemons. You can name your per-item price, and then specify how many of the items you'd like to purchase at that price. (You don't need to bid on all items if multiple items are offered.)

- *Number of bids.* Indicates how many users with unique email addresses have placed bids. Users who've placed more than one bid on an item are usually only counted once in this type of statistic.

- *Bid history.* Enables you to view the usernames of people who have bid on the item.

- *Starting and ending dates/times.* Specifies when the auction begins and when it closes.

- *Time left.* Shows the time remaining in an auction, typically in countdown form, such as 12 minutes and 41 seconds remaining.

- *Location.* Indicates where the seller resides.

- *Seller's name and rating.* Provides the seller's username along with a hyperlinked rating. On most online auction sites, you can click a seller's or buyer's rating number to view comments others have left about the user. We'll talk more about reviewing sellers' ratings in Chapter 5, then deal with leaving feedback/ratings for sellers in Chapter 7, and discuss feedback and ratings from a seller's perspective in Chapter 24.

- *Links to seller information.* Assists you in quickly gaining some background information about sellers, such as comments and other auctions offered by the seller (more about researching sellers in Chapter 6).

- *High bidder's name and rating.* Provides the name and rating level of the current "winning" bidder. If your username appears here, you're currently winning the auction!

- *Payment and shipping.* Specifies payment and shipping information. Frequently, sellers include more comprehensive payment and shipping information in the Description section of an auction listing, as described later in this chapter.

- *Notes/policies.* Lists any basic warnings or statements provided by the seller or the online auction.

While all of the header information is helpful in its own way, several items are of particular value. Therefore, when displaying a listing, you should take note of all the information, but especially review the following details:

TIP

When you review a header, you should also take note of the seller's location. If the seller is domestic, you won't have many mailing hassles to worry about. If the seller resides in another country, you'll need to consider shipping policies, exchange rates, and more. See Chapter 22 for more information about international shipping.

- *Current amount.*   Check the current price to determine whether the item is within your bidding price range. There's no use in wasting your time on overpriced or overly expensive items, unless you're just trolling for pictures!

- *Number of bids.*   This statistic gives you a rough indication of your competition or lack thereof. You'll want to keep an eye on this number. Further, keep in mind that an item's price can be inadvertently upped if bidding generates too much interest early in the game. We'll talk more about this statistic in Chapter 6, when we review bidding techniques.

- *Seller's rating.*   While the next chapter goes into more detail on how to run a full check on a seller, the seller's rating can provide a quick indication of the seller's auction experience. Common sense tells you that you're swimming in fairly safe waters if you bid on an item offered by a seller who sports a 1,034 rating instead of a −1.

- *Payment or shipping comments.*   Theoretically, this area should be used to indicate a seller's payment and shipping preferences, but more often it contains text instructing users to view the payment and shipping conditions in the description area of the auction listing. And, since we're talking about "payments" for the moment, here's a BIG hint: *If the payment and shipping comments area states that the only acceptable form of payment is cash or electronic check, run!*

As you can see, the function of the header area is to provide quick, summary information about the current auction. Always scan an auction listing's header before moving on to the more diverse description area. Later, after you have reviewed the description and are ready to bid, you'll definitely want to return to the header to more fully assimilate the information. For now, make it second nature to scan auction listing headers while you browse. If you have a dial-up connection, you can make good use of your time by scanning the header while you wait for the picture(s) to download.

MASTERING THE ART OF ICONOLOGY

When you browse through auction item search lists, category lists, and auction ads, you'll run across a number of small graphic symbols, or icons. Most auction sites use icons to quickly convey to viewers special information about items. The basic online auction icons include the following:

- *"New" symbols.*   "New" icons represent auctions freshly wheeled onto the auction block. "New" does *not* mean that the auction item is brand-new or factory direct; you'll have to read the item's description to find out that type of information.

- *"Hot" symbols.*   "Hot" comes in a couple of varieties in online auctions, so be sure that you know which variety is supported by the auction site. "Hot" can indicate that an item has received a particular number of bids, or the Hot icon can simply be an eye-catching graphic added by the seller (for a small fee, of course).

- *"Picture" or "Camera" symbols.*   "Picture" and "Camera" icons generally indicate that a picture accompanies the description.

- *"Star" symbols.*   Stars are frequently used to represent seller and bidder ratings.

- *"New user" symbols.*   Some sites flag new sellers or bidders for a set period of time (such as 30 days—after 30 days, the icon is automatically removed from the username).

- *"Gallery" symbols.*   eBay uses a picture frame graphic to indicate that an auction item also appears in eBay's photo gallery, an all-picture listing of auction items, organized by category.

- *"Lock" symbol.*   Auctions.com uses a "lock" icon to signify an insured seller. Other auction sites are planning verified user programs. For example, eBay is planning to start a Verified eBay User program, in which members will be authenticated and cleared by a third-party security company.

- *"Me" symbol.*   Any eBay user (seller or bidder) can create an eBay personal information page. You can then click on a "me" icon displayed next the username to open the user's eBay personal page.

- *"Holiday" symbols.*   Many sites offer a selection of icons to liven up listings and draw attention to items appropriate for specific holidays and events. Again, the seller pays a small fee to display this type of eye-catching symbol.

Icons provide visual cues that you'll quickly (and probably subconsciously) come to rely on. If you don't know what an icon represents, visit an online auction site's Help or FAQ pages to find an explanation.

THE DESCRIPTION—WHAT IT'S ALL ABOUT

After you scan an auction listing's header information, you're ready to dive into the description area. Most auction listing descriptions consist of text and photographs. See Figure 4.2 for an example. You'll want to review each component carefully before deciding whether to bid.

FIGURE 4.2

The description area in an Amazon auction listing.

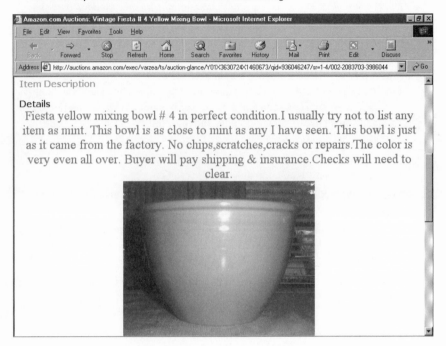

Reading Between the Lines

As you meander around online auctions, you'll find that description styles vary dramatically. Some sellers present long soliloquies describing their products, while others barely label the items. The most successful online auction sellers describe auction items both succinctly and clearly, highlighting notable points, and pointing out flaws and damage in "gentle" terms. Sellers and buyers both benefit from honest descriptions. Buyers want to get what they pay for, and sellers want to earn good feedback to create a successful online auction presence. As we'll discuss in future chapters, earning positive ratings from buyers is key to becoming a successful online auction entrepreneur.

While it's in the seller's best interest to describe items as honestly as possible, this doesn't always occur, and sellers don't need to be overly blatant about flaws. Furthermore, a seller's interpretation of a phrase or term may vary dramatically from your interpretation. Finally, some sellers genuinely don't have a way with words, or they don't feel an in-depth description is necessary. Therefore, the key to your online auction happiness is to learn how to work with what's presented.

First and foremost, read descriptions slowly and carefully. Stop every few words and ask yourself what a phrase or sentence means or what it *could* mean. Think about how descriptive words can be interpreted (or misinterpreted). For example, numerous online auction sellers label their goods as *vintage, retro,* or *shabby chic,* when in reality the items are simply old and worn out! Also, be wary of inaccurate or deceptive descriptions. If a description is too short or blatantly wrong, it could mean that the seller is unknowledgeable about the item or possibly trying to hide details. Finally, be cautious when viewing descriptions that are marred by numerous punctuation and spelling errors. You're taking an unnecessary risk when you do business with people who are sloppy and unorganized.

While you're perusing an item's description, pay attention to the shipping and handling costs included in the description area and ensure that the rates are reasonable. There are many online resources you can use to check shipping costs. (These are discussed in Chapter 7.) Further, if the seller lists unrealistic shipping terms, such as requiring that payment is received within five days, pass on the auction. You don't want to be held responsible for the slow U.S. Postal Service, be forced to spend extra for delivery, or risk unjustified negative comments on your bidder's profile.

A third way to ensure that you completely understand sellers' ads is to pick up on as much online auction lingo as possible while reviewing auction ads. As your auction experience grows, you'll notice that many sellers and bidders tend to use acronyms freely. Not only will you see common acronyms across the online auctions board, but you'll also probably notice some category-specific acronyms while you perform topical searches. To help get your acronym acumen up to speed, here are a few online auction abbreviations that you may run into:

DOA	Damaged On Arrival
FB	Feedback
HTF	Hard To Find
MIB	Mint In Box
MO	Money Order
MOC	Mint On Card
MOMC	Mint On Mint Card
NIB	New In Box
NRMINT	Near Mint
NR	No Reserve
NWB	New With Box
NWT	New With Tag(s)
OOP	Out Of Print
PC	Piece
PIC	Picture

PR	Pair
S/H	Shipping and Handling
SZ	Size
VHTF	Very Hard To Find
V/MC	Visa and MasterCard

There are many more acronyms embedded in online auction listings, but you'll have to add those to your arsenal on your own as you gain auctioning experience. The preceding list is just a sampler.

Finally, after critically reading a description, you're ready to get answers to your questions. Please note: If you do have any questions, *don't blow them off and bid on a whim!* Most online auction transactions do not come with a warranty. In other words, online auctions present the ultimate state of caveat emptor! It's *your* responsibility to become as informed as possible before bidding on auction items. If a seller states that an item is "slightly discolored" or has a "small crack on one side" or "needs to be cleaned" and leaves it at that, your job is to find out exactly what those statements mean. Fortunately, you can usually get answers by employing one of the following:

- Email
- Telephone
- Web pages

Emailing Before Bidding

The best way by far to gather additional information about an online auction item is to send an email message to the seller. Most online auctions provide seller information; at the very least, an auction site should provide each seller's email address. Usually you can click a link in an auction ad's header section to open an email message form preaddressed to the seller. (Yahoo! even provides a Question & Answer forum for each auction, as shown in Figure 4.3). *If an auction site does not provide some way for you to contact the seller, seriously consider using another site.* Having the ability to contact sellers is imperative to smart bidding. There are numerous instances when you might have questions for a seller. For example, you might want to:

- Request detailed shipping terms, if they aren't stated in the description or header (plus, sometimes you can get a shipping discount if you win more than one of a seller's auctions).
- Clarify whether a product is a particular brand or style.
- Find out if an item is new or used.
- Attempt to determine a reserve price.
- Gather more information regarding a flaw mentioned in the description.

You can click the Question & Answer link on a Yahoo! auction ad to view and post questions and answers about an auction item.

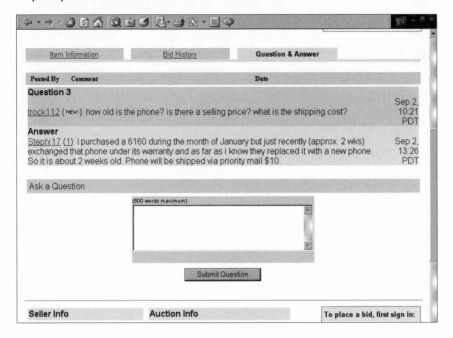

- Determine the size of a particular item.
- Verify whether an item works properly.
- Obtain further evidence of authenticity.

You get the idea. The main point here is that if you have a question, you need to contact the seller BEFORE YOU BID. Email, email, email!

Remember, you are in charge of getting the facts about items *before* you buy them. The old adage stands steadfast and true when it comes to researching auction items: There's no such thing as a dumb question. So fire off those emails, and get answers before you start bidding.

Calling All (or at Least Some) Sellers

While emailing should be your first method of questioning a seller, you can also call if a phone number is in the description. Sometimes (especially if the seller is also a streetside merchant or vendor) calling can expedite your quest for answers, and at times speed is of the essence in the online auctioning world. Receiving quick feed-

Everyone knows that 900 numbers are expensive phone numbers to call, but did you know that 809 (Caribbean) numbers are also being used to rack up your phone bill? Before you call a seller, be sure to check the area code to ensure that it matches the seller's listed location. Many online directories, such as Yahoo! (**www.yahoo.com**), Dogpile (**www. dogpile.com**), and other White/Yellow Page directories provide area code location services. You can also do a quick hard copy check in your phone book.

back comes in especially handy when an auction is going to close within the next hour or two. If you've emailed the seller but haven't received a response, it's time to activate Plan B—call the seller. Use common sense and simple courtesy when calling sellers. Don't provide personal information over the phone, and remember, if it's long distance, you're footing the bill.

Web Watching

A third way to gain further insight into an auction listing is to visit any seller's Web page addresses that may be listed in an auction listing. Frequently, sellers have business Web sites or they have created personal pages by using the auction site's Web page creation features (such as eBay's "me" function, which enables users to quickly and easily create Web pages). Sellers' Web pages can be business, personal, or a combination of both, and all three styles can provide useful background information. For example, before my friend bid on an autographed Neil Gaiman book, she clicked the seller's Web address link and learned that the seller was a bookstore in San Francisco. Furthermore, the bookstore's Web site advertised a number of upcoming author signings and events, which easily added to the auction listing's credibility. As you can imagine, when a seller lists a link to a business Web page—such as a music shop, bookstore, or clothing boutique—your successful-transaction quotient increases, especially if you verify the business via other means (Better Business Bureau, business directories, and so forth). After all, if the seller owns a business, you can easily check the legitimacy of the company's phone number and address, and you'll know where to find the business if communication breaks down after the sale (more about those topics follows in Chapters 8 and 9). In sum—visit seller Web sites before you bid. You'll be rewarded with information that will either bolster your prospects for success, or reconfirm your gut feeling that a transaction isn't for you.

At this point, we've theoretically perused the header, read some descriptive text, pondered the facts and claims, contacted the seller, and visited any linked Web pages. Now we're ready to talk about descriptive graphics. Most online auction listings are accompanied by illustrations, and such graphics play at least as big a role in auction sales as descriptive text.

Scanning for Visual Appeal

For the most part, auction listings with graphics present an advantage over those without photographs. Granted, there are some instances when a figure is unnecessary (do you *really* need to see a 600MHz Intel processor box?), but the majority of commodities are more salable when the listing is accompanied by a picture. Aside from other benefits, a photograph provides a modicum of assurance that the item actually exists.

Not surprisingly, the number-one benefit of pictures is that they can help you to avoid buyer's remorse. For example, let's say that a seller offers an item described as a "multicolored oriental rug." You can bet your next auction dollar that everyone who reads that description will picture an individualized version of that floor decor and that none of those versions will match the actual item. A picture can be the factor determining whether you want to bid on such an item. Some auction sites, such as eBay and Yahoo!, go so far as to provide all-picture listings. To see categorical groups of pictures in eBay, click on eBay's Gallery link; to view all-picture listings in a Yahoo! category, click on the Show Only Photos link within a category or search list. In both cases, you can click on a smallish thumbnail picture to access the auction item's listing.

TIP

Make sure a photo is a genuine photo and not the manufacturer's photo. A photograph should complement a description, not advertise a merchant's product line.

Now, before you go picture window shopping, remember to view photographs with the same critical eye that you use when you read item descriptions. Ask yourself questions as you view graphics, such as:

- Do the colors in the photograph match the colors listed in the description?
- Does there appear to be any damage that isn't listed in the description?
- Is the size clearly represented? For example, jewelry pictures often include an everyday item, such as a coin, within the picture to give viewers an idea of the size of the jewelry.

As with written text, if you have any questions regarding a picture, email the seller before you bid. We can't overstress that emailing questions to sellers before you bid is a perfectly acceptable and commonplace activity in the online auction world.

BIDDING AREA—GETTING DOWN TO BUSINESS

At the bottom of most online auction listings, you'll find the bidding area. Of course, you don't need to proceed to the bidding area until after you've studied the header and description areas and have received feedback from the seller answering your queries. Only proceed to the bidding area when you're comfortable that the item suits your preferences and falls within your price range. At this point, though, you are not ready to place a bid—you still need to evaluate the seller and determine your bidding tactic (as described in Chapters 5 and 6). But the bidding area is part of an auction listing, so it is mentioned in this chapter. Figure 4.4 displays the bidding area of auction listings on eBay.

As you can see in Figure 4.4, the bidding area mainly consists of a text box and a submit button. The act of bidding is simple—you enter a dollar amount, and you click "Bid Now" or "Review Bid" or other appropriately named submit button, depending on

FIGURE 4.4

The bidding area on an eBay auction listing.

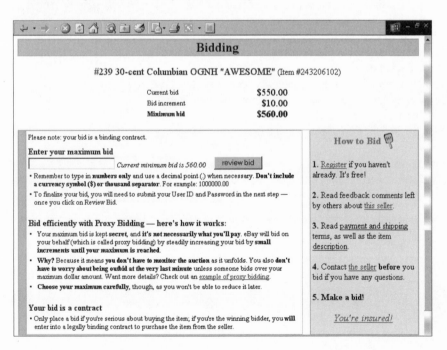

the site. Before you start bidding, ensure that you read the online auction's fine print (at least once!). On an eBay auction listing, the fine print appears on the listing page; on Amazon, you must click the "How Bidding Works" link to review Amazon's bidding policies. In any case, be sure to read the rules and regulations of any online auction site before you bid. While the temptation is great to bid at this moment, keep that mouse in check for a short while longer. In the next chapter, we'll check out sellers to make sure they're on the up-and-up. And then, in the following chapter, we'll cover bidding tips and tricks—*then* you'll be fully equipped to get in on the online auction action.

KEY POINTS

In this chapter, we started at the top of an auction listing and worked our way down. The key points in this chapter entail interpreting auction listings to the best of your ability with the resources available to you. To interpret an ad:

- Review header information.
- Critically read the descriptive text.
- Eye graphics closely.
- Compare graphics with descriptions.
- Contact sellers in search of clarification.
- Visit sellers' Web sites for additional background information.
- Read the fine print regarding bidding policies.

5

CHAPTER

EVALUATING A SELLER

ESTABLISHING YOUR MINDSET

It may seem slightly odd to start a chapter about evaluating sellers by talking about your psyche, but as you'll soon see, it makes sense. After all, as a buyer, you're basically in control when it comes to online auctions—you *choose* to participate. So, before you start bidding, sit back, do a little thinking, and make educated choices. In other words, establish a mindset that will enable you to avoid the bad habit of blindly bidding.

Online auctions provide an amazing selection of collectibles, hard-to-find items, and good deals. With all this at people's fingertips, it's no wonder that online auctions are a Mecca for impulse shoppers. You'll run across attractive items you never knew existed and enticing collectibles that you didn't even really want until they popped up on your screen. But it's a pretty safe bet that you don't *have* to have that cool cast-iron-cauldron-being-held-by-a-skeleton candleholder for Halloween—sure, it would be nice or make a perfect gift, but it might not be worth an unnecessary monetary risk. Therefore, before you bid, solidly ground your mindset. Stay rational. Do not let yourself get swept up by the action. Consciously decide that you'll only bid on an item after making a methodical choice—not yielding to a gut reaction. One of your overriding tasks as an informed online auction bidder is to rein in your impulse-buying DNA and critically evaluate an auction listing. And after checking out the auction site's risk level and the auction ad's details, the next fundamental step is to evaluate the auction ad's seller. There are a number of tactics you can use to evaluate sellers—and that's what this chapter is all about.

Your number-one resource for obtaining seller information is the seller's feed-back and ratings profile. Any reputable person-to-person auction site provides a seller and buyer feedback forum. We recommend avoiding any online auction site that doesn't offer a feedback feature. Additional ways for evaluating sellers include reviewing sell-ers' other auctions; knowing about verified user programs; visiting sellers' Web sites; and using other Web resources, such as the Better Business Bureau Web site, to check up on businesses and individuals. So, set your mind to click information-gathering links before you buy, and take a look at some ways you can profile sellers.

PROFILING A SELLER

An effective way to get a sense of the legitimacy of a possible transaction is to con-duct an auction background check on the seller. Most online auction sites provide a feedback and rating method to enable the auction community members to monitor each other. Generally, this rating scheme enables users to rank the sellers or bidders and add short comments regarding the sellers, bidders, and/or transactions. While the overall setup of ratings might seem a little subjective on the surface, the system is more effective than you might imagine, especially in online auctions that strive to generate a community feel, such as eBay, Yahoo!, and Amazon.

Positives and Negatives

Viewing a seller's feedback is as easy as clicking a link on an auction ad's page. The particular link that you click depends on the auction site you're visiting. For illustra-tive purposes, let's look at a couple feedback and ratings pages.

Viewing User Profiles

To see a seller's rating on Amazon, you can either click the seller's name on the auc-tion ad's page or click the seller's star rating. Figure 5.1 shows a typical feedback page for an Amazon auction member.

Note that the Amazon site enables members to specify a star rating (from one through five stars) as well as enter a short comment. For each transaction that you participate in, you can rate the seller (or the bidder, if you're a seller) from a not-so-hot single star to a nice-transaction five-star ranking. Notice that we said "for each transaction." You can only grant stars to an Amazon auction member if you're involved in a transaction with that member. The number of stars appearing next to a member's name represents an average of transaction stars the member has earned. The number in parenthesis after the star rating represents the number of people who have rated and commented on the Amazon auction member.

On eBay and Yahoo!, the feedback systems work a tad differently. On these sites, users can give other users positive, neutral, or negative ratings in addition to providing short comments. The number in parenthesis after a username represents a

FIGURE 5.1

A typical auction member's feedback and rating page on Amazon.

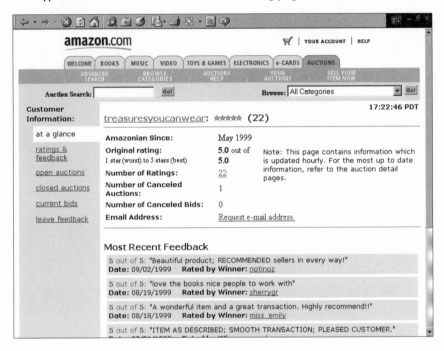

cumulative net score based on positive, negative, and neutral reviews. The number is tallied as follows:

- Positive (or Good) votes add one point (+1) to the auction member's rating.

- Negative (or Bad) votes subtract one point (−1) from the auction member's rating.

- Neutral votes neither add nor subtract a point. (Both positive and negative votes can be converted to a neutral vote if the person who provided the rating unregisters from the auction community.)

Leaving feedback on Yahoo! is similar to Amazon in that you can only leave feedback for transaction partners. Therefore, only sellers and winning bidders can leave feedback. To view a summary of a seller's feedback on Yahoo!, simply click the number that appears in the parenthesis following the seller's name on an auction ad. Yahoo!'s feedback summary looks similar to Figure 5.2.

Notice the sun and rain cloud icons in Figure 5.2, on the Yahoo! feedback page. You can click either icon, to display only positive reviews or only negative reviews.

FIGURE 5.2

A typical auction member's feedback and rating page on Yahoo!

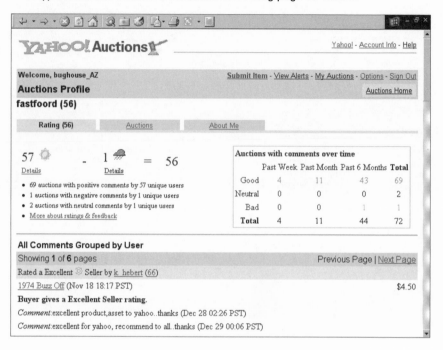

TURN TO THE ADVANCED SEARCH FORM

If you can't figure out which link to click in an auction ad to view a seller's feedback profile, you can always take note of the seller's user name and then turn to the auction site's advanced search form. Generally, advanced search forms enable you to search by an auction member's username.

On eBay, anyone can leave a comment about any other member, but there are some limitations. The most noteworthy limitation is that negative comments can only be left by the winning high bidder in an auction. Also, if a negative comment is not about an eBay transaction, it is not counted as a negative point on the overall rating score. Furthermore, while users can leave multiple comments in a member's feedback profile, any single member's feedback can only be counted once (regardless of the number of comments), thereby only adding 1 point to the overall rating total. This ensures that no one person can "tip the scales" in either (positive or negative) feedback direction.

Viewing a summary report of a seller's feedback on eBay is similar to viewing a report on Yahoo!—simply click the number that appears in the parenthesis following the seller's name.

At this point, you might be wondering what the stars on eBay feedback pages mean. The stars (which appear in various colors) next to user names indicate the number of positive feedback comments a user has obtained. Stars are like milestones. Each color signifies that a particular level has been achieved:

- *Yellow.*   Represents 10 to 99 positive comment points.
- *Turquoise.*   Represents 100 to 499 positive comment points.
- *Purple.*   Represents 500 to 999 positive comment points.
- *Red.*   Represents 1,000 to 9,999 positive comment points.
- *Shooting Star.*   Represents 10,000+ positive comment points. (In January 2000, eBay reported that parrothead88 became the first member to ever receive the shooting star.)

EBAY NEGATIVES

Viewing all of the negative feedback for an eBay community member is a little trickier than clicking Yahoo!'s rain cloud icon, but you can find negative feedback with a little ingenuity. The key is to display all of a user's comments on a single Web page, and then search for the word "complaint" using your browser's "Find On This Page" feature. The ingenuity comes into play when you're faced with listing all of the feedback on one page. By default, eBay breaks feedback into 25 comments per page. To show all of a seller's comments on one page, display the feedback page for the seller (click on the seller's rating number); click at the end of the Web address in your browser's address bar; type &page=1&items=all, then press Enter. If the user has hundreds (or thousands) of comments, you might have to twiddle your thumbs (or play some FreeCell) for a minute while all the information compiles onto a single page.

After briefly looking at a few samples of user feedback pages, you might be starting to understand how feedback can help you formulate an opinion about a particular seller. (We'll talk more about leaving feedback and reviewing your profiles in later chapters.) Let's look more specifically at how feedback profiles can assist you in determining whether to place a bid on an auction item.

Interpreting Profiles from a Buyer's Perspective

When you check a user's feedback profile, it feels a little bit like you're reading someone else's email. But never fear—the feeling quickly wears off, and soon you'll flash a user's profile page, scan for the information you need, and move on.

The key to using feedback profiles is multilayered. Namely, you want to discover the following:

- The total number of comments in the feedback profile.
- The positive-to-negative ratio of feedback responses.

- The number of positive comments associated with a transaction. (Most auction sites only enable you to comment if you participated in a transaction, but, on eBay, transaction-based comments are usually accompanied by the transaction number.)
- The seller's responses to negative comments.

The auction sites provide the tools for reviewing sellers' profiles—it's up to you to interpret the data. Interpreting the data is as simple as using common sense. If a seller has 6 positives and 6 negatives for a total profile score of 0, you should probably pass on the auction. On the other hand, if a seller has 100+ positive comments, and 5 negatives that are addressed by the seller with reasonable explanations, your odds are much more favorable.

Carding a Seller

Another way to pick up some quick information about a seller is to "card" the seller (i.e., check the seller's membership ID and find how long that person has been a member and whether he or she has changed IDs recently). The longer a seller has been participating in an online auction community, the higher your chances are that the seller is an auction site asset. Of course, keep in mind that length of membership doesn't hold a candle to a spotty feedback profile. Furthermore, if a seller has multiple IDs, you can run a feedback profile check on the other IDs for additional user information.

Here's how to card a seller on the big-three auction sites:

- *Amazon.*   Click the seller's username to display the member's ratings and feedback page. On Amazon, you can discover multiple nicknames and length of membership.

- *eBay.*   Click the seller's ID, enter your ID and password, and click Submit. You'll see the user's email address, ID history, and length of membership.

- *Yahoo!*   Click the seller's ID, and then click on the About Me link on the Auctions Profile page.

After you've gathered all you can from a seller's feedback profile, you're ready to move on to other research tactics.

SCANNING OTHER AUCTIONS

Another way to eyeball a seller is to check the seller's other active auctions. This is very easy. Auction ads usually include a link to the seller's other auctions. Click the link, and the auction titles unfold before your very eyes (okay—so it's not that dramatic!). If the seller's Other Auctions link isn't handy, bring up the handy-dandy advanced search page, and plug in the seller's ID.

Checking a seller's other auctions can lead to all sorts of pleasant surprises. You might be astounded at the number of auctions a seller is running, or you might discover that the seller specializes in a particular area—thereby possibly upping their reputation regarding the item you're considering. After all, wouldn't you feel more comfortable purchasing an antique rocking chair from a seller who deals mostly in antiques rather than specializing in Nintendo 64 games? Furthermore, if you like one item offered by a seller, there's a good chance you'll be attracted to other items that seller has on the auction block. Maybe, you'll even like the newly discovered item more (yep—auction shopping is most definitely fickle like that).

Other auctions to scan are auctions that offer similar items. You can search through current auctions as well as closed auctions (if the site enables you to search closed auctions—not all sites offer this feature yet). In this research phase, you don't need to limit yourself to a single auction site, either. Do a quick search on a couple of sites to see what you can find. In one instance, my friend Jake found similar items on eBay and Up4Sale, and both items were listed by the same person (the seller used the same user ID on both sites). The eBay feedback was impressive, but the Up4Sale feedback was a little anemic. Because Jake knew about the eBay information, he felt comfortable bidding in the Up4Sale auction. In the end, Jake won both auctions, and, through email communication, he got the seller to agree to ship the items together to eliminate one auction's shipping charges. If you ask me (or Jake, for that matter), it all worked out very nicely.

Another benefit of scanning a seller's active auctions is that you might find that the seller is running multiple auctions for similar items (such as my favorite printer toner seller mentioned in Chapter 2). Then, if bidding on one auction gets out of control, you can steer toward calmer bidding waters.

Finally, a benefit of scanning closed auctions is that you can see recent winning bids on similar items. This information may or may not come into play when it's your time to bid, but every byte of data helps. Besides, knowing the recent winning bid prices of comparable items might help you to avoid overbidding if the current auction's bids start to soar. (As we'll discuss in Chapter 6, when bids soar—bail! You'll have other chances down the road, and the exorbitant bidder(s) most likely won't be there the next time you start to bid.)

ACCESSING VERIFIED USER PROGRAMS

In a continuing effort to improve online auctions and the auction community atmosphere, auction sites are beginning to host block parties. Okay, not really. But they *are* starting to offer voluntary verified user programs. The verified user program concept is very straightforward. The premise is that online auction users supply additional, verifiable information, such as a Social Security number, driver's license number, phone number, and date of birth, to a specified security source. The security company verifies the information and "approves" qualified users. Approved users are then flagged as verified auction community members. Auctions.com was one of the first online auction sites to take advantage of verified users through its BidSafe program. eBay is following suit with its Verified User Program. To find out more about verified user programs, search the Help pages on online auction sites. Recognizing verified users can help you to determine whether you're willing to work with a particular seller (or buyer, for that matter).

LEAVING THE AUCTION FOR FURTHER INFORMATION

Finally, if you really want to go the extra step to check out a seller, you can temporarily minimize the auction ad page on your taskbar and visit other relevant Web sites. Namely, you can visit the seller's Web site(s) or personal pages associated with the online auction site (such as eBay's "About Me" sites). If the seller is associated with a business, check out the business as well. If you really get the Inspector Clouseau itch, you can visit the Better Business Bureau Web site or other consumer service Web site to check out the business. If a seller has related Web page links for you to visit, the auction ad will usually lead the way. If a link is offered, take a moment or two to peruse the site. When you visit related Web pages, though, remember to view the site with your critical auction eye—the same eye you use to judge auction ads. Not to sound overly pessimistic, but slick Web pages are a dime a dozen these days. Just because a Web page looks cool doesn't automatically mean that the sponsor is legit.

That about wraps it up for researching sellers. As you can see, it's not too difficult for you to find seller information. It's mostly a matter of clicking a few links and reviewing information before placing your bid. The added bonus is that knowing about a seller isn't your only safeguard. As you'll see in the next several chapters, there are a number of ways to keep your online auction experiences pleasant and safe.

KEY POINTS

Online auction success requires that you know what you're getting and who you're getting it from. In this chapter, we reviewed ways that you can add some substance to an online auction seller's identity. Knowing about a seller can help you to minimize your risk and bid with more confidence. In summary, when you're researching sellers, you should:

- Establish your mindset, and stay in control.
- Check seller profiles.
- Review positive and negative feedback ratings and comments.
- Uncover sellers' length of membership and ID backgrounds within an auction community.
- View sellers' other auctions.
- Look at similar auctions, both active and closed (if possible).
- Keep informed of auction sites' verified user programs.
- Pull up sellers' related Web pages.
- Use Web resources to verify businesses' legitimacy.

6

CHAPTER

BIDDING TIPS AND TRICKS

STARTING THE BIDDING PROCESS

Before you place a bid, you need to come up with a price you're willing to pay. With online auctions, you need to consider a number of factors when determining a price. Therefore, this chapter presents various pricing considerations to keep in mind, including shipping and payment fees. In addition to getting the shipping and payment details pinned down, this chapter discusses more directly related bidding topics, such as site policies, maximum bids, bidding to win, and tracking your auction activity.

SHIPPING STARTS BEFORE BIDDING

"Oh no!" you say, "Are they going to talk about shipping in *every* chapter?" Well, probably—but we won't go shipping crazy in this chapter (the detailed shipping explanations show up later in the selling chapters). There's no way around it, though—when you're working the online auction strip, shipping is a major topic for sellers and buyers. Understandably, as a buyer, your role in shipping is much more simplistic than the seller's role. Your main job (as a buyer) is to *understand the basics* about shipping, including shipping options, costs, and negotiations. With shipping knowledge firmly in hand, you can then more accurately formulate your bidding strategy. Therefore, let's look at some key shipping topics from a buyer's perspective.

Shipping Options

As we've all heard, there's more than one way to skin a cat—and this holds true for shipping. As a buyer, you need to know a seller's shipping preference, because the buyer almost always pays the shipping fees. Therefore, it's time to brush up on some shipping basics before you become a bidder.

Basically, sellers opt to ship packages via the following methods:

- U.S. Postal Service (USPS)
- United Parcel Service (UPS)
- Federal Express (FedEx)
- Airborne Express

By far the most popular shipping method among online auction sellers is USPS Priority Mail, which starts at $3.20 for packages weighing up to 2 pounds, plus an optional $.85 for insurance. Keep this weight and amount in mind. For most small items, you should pay no more than $4.00 (without insurance) for USPS Priority Mail shipping. The $4.00 amount is acceptable in cases where the seller has to purchase certain packaging supplies, such as packing peanuts or bubble wrap (keep in mind that boxes are usually supplied for free by shipping companies). On the other hand, if a seller is using USPS priority mail and charging $6.00 for a less-than-two-pound item, you should check with the seller to learn why the shipping fee is so high.

For more-detailed information about shipping companies and charges along with international considerations, see Chapters 21 and 22 in this book's selling section. As mentioned earlier, buyers need to be aware of shipping charges—mainly to determine whether the rates are reasonable and to be able take the shipping expense into consideration when placing a bid. You can easily figure out shipping rates, including mailing insurance costs (insurance is usually the buyer's option as well as the buyer's expense), by using online shipping calculators, as described in the next section.

Shipping Rates

As phone directories gather dust, the Internet continues to grow as a valuable research tool and reference guide. In the online auction world, you can use some of its resources before you bid. During your Net travels, you might have noticed that the Internet offers all sorts of calculators, including mortgage calculators, interest rate calculators, college expense calculators, life-expectancy calculators, compatibility calculators, and, most directly related to this chapter, shipping calculators. With the advent of shipping calculators, there's no excuse for blindly assuming that a seller's shipping rate is a fair rate. As with all other auction ad elements, shipping rates are "guilty until proven innocent"—it's in your own best interest to prove the facts.

You can check shipping rates using your ZIP code, the seller's ZIP code, and the item's weight. Most auction sites list each seller's location, and tracking a ZIP code can be as easy as using an online ZIP code finder. To find a ZIP code, go straight to the source by visiting the U.S. Postal Service's ZIP code finder at **www.usps.gov/ ncsc/lookups/lookups.htm**. If the auction ad doesn't list the item's weight, estimate the weight from similar auction ads or merchant sites. Also, if the seller seems reliable, you can email the seller to get a weight estimate.

After you've gathered your shipping facts, you're ready to plug the numbers into a shipping calculator. There are several shipping calculators on the Internet, including:

- *FedEx Shipping Calculator.* **www.fedex.com/us/rates**
- *iShip.com.* **www.iship.com**
- *UPS Shipping Calculator.* **www.ups.com/using/services/rave/rate.html**
- *USPS Shipping Calculator.* **www.usps.gov/business/calcs.htm**

In our opinion, iShip.com's service is the most useful of the preceding four calculators. iShip.com simultaneously shows shipping rates for USPS, UPS, FedEx, and Airborne in a printable table, as shown in Figure 6.1.

FIGURE 6.1

Reviewing an iShip.com shipping table.

Checking shipping rates takes only a minute, and, after a while, you'll get a feel for shipping rates that "look" reasonable. If there's ever a question regarding the shipping amount charged by a seller, email the seller and ask for an explanation. If the explanation seems weak, consider skipping the auction, or lower your projected maximum bid price to compensate for the extra shipping fees. (The art of generating a maximum bid price is described later in this chapter.)

So far, all of the shipping information in this chapter has been pretty cut and dried. But true to online auctions' form, shipping fees are frequently up for negotiation as well.

Cutting Deals with Sellers

Bargaining for better shipping deals? It's not as outlandish as it sounds. You have a number of shipping bargaining chips at your mouse-clicking fingertips. One of the most rampant shipping deals around is the multiple auction shipment. (As you may recall, we touched on this briefly in Chapter 5.) If you bid on multiple auctions offered by a seller and win the auctions, you can usually email the seller to try to get a shipping discount. In fact, if there's time, the best plan is to email the seller about shipping discounts *before* you bid. Combining auction items into one package works to the benefit of both the seller and buyer. The seller only has to pack one box, and the buyer only has to pay one shipping fee. As you may recall, Jake (our friend mentioned in Chapter 5) saved on shipping fees by bidding from the same seller on two sites (eBay and Up4Sale). Another friend of ours, Cale (the Hot Wheels collector), makes a habit of checking sellers' other auctions to try to create multiple-bid-single-shipping-charge opportunities. He often saves a few bucks this way as well as happily receives boxes containing four or more collectible Hot Wheels at a time.

Finally, when it comes to negotiating, keep in mind that auctions are literally turning into online communities, and paying shipping fees isn't a mechanical process like adding the shipping charge when ordering from the Sears catalog. Sellers aren't machine heads—they're real live people. If you treat sellers with respect and good humor, your efforts will almost always be rewarded. If nothing else, you'll eventually receive glowing feedback after the transaction completes. You never can tell where friendliness will take you. A good case in point involves another friend of ours, Jeff (one nice thing about writing an online auctions book is that it's really easy to get your friends, coworkers, and family members involved in the research!). Jeff won an auction, and when he emailed the seller, he mentioned that he lived in Arizona. After a friendly exchange of emails, the seller volunteered that if Jeff would send a postcard with an Arizona scene on it, the shipping price would be discounted. So, when Jeff went to the grocery store to pick up a money order to pay for the item, he also bought a postcard showing Arizona's Superstition Mountains. Then, he sent the postcard with his payment. Not only did Jeff save some money on shipping fees, he made the transaction an enjoyable experience all around.

At this point, we're going to assume that you've checked out the auction site, auction ad, seller, and shipping terms. You're just about ready to start the bidding process. But first, we should quickly review auction sites' bidding policies and procedures.

REVIEWING POLICIES AND PROCEDURES

When most people think about bidding in an online auction, they imagine an *English* auction. In other words, they imagine that an auction item goes to the highest bidder as of the auction listing's closing time. Well, most auction sites offer this type of auction, but there are some bidding variations, and you need to know what's up before you put your bid down. So, before you start to think about how much you want to spend for that vintage "Kramer" shirt (you know—one of those cool vintage shirts Kramer would wear on *Seinfeld*), read the following summaries about three typical auction bidding features: *proxy bidding, Dutch auctions,* and *reserve auctions.*

Proxy Bidding

Ahhh, *proxy bidding.* Most auction sites use it (but not *all* sites, so, at the risk of sounding redundant, we advise you to read the auction site's fine print), and most bidders are more than happy to take advantage of it. Proxy bidding means that an online auction holds your maximum bid in confidence and posts only as much of your maximum bid amount as is necessary for you to maintain the highest bid position.

For example, let's say that a *Star Wars* fanatic finds an original *Star Wars* Boba Fett figure. The buyer is willing to pay up to $25 for it, but the current bid price is only $10.50. At this point, the buyer has two options. The buyer can bid $11 and tediously sit at the computer, continuously refreshing the auction ad page, and outbidding each new bid that appears for the item (now, that sounds practical!). Or, the bidder can place a proxy bid. Luckily, proxy bidding provides a better way to bid. With proxy bidding, an auction site ups a buyer's visible bid to counter other buyers' bids as they occur. If the price rises above the buyer's maximum bid, the auction site stops placing proxy bids for the buyer and the buyer's out of the running unless he or she places a new bid. After placing a maximum proxy bid, the bidder doesn't have to be anywhere near the auction site for the automatic bidding to take place. In fact, the bidder's computer doesn't even have to be on.

To summarize, the process of proxy bidding is as follows:

1. You confidentially place a maximum bid.

2. You note the auction's closing time and surf to other waters or log off.

3. The auction site engages in bidding wars, if necessary, with other proxy bidders and a few live bidders, while you continue on with your life.

4. After the auction ends, you check back with the auction site to see how your proxy bid held up. If other bidders outbid your predetermined maximum, you don't win your item. But if your proxy bid is the highest bid, you're the winner—and the final price might even be less than your maximum bid.

As you can see, the proxy bidding system is a helpful feature that simplifies bidding. Be careful, though; not all online auction sites use proxy bidding, although the big three (Amazon, Yahoo!, and eBay) use proxy bidding, along with automatic notification when you've been outbid. As you'll see later in this chapter, proxy bidding is a helpful tool, but it doesn't replace artful bidding.

Dutch Auctions

In addition to English auctions with and without proxy bidding, you will find *Dutch* auctions on many online auction sites. Dutch auctions are for those who are selling or buying two or more identical items. You can recognize a Dutch auction immediately when you look at an auction ad's header information; the quantity number will be a number other than 1.

Sellers start a Dutch auction by listing a minimum price (also called a starting bid) and the number of items for sale. Then, when buyers bid, they must specify a price along with the quantity they want to buy. The winning bidders are those who bid the highest price, but with a twist. Only the top bidders whose quantity numbers add up to equal the total number of items available will win the auction, and all of the winning bidders pay the lowest price posted among highest bidders. Furthermore, among the winning bidders, larger quantity bids beat out smaller quantity bids at the same price. Sounds a bit confusing; so here's an example.

I just ran a quick search on eBay using the term *dutch*. I found that one seller is running a Dutch auction for three Munster Family Squeaky Doll sets at a starting price of $10 each. The actual auction doesn't close for a couple days, but we can use this setup for an example. Let's say that four buyers bid $10 per set—first Chris, then Matt, then Pat, and finally Mark. Each buyer only bids on one set. The first three buyers (Chris, Matt, and Pat) would each win a Munster Family for $10. (Remember, there are only three Munster Families up for auction.) Mark, the fourth bidder who bid later than the first three buyers, would not win a Munster Family (see Table 6.1).

TABLE 6.1

The Opening Bids for the Munster Family Dutch Auction

Bidder	Time	Bid Amount	Quantity	Winning Status
Chris	1:00 P.M.	$10	1	Wins one Munster Family for $10
Matt	2:00 P.M.	$10	1	Wins one Munster Family for $10
Pat	3:00 P.M.	$10	1	Wins one Munster Family for $10
Mark	4:00 P.M.	$10	1	Does not win

Now, let's say that Mark, the fourth bidder, bids $15 instead of $10. Because Mark bid higher than the others, Mark will jump to the top of the winning bidders list and will receive a Munster family set for $10 (which is still the lowest winning bid for the three sets). As bidding increases, the users with lower bids will systematically be bumped off (as shown in Table 6.2). So, as you can see, posting a bid higher than the lowest bid can increase your chances of winning a Dutch auction, but it also increases the risk of raising the winning bid price for all winning bidders.

Now, let's say that a bidder bids for more than one Munster Family. What happens? Well, the bidders toward the end of the list will be bumped off. Remember, in the case of a tie bid amount, the person who posted a bid first wins. For example, let's say a fifth bidder, named Dave, swoops in and bids for two Munster Families at $20 per set. The results (see Table 6.3) would be as follows:

- Dave, the $20 bidder, receives two Munster Family sets for $15 apiece.
- Mark, who bid $15, receives one Munster Family set for $15.
- Chris, Matt, and Pat, who all bid $10, win nothing.

Tables 6.1 through 6.3 show the progress of the Munster Family Dutch auction. You can quickly figure out who wins and who loses by starting from the top of the Quantity column and moving down the list, adding the quantity bid numbers up to three.

TABLE 6.2

The Munster Family Dutch Auction, After Mark Bids an Amount Higher than the Starting Price

Bidder	Time	Bid Amount	Quantity	Winning Status
Mark	4:00 P.M.	$15	1	Wins one Munster Family for $10
Chris	1:00 P.M.	$10	1	Wins one Munster Family for $10
Matt	2:00 P.M.	$10	1	Wins one Munster Family for $10
Pat	3:00 P.M.	$10	1	Does not win

T A B L E 6.3

Final Munster Family Dutch Auction Results, After Dave Bids a Higher Price for Multiple Munster Family Sets

Bidder	Amount	Quantity	Winning Status
Dave	$20	2	Wins two Munster Families for $15 each
Mark	$15	1	Wins one Munster Family for $15
Chris	$10	1	Does not win
Matt	$10	1	Does not win
Pat	$10	1	Does not win

Fortunately, the majority of Dutch auctions are simple. After you participate in one or two, you'll see what they're all about. In a last-ditch effort to adequately explain Dutch auctions, here's a quick rundown of Dutch auction facts based on tips provided in the eBay Help guide:

- Sellers list a starting bid and the number of items for sale.
- Each bidder specifies a bid price and quantity.
- All winning bidders pay the same price, which is the lowest successful bid price.
- If there are more buyers than items, the earliest successful bids get the items.
- Higher bidders get the quantities they've asked for.
- If bidders cannot get full quantities, they can refuse partial quantities and pass on the purchase.

Reserve Auctions

The final type of auction you should be aware of is a *reserve* auction. A reserve auction is an English auction with an undisclosed minimum selling price (which is different than a starting price). Sellers are not bound to sell an item if the highest bid doesn't meet the reserve price. Furthermore, sellers have the option of either keeping the reserve price hidden or of publishing the reserve price in an auction item's description. Of course, if you run across a reserve auction and the seller doesn't name the reserve price in the auction ad's description, you can email the seller and ask what the reserve price is—but you may or may not receive an answer.

You can easily identify reserve auctions, because most auction sites clearly flag auction items with reserve prices. Now, as mentioned, a reserve price is different than a starting price. A starting price is a published price on an auction ad page. The first bidder must bid at least as much as the starting price. You know you've run across an auction ad with a starting price when you see that an item is $15 (or some other amount) but no bids have been placed on the item. If a seller desires, an auction ad can have both a starting bid price and a reserve price.

Reserve auctions invoke mixed reactions. The upside for sellers is that if no bids meet or beat the reserve price, the seller is under no obligation to sell the item (although some sellers might volunteer to contact the highest bidder to see if the bidder is interested in buying the item at the reserve price). In this manner, sellers can protect their investment. For buyers, though, reserve auctions tend to carry negative connotations. From a buyer's perspective, reserve prices seem to convey that there's minimal room for a "good deal," or the reserve price presents an additional bidding barrier that the bidder isn't willing to negotiate. To help alleviate buyers' concerns, some sellers list "low reserve" in the auction ad's title, but most bidders would rather work with a higher minimum bid than a hidden reserve price.

Guess what—you're almost there. It's almost time to start bidding, but there's one more fee to keep in mind before you establish a top bidding price, and this fee involves payment methods.

DETERMINING A PAYMENT METHOD

You can pay for auction items in a number of ways. As a buyer, you have several considerations to keep in mind, as outlined here (in alphabetical order):

- *Cashier's check.* Cashier's checks are high-end money orders. Cashier's checks are generally used for amounts over $500. You can purchase a bank-drafted cashier's check for a fee, usually $2.50 to $5.00 per check.

- *C.O.D.* C.O.D. stands for "collect on delivery," and it means that you pay the delivery person when the package arrives. The drawback is that you have to be there when the delivery person shows up, with money order or check in hand. Many online auction sellers prefer not to work with C.O.D. purchases.

- *Credit card.* Paying by credit card gives you the benefit of stopping payment if a sale never comes through. If you plan to use your credit card for online auctions, consider setting up a credit card with a low credit limit (such as $500). Then, if your card number is ever used in a scam, you won't be out thousands of dollars. Also, whenever you supply your credit card information on the Internet, make sure that the site is secure and uses SSL (Secure Sockets Layer) technology.

- *Electronic transfer.* You can opt to transfer money electronically. If you do, use a bonded and reliable electronic transfer service, such as **www.paybyweb.com** or **bidpay.com**. For your own financial safety, don't provide your account information directly to sellers.

- *Escrow service.* An escrow service is an independent third party that holds a bidder's payment in trust until the buyer receives and accepts the auction item from the seller. This service charges a fee (of course), and is usually reserved for high-end transactions. I-Escrow, BidSafe, Trade-direct, and TradeSafe are some popular escrow services. See Chapter 23 for more information about escrow services.

- *Money order.* Many online auction transactions are completed with money orders. Buyers benefit because their account information is kept private, and sellers benefit because they don't need to wait for the check to clear (which is usually the case with personal checks). Buyers can purchase money orders at grocery stores and drugstores for fees as low as $.25 (banks easily charge the highest rates for money orders, so use a bank as a last resort). If you use a money order, save the stub and keep track of the money order's number in case you need to track it down later.

- *Personal check.* Writing a check is a quick and easy method for bidders to pay for auction items, but most sellers won't send out an auction item until the check clears. Therefore, using checks slows down the process and introduces unnecessary risks. The upside is that if it looks like a seller is going to run away with your check, you might be able to place a stop payment on the check before it's too late.

By and large, how you pay for an item is up to you. There are upsides and downsides to every payment method. Determine your payment method based on the value of the item. In most cases, paying by money order, credit card, or personal check presents a reasonable risk. Whichever payment method you use, remember to factor in the cost when you're bidding (especially if you're using an escrow service).

SETTING YOUR TOP PRICE

It's time. You see an item you want to bid on, but, before you put your user ID name up in pixels, stop. You need to name your top price, to yourself, before you place any bids. Determine a top price, and stick to it. Write it down as a reminder, if you have to. You don't want to end up paying $30 more than an item's worth just because you got caught up in the auction action. To help you determine a top price, work through these questions:

- How much would the item cost at a physical or online store (if possible)?
- How much is the item worth to you?
- How much would the item be worth in a collector's market?
- How much expendable cash do you have that you want to spend on the item?
- How much is the seller charging for shipping (*always* factor in shipping charges when placing an auction bid)?
- How much will the payment method cost?

Think about those questions, and come up with a reasonable top bidding price. If your price seems low—so be it. There will be other auctions if you're outbid on this one. And, if you're not outbid, you'll be pleasantly surprised.

Playing the Numbers Game

Now that you've carefully considered what an item is worth and what you're willing to pay, we're going to ask you to change your price. This is a winning tip, so pay attention. You probably have jars, ashtrays, or other containers holding extra pennies. The pennies are just sitting around, so take a couple of those Lincolns and add them to your top bidding price. If your top price for an autographed first edition copy of Allen Ginsberg's *Collected Poems* (1947–1980) is $35.00, then up your top bidding price to $35.02. Chances are that if you're willing to pay $35.00 for Ginsberg's poems, someone else probably thinks that's a good price, too. So, give yourself a slight edge by sneaking in your extra two-cents' worth.

BIDDING TO WIN

At long last, it's time to bid. First and foremost—are you registered? Before you can bid on any online auction site, you must register. Registering is as simple as clicking on the Register link and pro-

T I P

Notice *cash* isn't mentioned as a viable payment method. Sending cash for an item leaves you no recourse if the deal falls through.

T I P

One complaint repeated over and over among online auction sellers is that bidders win an auction and then state that they can't pay for the item until the next payday. If you can't cover the cost, you really shouldn't bid on an item.

You can track
auctions on Yahoo!
without bidding on
them by adding them
to your Watchlist.
Other sites have
similar features.

T I P

If you can't make it
to the auction site
just before an auction
listing closes (after
all, most of us have to
work sometime!), you
can simply bid your
top bid price when
you find the auction
ad and hope for the
best. Sometimes,
that's enough to
do the trick.

viding your user information. After you've registered, you're free to bid.

The act of bidding is simple. You enter your bid amount on an auction ad's page, enter your user ID and password, click a button to place your bid, then click another button to confirm your bid. While each site varies as far as when and how you perform these tasks, the basic bidding elements are universal—bid amount, ID, password, and confirmation.

While the act of bidding is straightforward, there are a couple of theories regarding successful bidding techniques, including the "bid high and bid early" tactic as well as the "bid at the last minute" scheme. You'll probably fall in between those two tactics for the most part, but the latter is decidedly more successful than the former. And here's why: *If you bid too early, you'll generate interest in an item and attract more bidders—and more bidders means higher prices.*

So, take your time. Note the time an auction ends, and then, if possible, check back shortly before that time. You can easily keep track of auctions by creating desktop shortcuts to auction pages. Or, copy the auction information onto a notepad or sticky note, or into a word processing file. Over time, you'll figure out what works best for you as far as keeping track of auction ads that interest you.

When you return to an auction ad just before it is about to close, you can place your bid. When you place your bid, bid once and bid your top bidding price. Earlier, you thought about the price you want to pay, so put your number to work. Bidding in minor increments is time-consuming and useless—it also opens you up to the possibility that you'll exceed your top bid price.

After you place your bid, you'll see a bid confirmation page that states whether you're currently the winning bidder or if you've been outbid by a proxy bidder (see Figure 6.2). If you're the current winning bidder, your user ID will appear on the auction ad page's header in the High Bid field and the auction listing will display on your user information page.

FIGURE 6.2

A bid confirmation page instantly tells you whether you're the top bidder or if you have been outbid by another bidder.

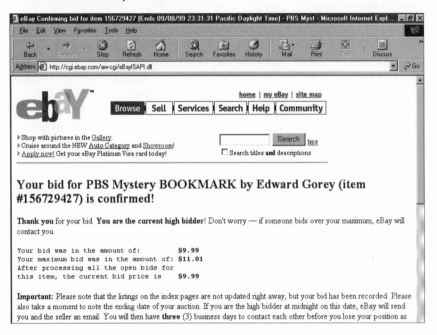

So, to recap, the key to successful bidding is simply to:

1. Find an item to bid on, do your homework, note the auction's closing date and time, and create a desktop shortcut to the auction (or save the auction information via some other means).

2. Return to the auction listing shortly before the auction is about to close.

3. Bid once, and bid your maximum bid (including the extra two-cent rule).

4. View the bid confirmation page.

This plan usually works because, when you bid late, other bidders don't have time to outbid you. Also, you'll never pay more than your maximum price.

The only way you can lose is if your maximum bidding price is less than someone else's maximum bidding price (posted before your last-minute bid). In that case, you lost happily because the item cost more than you were willing to pay anyway.

Now, if you find that you *absolutely* must win an item, there's a well-known bidding technique called *sniping*. To level the playing field, the next section describes how you can get in on the sniping action (with a winning twist, of course) when absolutely necessary.

Sniping—When You Absolutely Have to Win

Sniping is the act of swooping in during the very last seconds of an auction and out-bidding the highest bidder. The key to sniping is to bid so late in the game that no one else has a chance to outbid your bid. There are risks in this tactic, but, more often, there are rewards. It's a sneaky game that a lot of online auction bidders play.

The secret to outsniping the snipers is to open *two* browser windows that display the same auction listing. In one window, enter your bid amount, click the Enter or Review Bid button, and then STOP! Do not finalize your bid yet. In the other window, refresh the auction ad page every so often until there is less than 1 minute left before the auction closes. Subtract 10 seconds from the time shown, and watch a second hand for that length of time. When your countdown completes, click the Submit button in the first auction window. Your bid should slip in within the last few seconds of the auction. Refresh your second window to see if your bid made it in time.

Remember, auctions are auctions. Even using the most efficient sniping techniques, you still risk losing an auction. If someone else's maximum bid is higher than your maximum bid, even sniping won't deal you a winning hand.

T I P

It's never a good idea to bid high just to make the cut in a Dutch auction. For example, if you bid $300 for a $30 item, another bidder might come along who is willing to pay $75 for the item. In that instance, you might get stuck paying $75 for an item that is only worth $30.

Winning a Dutch Auction

Winning at a Dutch auction is a little different than winning an English auction. The key to winning a Dutch auction is to ensure that your bid price is among the higher winning prices—without being so high as to raise the winning price for all winning participants. In other words, you simply want your bid to be among the top winning bids. So, the best recommendation is to bid late and avoid being the lowest bidder. Remember, the lowest bidder is the first bidder to get bumped whenever a higher bidder arrives. When you bid in a Dutch auction, view the existing bid amounts, and strive to be somewhere in the middle of the pack without going over your maximum bid. This will ensure that you probably won't get bumped and that you won't inadvertently raise the price for all bidders or pay more than you're willing to pay for the item.

KEEPING TRACK OF ACTIVE AUCTIONS

Last but not least, bidding entails keeping track of your auctions. The next chapter goes into detail regarding what happens after an auction, but keeping track of your active auctions falls within the realm of bidding.

Most online auctions, and most certainly the big-three online auction sites, run an automated bidding notification service. This means that you receive an email message (or a beeper message or other notification if the site offers notification options) confirming each bid you place. Furthermore, you receive an email message or other notification each time another bidder outbids one of your bids. And, finally, you receive an email message or other notification each time you win an auction. These emails can pile up, and they can get lost in the shuffle. One way to keep track of auction email messages is to create rules within your email application that will filter auction-site-generated email messages into a separate folder. This cuts down on some of your Inbox traffic.

TIP

After you register on an online auction site, visit your user page to see what type of information the page stores. Then, you can use your user pages to help you keep track of your auction activities.

In addition, you should take full advantage of auction sites' user information pages. The pages help you to keep track of your active auctions. You can visit your user page on an online auction's Web site at any time. To do so, you simply click a link and enter your user information. Then, you can review your bids, auctions you're currently winning, auctions you're currently losing, and auctions you've recently won. For the big-three online auction sites, you can view your user information pages as follows:

- *eBay.*   Click the My eBay link, enter your user name, enter your password, and click Enter.

- *Amazon.*   Click the Your Account link.

- *Yahoo!*   Click My Auctions, enter your user name, enter your password, and click Sign In. If you are already signed in on Yahoo!, you won't need to reenter your user ID and password.

To see how your auction activity stacks up, visit your user information pages regularly and note your progress. If you've recently won an auction, move on to Chapter 7 posthaste, to find out what you should do now that you're a winner. After all, an online auction deal isn't complete until the seller receives the money and the buyer receives the goods.

KEY POINTS

In this chapter, we reviewed the basics of bidding. The preceding chapters led up to smart online auction techniques, and this chapter describes what you need to know to be a successful bidder. Namely, when you place a bid, you should:

- Consider shipping costs.
- Recognize auction types.
- Account for your payment method.
- Establish a top bidding price.
- Time your bid.
- Track your auction activity.

7

YOU'VE WON! NOW WHAT?

AFTER THE BIDDING

Time's up, the auction has closed, and your bid did the trick—you won! Now what? Now, it's up to you and the seller to complete the transaction. Whenever an auction closes, most online auction sites send an automatically generated email message to the seller and the highest bidder. Then, the online auction site steps out of the picture for the most part. (We say "for the most part," because if the transaction runs aground you can sometimes turn to the online auction site for assistance, as explained in Chapter 9.) After you win an auction, you need to ensure that the transaction completes. Don't wait for the seller to make it happen—be proactive. To guide you through your first couple of wins, this chapter takes you through the after-auction paces, which can be summarized as follows:

- Read your end-of-auction notices
- Contact the seller
- Make good on your bid
- Follow up
- Receive the goods
- Leave feedback

Keep in mind that as your online auction experience grows, you'll adopt methods that work best for you. Regardless of the details, as long as you address all the after-auction stages presented in this chapter, finalizing your transactions should be mostly smooth sailing.

END-OF-AUCTION NOTICES

Smack! The virtual hammer drops and you win. Shortly thereafter, you should receive a couple of emails. First, most online auction sites automatically send an email message to the seller and highest bidder when an auction closes. Second, you should receive an email message from the seller.

Auction Site Notices

As mentioned, when an auction closes most online auction sites generate email messages to the seller and top-bidding buyer. End-of-auction emails supply much of the pertinent information necessary for you to complete the deal, including:

- Seller and buyer IDs
- Seller and high-bidder email addresses
- Link to the auction ad
- Auction title or item name
- Final price
- Auction ending date and time
- Total number of bids
- Starting and highest bid amounts
- Link to the feedback forum

The preceding list depicts some of the types of information found in an automated email message. You will find that different online auction sites provide different types of information. The one bit of information all auction sites should provide is the seller's email address—if the seller doesn't contact you, you'll have to contact the seller to get the deal rolling (as explained later in this chapter).

Following are two examples of email messages sent to a winning bidder. The first example is a letter from eBay after the close of an auction, and the second example is a message from Amazon. It's interesting to note the subtle differences between the two messages, although much of the basic information appears in both formats. Notice that eBay sends the same message to both the seller and buyer:

```
************************************************************
Need help finding the perfect gift for even the hardest-
to-shop-for loved one? See http://www.ebay.com/givingguide
************************************************************
************************************************************
```

Dear dragon and *bughouse*,

Congratulations—this auction successfully ended.

Item Title: Alien Oil Lamp (Pewter & Crystal).....Cool! (Item #156512051)

Final price: $12.00
Auction ended at: 01/08/2000 16:46:32 PDT
Total number of bids: 4
Seller User ID: dragon
Seller E-mail: dragon@domain.net
High-bidder User ID: *bughouse*
High-bidder E-mail: *mcmail@primenet.com*

Here's what to do next:

*The buyer and seller should contact each other within three business days to complete the sale. Not getting in touch leaves the contract in limbo and can earn you negative feedback. If you have trouble, though, just visit *http://cgi3.ebay.com/aw-cgi/eBayISAPI.dll?MemberSearchShow*

*Help other eBay users by leaving feedback about your transaction, at *http://cgi2.ebay.com/aw-cgi/eBayISAPI.dll?LeaveFeedbackShow&item=156512051*

*This auction's results, including email addresses of all bidders, are available for 30 days at *http://cgi3.ebay.com/aw-cgi/eBayISAPI.dll?ViewItem&item= 156512051*

*If you've bought this item as a gift, you can let the lucky recipient know what's coming! As long as the seller has a positive feedback rating of at least 10, just visit *http://cgi3.ebay.com/aw-cgi/eBayISAPI.dll?ViewGiftAlert& item=156512051&userid=*bughouse*

*For further information and resources, visit *http://pages.ebay.com/help/ sellerguide/after-tips.html*

Note to Bidders: If you're a winning bidder, send your payment to the seller.

Note to Sellers: If you're a seller paying eBay with a check or money order, here's where to mail it:
eBay, Inc.
P.O. Box 200945
Dallas, TX 75320-0945

We're so glad your auction was successful, and we hope to see you at eBay again soon! And be sure to tell your friends about us—we'd love to see them here too.

Please let us know if you have any questions for us—but don't send an automatic reply to this email, as it may not reach a real person! Instead, please go to our online Help section at
http://pages.ebay.com/help/index.html

Trade On!

Item Description:

The flame comes from the top of the flying saucer, illuminating the alien! COOL! His eyes are GREEN CRYSTALS!. Awesome! Lift the top off the base to fill with lamp oil, permanent wick included.BRAND NEW. S/H $4.00.
GREAT*GIFT

Following is a sample winning email message from Amazon. Notice that this message is sent specifically to the winning bidder:

Dear bughouse,

Congratulations! We're pleased, tickled, and downright delighted to tell you that you were the winning bidder for:
POKEMON #25 PIKACHU PLUSH - MWMT at $14.95 per item.
To view the auction you've won, follow the link below:

http://auctions.amazon.com/exec/varzea/ts/auction-glance/Y01X6226814X8226821

As a winning bidder, you have agreed to complete this transaction with the seller. Now is the time to contact the seller to arrange payment and delivery. Please do!

Seller nickname: bay2city
Seller e-mail: *bay2city@host.com*
Item: POKEMON #25 PIKACHU PLUSH - MWMT
Auction ID: 08WWW228105

Please print this e-mail message and include a copy with payment. This will help the seller to efficiently process and ship your item.

Auction Details:

Item: POKEMON #25 PIKACHU PLUSH - MWMT
Auction ID: 08WWW228105
Quantity: 3
Seller's nickname: bay2city
Starting bid: $ 5.95

```
Highest bid: $ 14.95
Total number of bids: 5

Shipping fees:
----------------
Your current bid: $14.95
Quantity desired: 2
Your quantity allocated: 2
Auction closed on: 01/22/2000 16:29:07 PDT
```

Sharing feedback about this seller with other Amazonians is an important part
of making Amazon.com Auctions a great community in which to bid, buy, and
sell. Once you and the seller have completed this exchange, please remember
to share feedback in order to help other buyers and sellers. You have up to
30 days after this auction's close to do this.
Just follow this link:

http://auctions.amazon.com/exec/varzea/feedback-form/Y01X622AA6LME3QZEPN2

If you have additional questions about bidding, visit our Bidder's Guide at:

http://auctions.amazon.com/exec/varzea/ts/help/bidders/

(This message was sent to you by an automated e-mail system. Please don't
reply to it.)

Thanks for visiting Amazon.com!

Amazon.com
Earth's Biggest Selection
Find, Discover, and Buy Virtually Anything
http://www.amazon.com

While receiving an online auction site's automatically generated email is a
good source of information and a nice way to be notified that you've won an auction,
the "real" email you're waiting for is a message from the seller. After all, you need to
hear from the seller to learn where you should send your payment.

Seller Notices

After an auction ends, sellers generally contact the buyer within three days. Seller
notices typically provide the following informational tidbits:

- Auction number and item name
- Total purchase price (winning bid amount plus shipping)
- Payment preferences
- Mailing address

As you will see, sellers' messages range from two-liners to short stories, and they may or may not contain all of the necessary information. Don't be surprised if a seller forgets to include mailing information—it's happened more than a few times! Furthermore, because most sellers are regular people selling items on the Internet, messages may contain typographical errors, bad sentence structure, and miscapitalizations (including ALL CAPS, WHICH IS THE WRITTEN EQUIVALENT OF YELLING AND REALLY HARD TO READ). Try not to be critical, and keep in mind that the main purpose of a seller's notice is to get the ball rolling and to provide an address for you so that you can send payment—this is crucial to completing the transaction!

When you receive a seller's notice, you should reply to the seller immediately. Simply, read the message and then respond. It only takes a few seconds, and if you wait until later, you might forget to respond altogether. As you can imagine, forgetting to respond to a seller's end-of-auction email makes the seller verrry nervous.

CONTACTING THE SELLER

If you can't respond to a seller's end-of-auction notice immediately, you should be sure to at least reply within three days. On many online auction sites, a seller can contact the next-highest bidder if the seller is unable to verify the transaction with the high-bidder within three business days.

To reply to a seller's message, read the message and then click the "Reply" button in your email application. *Use the same subject line (which is inserted automatically when you reply to an email message) and do not delete the seller's message in the reply.* Type your message above the seller's existing text in the email window. You want to keep all of your communication as clear as possible. Enabling sellers to see the message they sent to you will help to remind the seller of the particular transaction.

In your reply, include the following information:

- Acknowledge that you realize that you've won the auction, and that you're a legitimate buyer.

- Specify the purchase amount, including shipping. This shows the seller that you agree on the purchase amount and shipping costs the seller listed in the originating email message.

- Restate the auction number and item name.

- Indicate how you plan to pay the purchase amount (money order, check, cashier's check, escrow service, electronic transfer, C.O.D., credit card, or other arrangement).

- State when you will be sending payment.

- Provide your mailing address. This enables the seller to prepare your package for shipping and also reassures the seller that you are a legitimate buyer who will be completing the transaction.

INSTIGATING A RESPONSE

If you are the highest bidder when an auction ends and the seller doesn't contact you, you need to contact the seller. You can obtain the seller's email address from the automated end-of-auction email from the online auction site, the site's user lookup feature, or the closed auction ad. Don't assume that the deal's off just because you didn't receive a notice. The seller may have overlooked contacting you. (As you'll see, some folks run 30, 40, or more auctions at once.) Email the seller and request a mailing address so that you can send payment.

MAKING GOOD ON YOUR BID

While online auctions are young in the grand scheme of the world, most participants take them very seriously, and this serious approach is what keeps online auctions alive and well. Therefore, if you bid on an item, you had better follow through, or you'll risk becoming ostracized from the community for a long time. As you'll see in the next chapter, online auction communities serve as a surprisingly strong self-policing force. The two keys to successfully paying for an item are to do so in a timely fashion and to send complete information with your payment.

Keeping It Timely

As already mentioned in Chapter 6, you should only bid on items if you have the resources to pay for them readily available. Therefore, if you follow that advice, keeping the payment timely is simply a matter of getting it done (as opposed to waiting for your next paycheck to arrive). For everyone's benefit, you should try make your payment within 10 days of the end of auction—send your payment, call with your credit card number, register with an escrow service, and so forth. If it looks like your payment might have to be delayed for a couple of extra days (who knew that your alternator was going to call it quits this week?), be sure to contact the seller, and read the fine print on the online auction site. Some sites very specifically dictate the maximum allowable length of time before payment must be received. Most sellers, however, are willing to work with buyers as long as the buyer continues to keep in contact with the seller.

TIP

If you win an auction and fail to honor your end of the bargain, some online auction sites have nonpayment buyer procedures. Ultimately, you could be suspended from an online auction site indefinitely.

Sending All the Information

If you're opting to mail your payment, such as sending a check or money order, be sure that you accompany the payment with the relevant auction information. More than a handful of sellers have made their collective frustrated voices heard in chat groups regarding receiving payments without any indication as to which auctions the payments were for. Remember, more and more sellers are moving well beyond the "dabbling" stage of selling an item or two found in the back of their closet, and keeping track of all their auctions can be a substantial task.

The easiest way to include all of the appropriate information with your payment is to print the seller's end-of-auction notification. Then, include a short message and write your name and address on a clear portion of the printout. That way, you have the auction title, auction number, and seller's address easily accessible to both you and the seller. For further assurance, ensure that your name, user ID, and auction number appear on your check or money order.

TIP

When following up after sending payment, be sure to include the check or money order number in the email. This will help to track down the money order if necessary.

FOLLOWING UP

So far, the auction has ended; the seller and the auction site have notified you; you've emailed the seller regarding your intent to honor the auction; and you've submitted a form of payment. At this point, you should notify the seller that you've sent payment (or simply verify in writing that you've called with your credit card number). Regardless of how you've paid, *email the seller.* This email message serves as a dated record of your payment for both you and the seller. As we mentioned earlier, it's always a good idea to print all communications between you and an online auction seller. So, print a copy of your message to the seller for your own records. If you don't regularly make a hard copy, the possibility exists that the one time you run across a lame seller, your hard drive will take a nosedive just when you're pulling up your old email records.

RECEIVING THE GOODS

The check is in the mail. That means that it's your turn to wait. The seller has been awaiting your action—now it's your turn. Most sellers will send you a message when they've received your payment and sent the item. If you *don't* receive any messages confirming your payment within a week or so after sending it, follow up with the seller. Your money's out there, so stay on top of the transaction!

If the seller doesn't have to wait for your check to clear, then you should receive your item within two weeks. And again, if you don't receive your package within two weeks or so—contact the seller.

After you receive your item (if you *don't* receive your item, turn to Chapter 9), open the package immediately. Check the purchase to ensure that it lives up to its description. If you feel that you've been misled or if the item is damaged, contact the seller to try and rectify the situation. As will be explained in the next section, you should not jump the gun and leave a negative feedback rating without first trying to work out a situation with the seller.

If the item arrives as described and you're satisfied that the transaction completed successfully, email the seller. (Do you see a trend here?) *In other words, after you receive and inspect an auction item, email the seller to confirm that the item arrived.* If you're planning on leaving positive feedback with the online auction (which you should do if the transaction completed successfully), mention your intention or email the seller *after* you've left positive feedback (feedback is discussed in the next section). Letting the seller know that you're satisfied with the transaction and that you've left or are planning to leave positive feedback might encourage the seller to return the favor and leave positive feedback on your behalf. Many sellers beat buyers to the punch and leave positive feedback for buyers as soon as they receive a timely payment.

TIP

Keep a list of sellers you've successfully worked with. Building a relationship with online auction sellers can help you ensure that you're dealing with reputable online auction participants.

LEAVING FEEDBACK

A buyer's final step in an online auction transaction is to leave feedback. You should make a point of doing so regularly. Many online auction sellers and buyers rely on feedback to bolster their online auction reputation, and feedback helps potential buyers and sellers evaluate whether they'll do business with a user.

You can leave feedback about a transaction by clicking the link in the online auction site's end-of-auction email message or by surfing to the site's feedback forum. In most cases, to leave feedback you'll need to know the seller's user ID and the transaction number, so have that information handy.

Leaving feedback entails filling out a short online form. You insert the seller's user ID information, your information, possibly the transaction number, and then you type a comment. Usually the comment area is limited to around 80 characters. That's not a lot of space, so make your words count.

To help you to start thinking about the types of comments you want to leave, read other people's comments and note the types of statements that help you to determine whether you want to interact with a seller. Often, specific comments are more helpful than general comments. Some samples follow:

When a transaction completes smoothly and in a timely manner:

- Positive/Good/5 Stars: "Smooth transaction. Fast payment/shipment. Highly recommend!"

When a transaction completes, but takes a little longer or requires extra emails:

- Positive/Good/5 Stars: "Item as described and transaction completed. Good seller."

When an item arrives damaged or isn't what you expected, but the seller resolves the issue:

- Positive/5 Stars: "Item was damaged (or Item was different than expected), but the seller made good! Honest and trustworthy. Recommended seller!"

When the transaction entails excessive nagging and the shipment is delayed for over a month:

- Neutral/3 Stars: "Took some time and extra emails, but deal eventually went through OK" (or opt to leave no feedback).

When a seller backs out with what seems like a good excuse to you:

- Neutral/3 Stars: "Didn't follow through on the sale, but seemed to have a reasonable excuse" (or opt to leave no feedback).

When an item arrives damaged or isn't what you expected, and the seller does not resolve the issue after you've repeatedly tried to contact and work with the seller:

- Negative/0 or 1 Stars: "Item received but was damaged (or Item was different than expected). Seller wouldn't resolve issue. Be careful."

When a seller backs out with a poor excuse, never responds to your email messages, or never contacts you after the end of an auction:

- Negative/0 Stars: "Did not complete transaction. Stay away!"

The preceding samples should provide you with some ideas regarding feedback. Other feedback tactics often used among buyers and sellers include grading a transaction (such as leaving an A++++++, the pluses sometimes fill the remaining space in the comment field), typing a recommendation in ALL CAPS for added emphasis, and stating that a seller or buyer is an eBay, Amazon, or other online auction site "asset."

SERIOUSLY NEGATIVE

A successful transaction, no matter how delayed, rarely warrants a negative feedback. One FAQ page about online auctions states that "people take feedback very seriously. Positive feedback is expected for every successful transaction. Negative feedback is like spitting in someone's face."

A good rule of thumb is to wait at least 24 hours before you post a negative comment—don't leave negative feedback in the heat of the moment. Feedback is permanent, and you'll have to deal with the repercussions of the feedback for as long as you're a member of the online auction community.

Above all else, leave honest feedback. If you are less than satisfied with a deal but the transaction progressed smoothly, leave a positive rating, but don't feel obligated to wax on about the deal in your comments. Instead, keep it plain and simple. Further, if you're unsatisfied but the cause is not directly due to the seller's actions (for example, maybe you didn't read the description well enough and you expected the item would be bigger or of a different material), you always have the option of leaving no feedback. Leaving no feedback is usually better than leaving neutral feedback, because, believe it or not, neutral feedback isn't really neutral. Most online auction users work hard for their positive numbers and take offense at neutral feedback. Neutral feedback doesn't affect a seller's or buyer's score, but no one likes to see that stray mark or two in the neutral zone. Therefore, instead of creating strife where none is necessary, it's better to leave no feedback unless a neutral comment is absolutely necessary.

After you leave feedback, your online auction transaction is complete. Thus, you'd think this chapter is complete, but there's one more topic to discuss—backing out of a bid. Backing out of a bid or sale is a major taboo in the world of online auctions, so this topic wasn't given equal time in this chapter's introductory text. But backing out does happen and is unavoidable in some instances, so before wrapping up this chapter the topic needs to be broached.

BACKING OUT OF A DEAL

Hopefully, you'll never need to know about backing out of an online auction bid, especially if you've won the auction. Retracting a bid is considered serious business in the online auction community. So, to purposefully restate for emphasis—*you should avoid retracting bids—especially after you win an auction—as diligently as possible.* But life is life, and someday there might be a legitimate instance when a retraction is unavoidable. Therefore, this section presents some information you can use when you need to retract your bid.

Technically, most online sites state that bids are binding. If bidders could retract their bids willy-nilly, online auctions would fail. But you *can* retract your bid if you have a really good reason, such as:

- The seller added new information that altered your impression of the item.
- You made an obvious typographical error (such as, bidding $30,000 when you meant to bid $30).
- The seller's email address is invalid.
- The seller's feedback rating changed negatively after you placed your bid.

If you have to retract a bid for personal reasons or any of the preceding acceptable ones, try to retract before the auction ends. You retract a bid by using the online auction bid retraction form provided by the online auction site. When you retract a bid, be sure to contact the seller, in addition to filling out the proper form. Sellers are people, and most sellers appreciate an explanation.

Regardless of your explanation, a seller has every right to leave negative feedback when you retract a bid, and some sites list bid retractions and retractors. So you might have to deal with the consequences of a bid retraction, no matter how legitimate your explanation. Furthermore, many people in the online auction community view bid retractions as the sign of a novice or someone who lacks responsibility and commitment to making online auctions a viable market.

TIP

If you absolutely must back out of the deal after you've won an auction, try to make amends. Contact the seller as soon as possible, explain your reason for backing out, tell them you're very sorry, and *offer to pay the auction listing fees and other online auction charges.* There are no guarantees, but acting in good faith might help you to avoid earning a negative feedback rating.

KEY POINTS

This chapter reviews the process of completing an online transaction. The overriding keys to successful transactions lie in clear, frequent communication and timely actions. If sellers and buyers send frequent emails, provide payments and shipments in a timely manner, and leave honest feedback, the online auction communities will continue to thrive. The specific steps a buyer takes to complete a transaction can be summarized as follows:

- Read end-of-auction notices.
- Contact the seller.
- Submit payment to the seller.
- Notify the seller when payment is sent, and follow up a week later, if necessary.
- Check out the goods as soon as they arrive.
- Leave feedback.
- Email the seller to confirm that you've received the goods and left feedback.
- Avoid retracting bids at all costs.

8

CHAPTER

HANGING OUT WITH THE ONLINE AUCTION CROWD

THEORY OF AUCTION COMMUNITIES

Online auction sites recognize the benefits of building online communities. Actually, online communities aren't limited to online auctions—take a look at sites like AOL, GeoCities, and Tripod. Building online communities has been a topic among Web developers for several years now. Basically, building an online community is an attempt to involve users who share common ground with other people visiting the site.

The theory is that even though Web pages are accessible from around the world, people will return to a particular site if they can relate to it and experience a sense of belonging. Not surprisingly, the success of most Web sites relies on repeat visits from users. Online auctions subscribe to the same sense-of-belonging theory and stretch the community concept to encompass even more site-specific services. Namely, online auction communities play the following roles:

- *Self-policing of unethical and illegal activities.* This is the most significant benefit of online auction communities. When online auction users feel a sense of community, they are more apt to ensure that their stomping grounds are kept free of shysters and scam artists.

- *Providing assistance to others.* Sellers and buyers in an online auction community have a forum where they can turn to others for opinions and answers.

- *Generating increased interest in the site and auctions.* Increased interest ensures the health of the site and enlivens the auction action.

- *Vesting users.* No, we're not talking about tacky clothing here. *Vesting* refers to the concept that when a person becomes personally involved in a site's issues, welfare, and membership, that person is more prone to invest time, effort, and resources to benefit the site.

- *Increasing user benefits.* Online auction communities often provide ways for users to build friendships, engage in side deals, and develop repeat customers. Further, users have a sounding board when frustration and confusion set in.

As you can see, online communities are beneficial to both the sites and users; and the nice part about it is that you can participate only when you want. All in all, communities can be viewed as good to have around. Better to have too much information and communication at your fingertips than not enough. That's enough theory; let's look at some practical applications.

COMMUNITY BANDING

Don't underestimate the power of online auction communities. In more than a few instances, we've watched as buyers band together to track down a deadbeat seller. What tends to happen is that one buyer gets frustrated that the money has been sent, but the seller won't respond to email messages and there's nothing to show for the buyer's expense. So, the buyer gets proactive and contacts all other bidders who've recently "won" auctions offered by the seller in question. The bidders compare notes, and then the action begins. Soon, the seller gets swamped with email messages and phone calls (if a phone number is available), and the bidders submit complaints to the appropriate resource (such as eBay's Safe Harbor). In most cases that we've observed, the seller finally acquiesces and either reimburses the money with some semblance of an excuse or sends the products to the winning bidders. If you're ever included in one of these vigilante-type escapades, you're in for some interesting email as you watch the events unfold.

BENEFITTING FROM AUCTION COMMUNITIES

All right, auction communities are good, but just what are they? Well, like any community, an online auction community is developed through communication, and communication happens to be the Web's forte. Online auction communities offer ways to communicate among users as well as between site developers and users. The most prominent means of creating a community is to use user-to-user communication.

Touching Base with Others Online

User-to-user communication can occur in a variety of fashions. Further, you can "listen" in (more aptly called *lurking*) or participate in auction community communication in any number of ways, including:

- *Chat groups.* Chat groups are areas on online auction sites and auction-related sites where people can post messages in real time to get quick feedback from others. Generally, everyone logged into the chat group can participate in these typed conversations. Many sites have very specific topic-related chat groups.

- *Mailing lists.* Participating in a mailing list is like rounding up a group of people and picking a topic to talk about via email messages. When you join a mailing list, you receive an email message each time a participant sends a message. In other words, one person sends an email, and all participants receive a copy of the email; then, someone else responds and all participants receive a copy of that email; and so on. You can find a large number of mailing lists to join at **www.onelist.com**. Search for lists based on the word *auctions*, and you'll have over 300 mailing lists to choose from. Sign up, and watch the email messages arrive.

- *Message boards.* Message boards are areas on online auction sites and auction-related sites where people can post messages that other users can read at their convenience. (Sometimes it is difficult to distinguish between message boards and chat groups.) Other message board participants can post replies for all to see. A great place to find message boards for the big auction sites as well as general auction topics is **www.auctionwatch.com/mesg**.

TIP

Recently, eBay held a "free listing" day. The number of auction items jumped from the average 3 million to 4.1 million *in one day!* With that many auctions happening on a single site, you can bet there are lots of people out there willing to chat with you about online auction activities and topics.

- *Newsgroups.* Online auction newsgroups work on the same premise as other newsgroups. You use your newsreader application (which is generally the same as your email application) and participate in newsgroups offered by your Internet Service Provider (ISP). You will find varying degrees of participation in auction newsgroups. For auctionites, the most prominent methods of communication seem to be via chat groups, message boards, and mailing lists.

As you can see, there are a number of ways to touch base with other auctionites. If you're planning to participate in auctions, you should click around and see what's going on in the community. You'll find deadbeat seller lists, scam alerts, great deals, items-wanted forums, HTML tips (for sellers), and more—probably way more than you want! As we previously mentioned, along with user-to-user communication, some sites are starting to offer site-specific community benefits.

Site-Specific Community Resources

Some online auction sites take community very seriously and offer auction community members a number of services. For example, both Yahoo! and eBay provide a community page, with links to various helpful features that include chat groups, news announcements, message boards, and more. Figure 8.1 shows Yahoo!'s community home page. You can find eBay's community page at **pages.ebay.com/ community**. Click around to see what each site offers. You'll pick up tips that you can use on any number of auction sites.

Because auction communities are highly site-specific, we won't go into detail here. We just want you to know that community pages exist, and that you should check

FIGURE 8.1

Yahoo! Auctions Community page (**auctions.yahoo.com/html/features/ community.html**).

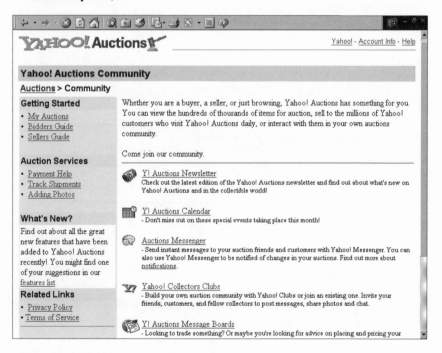

out the services. Plus, you'll find news items, charity auction schedules, auction tools (such as Yahoo!'s Auctions Messenger tool that you can download for free), and so forth.

NEWSLETTERS AND MAGAZINES

Another way that auction sites try to build a sense of community is to offer newsletters and magazines. Newsletters and magazines give sites a channel for sending information to users (instead of users having to search out the information). Currently, eBay is the only popular online auction site that provides a hard-copy magazine that you can subscribe to. (To subscribe, visit the eBay home page and click the eBay Magazine link.) The first issue came out in September 1999, so this online community tactic is still in its infancy. Time will tell if magazine subscriptions will play a role in fostering the success of online auctions.

A more widespread news distribution method among online auction communities is the use of newsletters. On many sites, users are invited to sign up for free newsletters. In most cases, the "free newsletter" is a newsletter-like email message that you receive once or twice a month. In our opinion, you should sign up for the *free* newsletter when you visit an online auction site. (If there's a fee, consider passing on the newsletter unless you become a regular site member.) After you receive a copy or two of the newsletter, evaluate its worth. If it's more of an annoyance than an informational source, cancel your subscription. For example, some newsletters are more similar to advertisements than newsletters. (Auctions.com used to fall into that trap.) On the other hand, if a newsletter provides a good hint or tip here and there, you might as well let it continue to arrive in your Inbox.

WHAT IT ALL MEANS

While participating in online auction communities isn't imperative to successful auction bidding, the community resources are often good places to turn to when you need or want information. You should spend a few hours surfing the resources on various Web sites. You'll see where online communities exist, friendships are nurtured, queries are answered, and topics are addressed (including informative discussions about shilling, deadbeat sellers and bidders, shipping fees, scams, and so forth). The good news is that while there undoubtedly are people out there who attempt to take advantage of the online auction market, the communities show that there are even more peo-

TIP

Most auction sites that have a community page provide a community link on the site's home page. If you're not sure whether an online auction site has a community page, check the site map link.

TIP

As we mentioned in previous chapters, a number of non-auction-site-specific Web sites offer newsletter information as well, including Auction Watch (**www.auctionwatch.com**), Auction Insider (**www.auctioninside.com**), and Auction Guide (**www.auctionguide.com**).

ple who are working diligently to make online auctions a success. The majority of users realize that anyone with true integrity doesn't want to poison the online auction pond. So, if nothing else, you can turn to the community features for added reassurance that successful transactions with honest sellers are more the norm than the exception, and that online auctions can and generally do work as planned.

KEY POINTS

This chapter takes a brief look at the phenomenon of online auction communities. It isn't designed to be rah-rah about auctions and auction participants. Instead, this chapter points toward areas and resources where you can find the auction community serving real needs among online auctionites. Specifically, you can find evidence of community interaction in the form of:

- Chat groups
- Community pages
- Magazines
- Mailing lists
- Message boards
- Newsgroups
- Newsletters

9

WHEN FRAUD STRIKES— FIGHTING BACK

FACTS AND FRAUDS

Most of the Buying section in this book talks about ways to keep your online bidding safe, including:

- Checking out sellers.
- Keeping copies of all correspondence.
- Possibly designating and using a low-maximum credit card. (Under the U.S. Fair Credit Billing Act, you can only be held liable for $50 on a credit card scam.)
- Employing escrow services for high-ticket items.
- Avoiding cash transactions.
- Getting to know the auction community.

Regardless of your precautions, online auction scams do exist, and fraud might scratch at your door when you least expect it. Therefore, this chapter takes a look at fraud, how online auction sites address it, and what you can do if fraud strikes.

An Awakening

According to the National Consumer League's Fraud Information Center, online auction fraud accounts for nearly 9 out of every 10 Internet-related complaints filed with the center, and the average auction loss is $248 per complaint. That's the bad news.

The good news is that you don't have to sit idly by while your money evaporates, because the word is getting out and knowledge serves as a strong deterrent.

In the early part of 1999, the newswires were glutted with stories about online auction fraud—*U.S. News & World Report, USA Today, The New York Times, Newsweek, Wired, MSN,* and just about every other news source made a point of addressing online auction risks and scams. Online auctions were starting to take off, and fraud had become a marquee issue. By early 1999, online auction fraud held a comfortably rooted position as the top Internet fraudulent activity.

While online auction fraud continues to cast a noticeable shadow over other online scams, heightened consumer awareness has resulted in a growing number of tactics, resources, and organizations that fraud victims can rely upon. Namely, fraud victims can turn to online auction sites, state and federal government organizations, law enforcement agencies, fraud services, public interest groups, and privately hosted fraud information Web sites. Probably one of the most significant changes in the online auction community is that online auction sites—especially the larger ones like Amazon and eBay—are starting to take a firm interest in countering fraudulent activity.

eBay's Take on Fraud

We believe people are basically good.
We believe everyone has something to contribute.
We believe that an honest, open environment can bring out the best in people.
We recognize and respect everyone as a unique individual.
We encourage you to treat others the way that you want to be treated.
—eBay

As you can see, eBay stands firmly grounded in the "honesty is the best policy" approach. But, that's not to say that it blindly gazes past fraudulent activities through rose-colored Vaurnets. Meg Whitman, eBay's chief executive, affirms that eBay has "zero tolerance for fraud." She says that eBay takes fraud extremely seriously, and estimates that "about 27 out of every million transactions are reported as fraudulent." You can see evidence of eBay's commitment to fighting fraud by visiting eBay's Complaints page at **pages.ebay.com/help/myinfo/complaints.html**.

If you think you've been victimized by online auction fraud on eBay, visit the Complaints page to find links pertaining to reporting and dealing with fraud. Furthermore, eBay offers users limited free insurance. You can file a formal complaint on eBay using the Fraud Reporting and Insurance Claim Form. You must file the complaint within 30 days from the auction's closing date (which is another good reason to contact sellers frequently throughout the auction process). eBay's insurance has a maximum coverage of $200, with a $25 deductible. Later in this chapter, you'll see how eBay's (and other online auction sites') fraud reporting services come into play when you're dealing with a deadbeat seller.

Amazon's Take on Fraud

Amazon takes fraud seriously as well, which is understandable because Amazon's auction site is a facet of a much larger business. Tom Holland, director of fraud detection and prevention at Amazon, says that the company regularly monitors certain auctions that would be likely targets for counterfeit items. "We have to be very proactive in spreading the word about fraud . . . we work together with law enforcement, government agencies, and public interest groups to set standards for policing sites and combating fraud vigilantly."

To help ensure buyer security, Amazon offers online auctionites the following services:

- *Safe shopping guarantee.* This guarantees to cover any amount up to $50 that a banking institution holds a buyer liable for when a credit card scam occurs.

- *Auction guarantee insurance logos.* Indicates to buyers that an auction item carries a money-back guarantee from $250 up to $1,000 if fraud occurs.

- *Valid credit card identification.* Requires all participants to present valid credit card information before they can participate in Amazon auctions.

- *Escrow services.* Enables buyers and sellers to use a "middleman" to ensure that the deal goes through.

- *Fraud investigation staff.* Patrols Amazon auctions on a continuous basis.

- *Zero-tolerance fraud policy.* Boots a buyer or seller off Amazon auctions instantly if one fraudulent incident occurs. As stated on the Amazon site, "If we discover fraud, there will be no suspensions, no warnings, no slaps on the wrist—frauds are not welcome."

The small sampling of online auction fraud-fighting tactics presented illustrates how auction communities are starting to share the responsibility of ensuring reasonably honest trading. In addition to the special fraud insurance programs and reporting features offered by the bigger sites, almost all sites offer feedback forums, and many provide message boards, member information areas, and more. The main point to walk away with is that sites are starting to take notice of fraudulent activities, and they are attempting to offer members some safeguards.

Ultimately, though, you're in charge of your own online safety. Therefore, to further add to your bag of fraud-fighting tricks, the next section presents a resource guide that outlines the steps you can take when you suspect fraud.

TAKING ACTION

Basically, online auction fraud takes two forms:

- Buyers don't receive the items they've paid for.
- Items are misrepresented as being in better condition or more valuable than they really are.

If you fall prey to fraud, you can and should do something about it. Remember, if you're being ripped off, other buyers are or will be ripped of as well. So it's in everyone's best interest for you to take action when fraud strikes. Following is a progressive presentation of steps you can take to counter fraud.

TIP

Obtaining a copy of a money order can take several weeks or even months, and will cost you a fee. If you suspect foul play, request a copy of the money order as soon as possible. You'll need it as you continue to pursue the issue.

Email the Seller

First things first: We know you've heard this before, but if you haven't received your item after a week or two, *email the seller (a few times!)*. Maybe there's been a mistake, or your auction got lost in the shuffle. In one instance that we personally experienced a seller accidentally sent an item to the wrong buyer. It took over four weeks and numerous email messages to straighten out the mix-up, but the deal eventually completed, and, through frequent email exchanges, it became clear that no fraud had been intended. In this case, the seller's overwhelming positive feedback rating helped to calm fears while we waited.

When you email a nonresponsive seller, keep your emails short, to the point, and, most important, *civil*. There's no need to threaten the seller with legal action or negative ratings just yet. If the seller doesn't respond within a day or two, prepare to file a fraud claim.

Gather Your Documentation

Just as with the ol' "email the seller" mantra, you've seen the "print hard copies" adage. That means, you won't be surprised to read it again! Before you start to file fraud complaints, gather hard copies of your documentation. Print out all email messages, the auction ad, and your end-of-auction notice from the online auction site.

Furthermore, if you sent a check or money order, gather evidence indicating whether the seller received the payment. Get a copy of the cancelled check or money order. You can obtain copies of cancelled checks from your bank. If you paid by money order, you'll need to contact the institution that sold you your money order (you saved your stub, right?). The money order stub should provide the address and phone number of the institution. Simply call or write to the institution and request a copy of the cancelled money order.

Obtain the Seller's Registration Information

If you haven't heard from the seller since you sent your money, you can usually turn to the online auction site to get the seller's user registration information. On some sites, such as eBay's, whenever you request a user's registration information, eBay automatically notifies the user that information has been requested. This official eBay notice might help to jumpstart communication between the seller and you. After you obtain the seller's information, attempt to contact the seller by phone or snail mail. Keep in mind that you'll be footing the bill for phone calls and postage, but it could be that a single phone call will clear up the issue. Again, keep your correspondence civil; the seller could have a plausible explanation. If your attempts to contact the seller via phone and mail are unsuccessful, it's time to upgrade your effort by involving the USPS.

Contact the USPS

If your attempts at communication have been futile and your transaction involved the U.S. Postal Service in any way (for example, you mailed your payment to the seller), you can file a complaint with the Postal Inspector's Office. The USPS provides a simple complaint form. You can get a form by calling 1-800-275-8777 (you'll even receive a postage-free envelope along with the form); by requesting a form via email at **fraud@uspis.gov**; or by downloading a form from the USPS Web site (**www.usps. gov/websites/depart/inspect**).

The Mail Fraud Statute (Title 18, United States Code, Section 1341) is the nation's oldest federal consumer protection statute, and it defines fraud as "a scheme or artifice which uses the U.S. Mail to obtain money or property by means of false or fraudulent representations." Therefore, if you used the USPS to send money for an auction item, the deadbeat seller can be charged with mail fraud. Furthermore, because of the rapid growth of the Internet and online auction activities, the Postal Inspection Service has formed the Internet Fraud Subgroups as part of its Consumer Fraud Working Group.

Another instance in which the USPS can come into play is when you have contacted a seller and the seller claims that your payment never arrived (and you don't have a copy of the cancelled check or money order). In that case, you can file a Lost Mail Claim at your local post office. You must fill out your

TIP

If a seller lies to the Postal Service about receiving your payment, or if your mail fraud complaint investigation pans out, the seller will be charged with both perjury and mail fraud.

part of the form as a buyer and turn it into the post office. Then, the post office will search for your item, send a Lost Mail Claim to the seller's neck of the woods, and require the seller to complete the form as well. All of this might not result in finding your payment, but it certainly will indicate to the seller that you're seriously attempting to resolve the transaction.

Turn to the Online Auction Site

If contacting the seller and the USPS doesn't do the trick, it's time to report the transaction to the online auction site, and, if it's closing in on the 30-day deadline imposed by some online auction sites' insurance coverage, file an insurance claim. Keep in mind that not all auction sites have fraud forms or insurance coverage—you'll need to read a site's fine print to find out what actions are available. At this point, take the time to use any reasonable fraud resource offered by the online site. One caveat—if you have to pay a fee for a service, forget it. You're trying to recoup money, not spend more!

TIP

You can help to prevent future fraud by filing your claim with the NFIC. Plus, several people who filed a report with the NFIC reported that they received a refund from deadbeat online auction sellers.

Contact the National Fraud Information Center

For general information and assistance, you should also visit the National Fraud Information Center at **www.fraud.org**. The NFIC was established in 1992 by the National Consumers League, the oldest non-profit consumer organization in the United States. Initially, the NFIC campaigned against the growing menace of telemarketing fraud, but the organization has since grown to counter a wide range of fraud activities, including Internet fraud. According to NFIC, the "Internet Fraud Watch was launched in March of 1996 enabling the NFIC to expand its services to help consumers distinguish between legitimate and fraudulent promotions in cyberspace." To file a possible scam with the NFIC, or to obtain information about online auction fraud, click the "Online Reporting Form" link on the NFIC Web site or call the NFIC hotline at 1-800-876-7060.

Contacting Other Organizations

In addition to contacting the USPS and NFIC, you can turn to a number of agencies when you suspect fraud. Instead of describing all of the agencies here, we'll provide their contact information. The key is to get your complaint heard. The more agencies

Online Auctions

you have working for you, the better chance you have of recouping your loss or at least making others aware of fraudulent activity. Agencies you should contact include:

- *Better Business Bureau* (**www.bbb.com**)
- *International Web Police* (**www.web-police.org**)
- *National Consumer Complaint Center for Internet Fraud, False Advertising, and Breached Warranties* (**www.alexanderlaw.com/nccc/cb-ftc.html**)
- *Your local district and state attorneys' office fraud groups* (see **janus.state.me.us/states.htm** for a clickable map to state government resources, and then file a written complaint with each office).
- *The seller's district and state attorneys' office fraud groups* (file a written complaint with each office in the seller's jurisdiction).

Bring in the Feds

Finally, while you're contacting agencies, don't forget to contact the feds—particularly the Federal Trade Commission. Your best bet is to file a complaint on the FTC's Web site at **www.ftc.gov**. The FTC compiles complaint data on Internet scams, so don't fall for that lame voting mentality of "my one voice doesn't count for much." Who knows? Maybe your complaint added to a few others will spark a federal investigation.

FEDERAL TRADE COMMISSION

Here's some evidence that the FTC is at work. Before February 1999, Craig Lee Hare, an "online merchant" in Florida, was cashing in on eBay and Up4Sale online auctions. Hare used eBay and Up4Sale to advertise new and used computers. He attracted bids as high as $2,700 each, but never delivered the goods or issued refunds. But the U.S. Federal Trade Commission caught up with Hare and convicted him of wire fraud. Hare was sentenced by the U.S. District Court in the Southern District of Florida to six months of home detention and three years of probation. Furthermore, he was ordered to pay restitution of over $22,000.

On a more widespread note, the FTC has launched Project SafeBid to work with auction houses and law enforcement agencies around the country. The FTC offers a toll-free consumer help line (877-FTC-HELP) where victims can report frauds.

Another reason to turn to the FTC is that, like most government agencies, the FTC offers a slew of pamphlets and informational resources designed to help consumers recognize scams (**www.consumer.gov**).

Finally, if you're really gung ho and would like to find some additional fraud assistance (including international help), visit InterGov (**www.intergov.org**), and InterGov's long list of resources at **www.intergov.org/public_administration/information/view_assistance.html**. InterGov's list of resources and links on its "Agencies" page is almost as long as the Web page's URL!

When You're Sure It's Fraud

After you've exhausted your resources and there are no more agencies to contact, it's time to move on. But before you wash your hands of the fraudulent transaction, you should follow through with some cathartic action, including:

- Contacting the seller's Internet Service Provider to notify it that the user is practicing fraudulent behavior on online auction sites.

- Leave negative feedback. Remember, don't be vindictive, be honest. Clearly warn others to stay away without jeopardizing your credibility with nasty remarks.

- Visit the online auction site's chat groups or message boards and freely talk about your negative experience. Let others know the seller's user ID so they can avoid those auctions. Frequently, auction community members create "bad seller" and "bad buyer" lists, and your bad seed's user ID could be listed among the undesirables.

Although none of these cathartic activities will get your money back for you, at least you'll know that you've done all you can to fight fraud and notify others. By continuing to have community members actively pursue fraudulent sellers (and many community members *do* actively pursue deadbeats), online auctioning can continue to gain in its fight against fraud.

ON A LIGHTER NOTE

With online auctions bringing so much enjoyment and success to millions of people, it's a shame to end this book's Buying section on a pessimistic note. Therefore, I present the following (with permission) to counter the deadbeats—an actual post from an active eBay mailing:

"My wife Jeanette just concluded a transaction with someone who may qualify for eBay sainthood. The seller is a-paleodude (Gordon G. Byrn). My wife bid on a small piece of fossilized coral. The seller immediately contacted us after the auction with an address and a shipping quote. I quote from the letter enclosed with the specimen:
****

Hello!
I hope you enjoy the goodies in this box. I truly appreciate your patience with me in estimating the shipping, but I realized that I quoted a bit too high, so I added quite a few additional specimens to your order. Included within are:

—the Devonian coral Dysphyllum (your original bid)

—a second, much larger specimen of the same coral type

—the Devonian coral Thamnophora, also known as Coenites, and old references refer to this as "Cladopora." All of these specimens are from the Martin Formation in central Arizona.

—a specimen of Cretaceous petrified wood, from the Dakota Formation of eastern Arizona (most petrified wood from AZ is Triassic in age, so this is a rarity)

—an as yet unidentified Cretaceous freshwater snail. This was found attached to the carbonized debris of a log (unrecoverable) in a terrestrial deposit. The locality that this came from is the Western-most extent of the Dakota Formation, and indicates a shoreline transition of the Pierre Seaway.

—just for fun, I added a garnet in (rhyolite?) matrix. This was found near Wickiup in western-central Arizona.

I hope you enjoy the contents! I have gone out and bought a scale, so I should not have this problem in the future.
Good luck with your collection, and may you find your treasures everywhere!!

Sincerely,
Gordon G. Byrn
a-paleodude
****

By the way folks, all of this detailed data makes the specimens MUCH more valuable for teaching.
Oh, yes! The bid price for the original specimen was $3.25!
Need I say more?"

end email

KEY POINTS

This chapter arms you with some fraud-fighting tools. Hopefully, you won't need the tools presented in this chapter, but at least you'll know where to turn if the need arises. Specifically, when you fear you've been had, you can:

- Email the seller—repeatedly.
- Obtain the seller's registration information and then call and send mail to the seller.
- Report the seller to the USPS.
- Use the online auction site's fraud resources.
- Contact the NFIC and other organizations.

- File a claim with the FTC.
- Notify the seller's ISP of the user's fraudulent activity.
- Leave honest negative feedback.
- Make your story known on chat groups and message boards.
- Finally, realize that fraudulent auctions are in the minority. Most transactions go through without a hitch. For successful auctioning, strive to work with people like a-paleodude—people who bring out the best in online auction communities.

PART THREE

THREE

GUIDE FOR SELLERS

10 CHAPTER

RESEARCH BEFORE
YOU SELL

RESEARCH: THE FIRST SELLING STRATEGY

Whether you are planning to sell a Sammy Sosa autographed baseball or your life-time collection of *TV Guides,* you'll have to find a place to sell your stuff. The first decision: where to sell. You may make a choice between specialized auctions such as AutographAuction.com (**www.autographauction.com**) or the Hollywood Auction (**www.thebroadcaster.com**), or auctions known for carrying a large variety of merchandise, like eBay or Amazon Auctions. Specifically, if Sammy is at the plate, your choices should be narrowed to sports memorabilia auctions like SportsAuction (**www.SportsAuction.com**) or SportsTrade (**www.sportstrade.com**) or to a major auction such as eBay.

Whether selling an Andy Warhol print or figure skates, you'll need to consider the following:

- *Auction fees.* When you know how much you'll profit, you'll be able to determine a fair level for auction fees.

- *Traffic at the site.* Lots of traffic is great for attracting bids on a wide variety of merchandise.

- *Good merchandise match.* Have other skates sold there?

- *Good prices.* Did the skates bring a good price?

The first step in maximizing online auction sales is research, research, and more research. You may think that an item is only worth $25 but with a bit of research perhaps you'll discover that something similar just sold for $47. Your goal: Find the best-fitting auction, where items like yours sell for top dollar, with a minimal or reasonable seller's expense.

Through the process of researching and selecting a venue, you can learn how to best position your Rawlings Catcher's Mitt or Cuisinart Pasta Maker. Conducting research on auctions that have closed will help you to plan your auction. When looking at closed sales you'll want to note the following:

- How individual auctions were categorized
- Whether the sellers had set reserves
- On what day of the week (and at what time of day) the most successful auctions closed
- The prices set for opening bids

Don't sell 1929 ticker tape or a rare stock certificate during market hours. If brokers are your audience, they'll be pacing the floor of the stock exchange while your auction gathers dust. Make sure that your audience is available when your auction is about to close.

Office supplies sell well during afternoon business hours on both coasts. If you are selling an item for home use, consider evenings. For most auction sales, select closing times that include both coasts. Tickets to a regional event should be timed for that region. One of the best examples of timing relates to Saturday concert tickets. When do they sell? Tuesday, Wednesday, and Thursday! We do know one thing, it won't be on Saturday. Nor Friday or Sunday.

T I P

Regifting Revised

Did you receive one too many cake plates for your wedding? Sell one at auction. You don't have to tell Aunt Lucy.

Research Plan

Spend some time visiting auction sites to see what other people are selling. Research is important once you have selling items in mind, but that first research step may also provide the kick you need to raid the closets and clean the basement. You may even want to return to your parents' house to finally clean out your childhood bedroom. Old Barbie dolls, bobbing-head baseball players, pristine Gumbies, and Pez dispensers are now valuable treasures sought by collectors.

I (Luanne) now regret having given away numerous saleable items before online auctions became popular. I've not yet joined the avid sellers who raid yard sales on Saturday mornings, and then list auctions all week. But my priority list of salable possessions includes name-brand clothes, baby clothes and equipment, cookbooks, software, my brother's Lionel train, my other brother's baseball cards, kitchen appliances, roller skates, modems, steam irons, candlesticks, wine glasses, watches, and more.

How Much Traffic Is There?

Traffic matters to both buyers and sellers. Buyers can get their best bargains where there's little competition. But that's no advantage to you. Sellers get the most from auctions where traffic is heavy. With lots of bidders, there are more opportunities for *someone* to start the bidding. After the first bidder bids, more will jump in to the bidding excitement. In total thrill bidding, the excitement is contagious.

My grandmother's 1940s chrome toaster provides an auction seller's opportunity. But where should I sell it? I look at the kitchen appliances offered by the biggest auction sites. A quick search reveals (as seen in Table 10.1) that eBay's Home Furnishings category and Excite's Appliances category are both worth consideration. From the research I've done, I've concluded that my grandmother's chrome toaster should bring $25.

KNOW YOUR SITE

As you enter the auction world, take a few minutes to get to know each auction site. Investigate site maps and search tools. Become familiar with the search engine so you'll know whether the default search "reads" titles only or titles and descriptive listings. Amazon's engine searches titles and listings, while eBay's searches titles. eBay's engine returns more pertinent search lists.

Search engines generate the fastest responses when queries return the fewest matches. Each word in a search string is called a *keyword.* As you add keywords to the search string, the engine will return fewer (but more specific or closely matching) responses. Once you've gotten a general feel for a site, its time to get specific.

TABLE 10.1

Auction Sites and Kitchen Appliances

Auction	Category	No. of Items
eBay	Home furnishings	1700
Excite	Appliances	1453
Amazon	Household items	266
Yahoo!	Kitchen appliances	164
CityAuction	Electronics and appliances	60
Auctions.com	Kitchen items	20

Research Checklist

When you've gotten a feel for items that sell well at auction, focus your research. Take stock of each item's characteristics for use in the auction title and description:

- Size
- Weight
- Color
- Characteristics
- Features
- Age
- Condition

Is that item a large blue vase or an antique 9-inch Wedgwood Jasperware cachepot? Are those casements colored residential windows or 1920s leaded stained glass church windows? Do you have a black golf bag or a New Titleist Lightweight Golf Bag? You'll want to search the sites for sales of items like yours—knowing the details will make your research more efficient. Once you've made a list of the details above, you'll need to know how to use them to do a search.

Search Techniques for Sellers

Search competitors' auctions and closed listings to find the most successful terminology and the best ways to position the postage stamps or Springsteen tickets. A few minutes of work can generate more dollars for you. By studying other auctions, you'll quickly see which were most successful in attracting bidders and in closing at high prices.

While there's always more than one way to search, it's most efficient to search closed auctions from well-designed search pages. Buyers and sellers can quickly apply their knowledge of closed high bids to their auctions. Review Table 10.2 for the fastest access to closed auction searches.

It's not possible to conduct a general search of closed auctions at Yahoo! You can track specific auctions by seller or item number, but the task may be tedious.

Search Tools and Techniques

Auction *search tools* are search engines that work the same way as Internet search engines. You may be familiar with those under the names Yahoo!, AOL, Excite, and Go Network (Infoseek).

The words you type into the text boxes are called *keywords,* and they get the search rolling. Most search engines use "boolean logic," and that simply means they allow the words *and* and *or* in the keyword search. The following examples (Table 10.3) are from eBay, which has the most advanced auction search engine. Most auction search functions work similarly.

T A B L E 10.2

Completed Auction Searches

Auction Site	To Search Completed Auctions . . .
Amazon Auctions	Choose Auction Search from the menu bar to reach search page. Choose the Completed Auctions button.
Auctions.com	Choose the Power Search link to get to the search page where you can select Closed Auctions in the Auction Status box.
CityAuction	Select Search and choose completed auctions from the last two days, last two weeks, or all completed auctions.
eBay	Use the Search button at the top of most pages to access the search page. Use the Completed Items link. Alternatively, whenever a search list of active items is generated, clicking the "Search Completed Items" link results in a closed auction for the same search criteria.
Excite	From the home page, select a category, and if available, a subcategory. A search page for the category will appear. Scroll down to Advanced Search Options and select Closed Auctions.
Yahoo!	Closed auctions can only be searched by auction ID number.

T A B L E 10.3

eBay Auction Search Techniques

If You Enter . . .	Search Will Find Items That . . .
Travel book	include both of the words *travel* and *book*
(travel,book) (no spaces after comma)	include either the word *travel* **or** *book*
"travel book"	include the exact phrase *travel book*
travel −book	include the word *travel* but **not** *book*
travel +book	include the words *travel* **and** *book*
foot*	include foot: *football, footed bowl, footprints,* etc.
travel −(book, magazine)	include the word *travel,* but **not** *book* or *magazine*
#1865	include the year or number *1865*
"Adirondack chair"	include the exact phrase *Adirondack chair*
@0 travel book	include either the word *travel* **or** *book*
@1 Europe travel book book	include at least two of the words of *Europe, travel,* and *book*
Doll clothes	include both of the words *doll* **and** *clothes*
silver $5	include both of the words *silver* **and** *$5*

When selecting to search auction titles or titles and descriptions, we strongly recommend that you search titles only. This will keep your search at a manageable size. It will also be the most efficient procedure for you and the search engine.

Sales Recon Secrets

When an auction site makes it possible to search closed listings, that smartly facilitates deals. Knowing an item's potential value can be a big help when preparing to auction an item. Recent sales are the best "comparative" price resources. Last week's Cuisinart DLC-7 food processor sold for a high bid of $150, and there were 15 bidders. There's a good chance that 14 bidders are wondering if they should have bid $150.01. Those bidders are waiting for you to post the next DLC-7.

Auctions that have closed in the past 30 days provide a realistic estimate of what you can garner for your gizmo. Within that window of time, many of the same bidders will still be active and looking.

Using Search Options

There are three main methods for conducting searches on auction merchandise:

- *Category search.* The first option is to navigate to the category and page through the lists. But just imagine searching through a list of 93,601 baseball cards to find the near-mint 1960 Topps #350 Mickey Mantle card! To conduct a category search, select the Category link from the auction home page and continue selecting links until you reach the desired subcategory.

- *Searching within a category.* A second option is to use the search engine to focus exclusively on a certain category. If you are quite sure, for example, that all porcelain figurines fall into the Porcelains category, use the category level search engine. In some cases this may even be the subcategory search. To search within a category, select the Category link from the auction home page. At the appropriate category or subcategory page, use the search tool. Enter keywords and be sure to check the box indicating a search only within that one category.

- *Top-level searching.* The third option, and the one I use most frequently, is to begin the search from the Search box on the home page or from the auction site's main search page. A 50-year-old A&P clove spice tin may be categorized with Collectibles or with Kitchen Décor. Begin with a top-level search and you'll be able to develop a list of possibilities—no matter how categorized. To conduct a top-level search, enter the keywords in the search box on the home page or the main search page. As you review the list of auctions, take note of how each was categorized. This search will help you decide which category is best for your grandmother's spice tin.

Closed Searches

The same three search methods can be used as starting points to conduct searches on closed auctions:

- *Closed category search.* From the auction home page, select the Category link, and continue selecting links until you reach the desired subcategory. Toward the top of the category listing, select the link for Closed Auctions.

- *Closed auction searches within a category.* From the auction home page, select the Category link. At the appropriate category or subcategory page, use the search tool. Enter keywords and be sure to check the box indicating a search only within that one category. Select the link to search completed items.

- *Closed auction searches within top-level searching.* From main search page, enter the keywords in the search box. On eBay, type keywords into the Completed Auctions search box. At other sites, select the Completed Auctions checkbox or radio button.

The Power of Not

An eBay search for just the term *not* yielded 3237 results. Some were employed in titles to attract crossover sales. An example is a common finding in children's clothing listings: Gymboree not Gap. This attracts two classes of bidders; those who specify Gymboree in their searches, and those who specify Gap. Such crossover, or spam, listings are often in violation of a site's guidelines, but they are rarely detected by auction site management. Some bidders, however, find them annoying and won't bid on auctions with crossover titles. They can be effective advertising, though, so consider using them.

T I P

Like Gap!

"Like" is similar to the use of "not" in attracting crossover buyers. An example is **Old Navy like Gap.**

A more quizzical use of "not" is that which generates "not working." Believe it or not, there are bidders who are happy to buy all those "not workings" in the basement. In a quick check, I found this watch listing:

Gold Seth Thomas Pocket Watch Not Working

The search string to find this was:

watch "not working"

Isn't this interesting? Someone sold a watch described as, "It doesn't run and the face is cracked and the lense (sic) is missing. Use for parts or whatever . . ." There's a seller who received $17.52 for something that had been sitting in a drawer. Go check that junk drawer!

It's best to put quotes around **not working** so that the search returns those words used together. I've experienced some inconsistency in the results from this string when I've not used the quotes. Without the quotes, eBay's search engine has interpreted it as minus **working,** meaning that it removes all listings with any reference to working.

Another way to enter this search is to type **watch working not** in the search box. Since no word is listed after "not," no search words are excluded. Other terms to try are **doesn't work, does not work,** and **not running.**

For the sake of efficiency, "not working" searches should be conducted only on titles. The following examples (Figure 10.1) demonstrate the treasures that can be found with this search.

Resources

There's no better resource than an auction search engine that can perform searches on completed sales. Get to know the ins and outs of the search engine at your favorite site.

F I G U R E 10.1

A completed search on "working not," sorted by high bid.

	Search Result			
	Completed Auctions			
	08:01:59 PDT			
Item#	**Item**	**Price**	**Bids**	**Ends**
97623457	Marantz 10B Not Working--No Reserve!	**$500.00**	1	05/04 10:29
94999801	Tempest video arcade game (not working) **PIC**	**$305.00**	16	05/01 13:34
99257305	**HOT!** Toshiba Libretto 30CT Notebook "Not working" **PIC**	**$303.57**	40	05/06 11:00
99031853	AS - IS Minolta XK with AE Prism, not working **PIC**	**$222.50**	16	05/09 17:31
98282128	Motorola HT1000 VHF 16 Channel Not Working	**$192.50**	18	05/07 22:38
96092060	"Compaq Presario 4712" Not working....	**$187.50**	23	05/02 20:00
92649925	Hitachi VM-H39A Hi8 camcorder-not working	**$153.50**	15	04/25 05:41
93125313	ATTRACTIVE WORKING STIRLING ENGINE~Not Steam **PIC**	**$152.50**	13	04/23 21:18
93781351	IBM 350c NOT WORKING, BUT HAS USEABLE PARTS!!	**$103.00**	25	04/27 15:12
97895877	Marantz Model 4230 Quadradial 4 NOT WORKING **PIC**	**$102.50**	18	05/06 20:21

KEY POINTS

In this chapter we talked about the importance of conducting research before you sell. This research forms the backbone of your selling strategy.

- Develop a research plan.
- Determine the characteristics and selling features of your auctionable item.
- Find the best site for your goods.
- Use a variety of search options.
- Search for items like yours that have recently sold.

11
CHAPTER

WHICH AUCTION
VENUE IS BEST?

What makes a top auction site? Lots of traffic, lots of buzz. Closely related to the traffic at each site is the organization of the site. Bidders bid where auctions are well organized and the search tools are efficient.

FINDING THE BEST LOCATION

"Location, location, and location" are the top three buzzwords in real estate. Those same keywords are equally crucial to online auction sellers. Auction sellers must have traffic, and in the online world, prominent sites possess the attribute known as *location*.

Amazon Auctions, Auctions.com, CityAuction, eBay, Excite, and Yahoo! Auctions are the largest person-to-person auctions. The flea markets and garage sales of the Internet, these are exactly what you need. Individual buyers and sellers come together here and enjoy transactions with technology:

auctions.amazon.com

auctions.com

cityauction.com

eBay.com

auctions.excite.com

auctions.yahoo.com

Amazon Auctions

Amazon's power in the online marketplace carries over to its auction site. This site is immediately compelling and has quickly gained a dedicated base of buyers and sellers. Amazon's default search looks both at titles and the descriptive text, which can lead to confusing results if you are accustomed to other sites whose default search pattern is titles only. An interesting aspect for sellers is the cross-selling that Amazon attempts. The software that I auctioned there was cross-linked to books within the Amazon bookstore. At the time of my sales some cross-links were not appropriate, but constant improvement is a hallmark at Amazon.

Just for fun, I looked for Elvis. He was sighted 155 times across several Amazon categories.

Need sales ideas? Amazon has a weekly newsletter of wacky and unusual items for sale. From the home page, select the "Amazon.com Delivers" link to sign up for a weekly newsletter tailored to your tastes. The first two columns of selection cover Amazon books. Auction fans make selections from the third column. "Bizarre Bazaar" brings the way-out auctions. Blooper videos, toys for cats, and odd cookie jars have been seen on this list. "What's Hot" conveys the hottest auctions! One recent issue contained hot movie memorabilia, digital cameras, and audio equipment.

Auctions.com

Snooze and lose. How *does* one win here? This is a sparsely populated town. Auctions.com has created its own directory of category headers, making it hard to compare activity with competitors' auction sites. Its (few) followers must be very loyal, because there's little reason to return. Bidders may find bargains here, as there are few bidders to compete with, but I'd compare prices before making the effort to sell here.

Elvis is having a near-death experience at Auctions.com. A search of the Elvis subcategory reveals only 28 items for sale, including five records. In the Elvis subcategories more are empty than occupied.

CityAuction

With most person-to-person auctions, users can trade in a large national or international marketplace. CityAuction also offers local users the opportunity to trade online. Traders can take part in the local or global marketplaces. When sellers start new auctions, they are asked where they want their items to be advertised. On the first visit to CityAuction, bidders also select a home region. CityAuction's software shows everything that's for sale, whether it's local, or anywhere in the world.

One of the best reasons for the existence of local auctions or local "options" within auctions is the tricky problem of shipping bulky items. While local auctions necessarily attract a smaller bidding pool, some bidders are more likely to trust—and therefore bid in—local auctions.

There were nine Elvis sightings at CityAuction, with collectibles that included driver's license replicas, key chains, and signs.

eBay

This is the biggest and best of the online auctions. As of this writing, eBay has the most buyers, the most sellers, and the largest advertising budget. eBay is the granddaddy of online auctions (in the short life of the Internet). For general merchandise—and many specialized items—it should always be at the top of your list. eBay's "Personal Shopper" feature tracks three designated searches and reports the results to you by email. As a seller, before adding your items to the bidding use the "Personal Shopper" to track similar ones.

There's a virtual Graceland at eBay. Elvis rules, with 2309 sightings just within Memorabilia: Rock & Roll category. In all, Elvis has been seen 4048 times in the current auctions.

Community is a big word in the online world. It may be the biggest word at eBay. Huge numbers of bidders have spawned innumerable communities. Many of those communities have formed mailing lists to help users share information on how to make the most of eBay's many opportunities and features. In Resources at the end of this chapter, you'll find more information on locating communities.

Excite

This alias of Classifieds2000 falls short with bidders. Excite's "Cool Notify" can be used as a wishlist for tracking items when they become available. Searching Excite's auctions can be annoying when searches return unrelated classifieds. Thinking of the American Girl dolls, I typed just *American Girl* into the search function. While the first item on the list *was* an American Girl doll, the others were personal ads.

A handy feature on Excite is the way top-level searches are returned. The list shows the category adjacent to the title of each listing, making it easy to see which

---

e B A Y   T I P

Are you thinking of selling Grandmother's china, but you'd like to monitor the action first? Try eBay's Personal Shopper. Enter up to three searches, and they will automatically send an email (at the frequency you set) for up to 90 days. You'll receive notices of new auctions added that match the criteria on your wish list. Personal Shopper was created for bidders, but it can also be a great research tool for sellers.

FIGURE 11.1

Excite's Elvis population can be sparse.

Auction Keyword Search Results

Search for [Elvis] in [All Categories ▼] [Search]

We found 37 ads. Displaying ads 1 - 10.

[◄◄ Prev 10] [Next 10 ►►]

75% **Dolls: ELVIS PRESLEY - 3 Doll set, Vinyl/Plastic, $199.95, Victoria,.....**
AUCTION ENDS 06/04/99 08:00 PM PST. Mint, ELVIS PRESLEY COLLECTORS...here
are 3 seperatley dressed Elvis dolls and in original boxes(never opened)...the dolls...
Detailed search form: > Dolls

73% **Audio Media: Record, ELVIS PRESLEY, HIS HAND IN MINE, $8, Fort Smith,.....**
AUCTION ENDS 06/06/99 09:00 PM PST. Elvis Presley, His hand in mine, RCA label,
Stereo ANL1-1319-A. Orange Label, with white lettering RCA. Song selections...
Detailed search form: Merchandise > Audio Media

73% **Memorabilia (non-sport): Elvis Presely...1st. in series, Music, $75,.....**
AUCTION ENDS 05/31/99 08:00 PM PST. Mint, Certificate of Authenticity, Mattel-20544.
Mint Collector Edition and never removed from window front box. 1st. in the...
Detailed search form: > Memorabilia (non-sport)

73% **Paper: ELVIS PRESLEY, Other Type, $9, Charlotte, NC**
AUCTION ENDS 05/31/99 02:00 PM PST. ELVIS PRESLEY- A COURT-OBTAINED
LAST WILL & TESTAMENT OF ELVIS A. PRESLEY. THIS DOCUMENT, FILED JUST 5

categories are most likely to have the Elvis items. As seen in Figure 11.1, Elvis was
spotted 37 times in Excite in a wide variety of categories.

Yahoo!

Yahoo! Auctions was *the* site to watch before Amazon entered the race. While Yahoo!
has its hand in large numbers of auctions, the marketing prowess of Amazon threat-
ens to drop Yahoo! to third position. The number of items for sale makes this an interesting place, but there are more bargains for bidders than strong opportunities for
sellers. Still, it's a good place to list auctions free of charge.

Elvis has his own subcategory of Rock & Roll Memorabilia here. He was
sighted more than 250 times. Yahoo!'s volume remains second to eBay's.

FEE VERSUS NO FEE

When choosing an auction venue for Beatles LPs, nose hair clippers, and Chatty
Cathy dolls, you'll need to consider auction fees. There are two basic types of auc-

tion fees: *listing* fees and *final value* fees. Taking a page from classified advertising, listing fees may alternatively be called *insertion* fees.

Listing fees are the prices you pay to advertise your wares on major auction sites. Listing fees are nonrefundable, and they are determined by the initial bid or reserve level set by the seller. Where listing fees are charged, most sites' fees are comparable. Be sure to check the fee list for each site before listing high-value items like cars or real estate. In this Monopoly game, you'll find flat-rate fees for these items on eBay.

In a Reserve Price auction, the listing fee is based on the Reserve Price set by the seller. When an auction has a reserve, the seller is not obligated to sell if the high bid is less than the reserve. A Schwinn beach bike may be listed for $10, with a reserve of $75. The low initial bid is set to encourage bidders to get the bidding started. The reserve fee is not revealed to the bidder, but acts as insurance to the seller.

Dutch auctions are auctions where several of the same item are placed for bid. The insertion fees for Dutch auctions are a multiple of minimum bid. Place 15 identical disposable cameras up for auction, with an opening bid of $4.00. The insertion fee is 15 times the insertion fee for one item of the same value.

Take a look at Table 11.1 for types of auctions and listing fees.

Final-value fees are just what you'd expect. They are commissions calculated on the final selling price—the high bid. Final-value fees can be refunded by the auction venues when a seller encounters a bidder who fails to pay for the merchandise. On these rare occasions, sellers can relist the items in addition to requesting a refund of the final-value fee. After the completion of the second auction, fees are adjusted so sellers pay only one listing fee and one final-value fee.

Consider whether it is worth paying a listing fee and a final value fee for an antique teapot in the $200 range or for an unsigned, third printing of a Tom Clancy book, likely to sell for $3. One strategy is to alternate the sale of a low-priced item between a free auction and an auction with fees. I auctioned several children's software titles individually on free auctions. When three packages remained, I bundled

TABLE 11.1

Auctions and Listing Fees

Type of Auction	Listing Fee Is Based On
General auctions	opening bid set by seller
Reserve price auctions	reserve price set by seller
Dutch auction	opening bid set by seller multiplied by the quantity of items offered
Real estate	Flat rate (on eBay)
Automobiles	Flat rate (on eBay)

TABLE 11.2

Fee and Free Auctions

Fee	Free
Amazon	Excite
Auctions.com	Yahoo!
CityAuction*	
eBay	

*There is no listing fee at CityAuction. Users incur a final value fee on items sold, but pay no fee on items that fail to attract bidders.

them and placed them for auction at Amazon. I was very satisfied with the final bid! By grouping them, listing and final value fees were incurred on the *group* (or *lot*) rather than on each item. The mechanics of paying the auction sites are discussed in Chapter 13, "Decide Your Price."

Sites without fees may have a lower volume of traffic. That can be bad news for sellers. Research these sites carefully to determine if the fee-frees are worth it. Such auction sites (see Table 11.2) may not be the best places to sell your high-value treasures, but they may be the perfect places for $3 or $4 items. Auctions.com charges a flat 25-cent listing fee. At CityAuction, there is no listing fee, but users incur a final-value fee on auctions that attract bids.

Look for other fee-free sites in specialty auctions (e.g., Mother's Nature—**www. mothersnature.com**) or at advertiser-supported sites (e.g., Yahoo!), where auction traffic is exposed to advertisements. Yahoo! is a site that charges neither insertion fees nor final value fees. CityAuction charges only final value fees on auctions that close with winning bids.

TABLE 11.3

Comparing Reserve Auction Fees

Opening Value or Reserve Price	Amazon Insertion Fee	eBay Reserve Auction Fee +	eBay Insertion Fee
$0.01–$9.99	$0.25	$0.50	$0.25
$10.00–$24.99	$0.50	$0.50	$0.50
$25.00–$49.99	$1.00	$1.00	$1.00
$50.00 and up	$2.00	$1.00	$2.00

TABLE 11.4

Final Price Commissions

Range of Final Price	Amazon Auctions	eBay
$0.00–$25.00	5.00%	5% of the amount of the high bid (at the auction close) up to $25
$25.01–$1,000.00	$1.25 plus 2.5% of any amount over $25	plus 2.5% of that part of the high bid from $25.01 up to $1,000.00
$1,000.01 and up	$25.63 plus 1.25% of any amount over $1,000	plus 1.25% of the remaining amount of current high bid that is greater than $1,000.00

Calculating the Fees

Let's take a look at the fees related to a new Polaroid One Step camera recently sold on eBay. The opening bid was $5.00. For this illustration, please assume the reserve was $9.99. eBay does not reveal reserves. Referring to the listing fees in Table 11.3, we see that the seller incurred seventy-five cents. If he had opted to list his camera on Amazon, he would have incurred a lower fee—but many sellers are willing to pay that difference in order to reach eBay's larger market.

Now let's compare the final value fees across the same three auction venues. (See Table 11.4.) After eight bids, the bidding closed with a high bid of $20.50. The final value fee is $1.03 whether sold on Amazon or eBay. The total fees for this transaction are $1.28 ($0.25 plus $1.03) on Amazon, with the same net cost on eBay. eBay refunds the Reserve Fee when the reserve price is met.

If the camera auction had not met the seller's reserve, the eBay seller would have incurred seventy-five cents, while the Amazon seller was out only twenty-five cents.

If the selling price had been $100, the final value fee on both eBay and Amazon would have been $3.12 ($1.25 + $1.87). Amazon's total fees for the Polaroid would have been $3.37. With the refundable reserve fee, eBay's total fees would also be $3.37.

In general, sellers are not charged a final-value fee if:

- There are no bids on the item, OR
- There are no bids meeting the reserve price in Reserve Price Auctions.

BONUS! MORE FEATURES FOR SELLERS

You can attract more bidders through the use of special advertising features. The major auction sites include advertising-type features for those sellers who are willing to pay additional fees for the added exposure. These may appeal to high-volume sellers and sellers of high-value items. Not everyone can use them, however. Premium features are often reserved for sellers who have achieved a certain feedback rating or a set number of sales. A review of these fees and benefits appears in Table 11.5.

eBay's very reasonable "Gallery" fees may be worthwhile for items that have significant visual appeal. Buyers of clothing or jewelry are often window shoppers attracted to the thumbnail views in the Gallery. Exposure in the Gallery may help well-photographed items stand out in a crowded marketplace. Since the thumbnail offers only an initial view of an item, first impressions count. Don't incur the Gallery fee if the image is not top-notch.

TABLE 11.5

Feature Fees on Amazon and eBay

Feature Fees	Benefit	Amazon	eBay
Boldface title	Prominent appearance on category and search lists	$2.00	$2.00
Reserve auction fee	Price insurance for the seller		$1.00
Category feature auction	Appears on the feature list at the beginning of designated category	$14.95	
Featured category auction	Appears on the feature list at the beginning of designated category		$14.95
Auctions home page	Very prominent position; rotates with others on auction home page	$99.00	
Featured auction	Very prominent position; rotates with others on auction home page		$99.00
Gift icon	Attention-getter icon; appears with auction title		$1.00
Gallery	Thumbnail sized image appearing in a category style list		$0.25
Featured in gallery	Larger than thumbnail; appearing at the "top" of the gallery category		$19.95

Note: For eBay's Featured Auction and Featured Category auction, sellers must have a feedback rating of at least 10.

MEGA-SEARCHING

When it is time to branch out to unique auctions, we usually don't have time to prowl the Web. Instead we can turn to a group of sites that offers links to hundreds of specialty auctions. At other times, we turn to sites that conduct auction searches for us. With the right search tools, I can find the sites to sell an axe, apple tree, and juice machine.

Look at Table 11.6 and you'll see 13 sites representing the variety of auction specialty sites. Consider selling at these sites, or use them as price guides. More sites like these can be found through AuctionWatch, the Internet Auction List, and Yahoo!'s Auction List.

First, we'll take a look at how to find specialized auctions. Scores of specialized auctions can be found through Web search engines. Enter **auction list** and you will be greeted with a compilation of great starting points. When using the search tools, please be aware that some of the results generated will not be person-to-person auctions.

AuctionWatch

The AuctionWatch (**www.auctionwatch.com**) site is a terrific resource that brings together a directory of auction sites, auction news, message boards, and image hosting. General and specialty auction sites are arrayed into categories with an easy to navigate layout, linking users to the auction sites. We'll cover more about Auction-Watch's image hosting services in Chapter 14, "Preparing a Great Ad."

T A B L E 11.6

Leading Specialty Sites

Category	Representative Sites
Car memorabilia	www.mobilia.com
Coins	www.coin-universe.com
Computer products	auctions.cnet.com
Golf clubs (only)	www.golfclubexchange.com
Historical documents	www.collectingchannel.com,
	www.galleryofhistory.com
Horses	www.cyberhorse.com
Quilts	www.quiltcollector.com
Sports cards	www.curranscards.com
Stamps	www.collectors.com/stamps
Travel	www.Bid4Travel.com
Wine	www.winebid.com

The Internet Auction List

One of the best of the all-auction sites is The Internet Auction List (**www.internetauctionlist.com**). The list's site is packed with news about the online auction world and features access to innumerable specialty auctions. Publications, directories, schools, and software are linked from here. This site maintains the largest list of auction company web sites found on the Internet.

Yahoo!'s Auction List

Once you get to Yahoo!'s Auction List (see below) you'll be rewarded with a comprehensive list of over 400 auction-related links, and over 200 directly related to online auction sites. Yahoo! generates this list at the difficult URL:

> **dir.yahoo.com/Business_and_Economy/Companies/Auctions/Online_Auctions/**

Alternatively, from Yahoo.com's home page, choose the Business & Economy link, followed by the links for Companies and Auctions.

COMPARATIVE SHOPPING

Too much searching, not enough time? Lighten the load by employing search engines that conduct multiple auction searches.

BidStream

BidStream (**www.bidstream.com**) conducts multiple auction searches. While not all auctions—nor all categories—are included, it is still a good first stop to find out which site is selling treasures like yours. BidStream's category list includes a large number of small auctions, certainly sites that would take too long to visit sequentially. One entry in BidStream's search box results in a review of the inventory in all of the participating auction sites. For sales of items in one of these categories, check BidStream first:

- Antiques and collectibles
- Books, music, and videos
- Business goods and services
- Clothing and jewelry
- Computers
- Electronics and cameras
- Home and garden
- Sports and recreation
- Toys and games

- Travel and vacations
- Vehicles
- Other goods and services

Bidder's Edge

Bidder's Edge (**www.biddersedge.com**) is a Web site that provides "buying tools" for people shopping at online auctions. You can search its continuously updated database for auction product and pricing information. Bidder's Edge searches for items across multiple auction houses at once. The database is organized by category, and is updated as new auctions are opened and others are closed. Bidder's Edge provides detailed historical information on items that have appeared for sale before. "My Auctions" list provides detailed auction searches—across multiple auctions. "The Deal Watch" list ensures that you are notified quickly when an item you are interested in comes up for sale again.

TIP

Mirror, Mirror . . . The sales located through Lycos' Auction Connect (www.lycos.com/ auctions) are the same as those found at Bidder's Edge.

iTrack

iTrack (**www.itrack.com**) searches eBay, Yahoo!, and Amazon for specific items that you designate. ITrack automatically searches the site you designate, for the items you specify, and delivers the results to your email account. eBay's "Personal Shopper" is similar, but it only searches for new auctions on eBay. iTrack searches over a dozen auction sites. There are three levels of iTrack membership, with a free (advertiser-supported) level of five searches open to all. There are two paid membership levels, allowing ten and 20 concurrent searches. Free users encounter brief advertisements in their iTrack email.

DECIDE YOUR CATEGORY

Once you have selected the best site on which to auction your items, it's time to select the best-fitting category.

Closely related to the traffic at each site is the site's organization. Bidders tend to return to sites where auctions are well organized and the search tools are efficient. Each auction site's order (or disorder!) can be seen in how effectively categories and subcategories are defined.

Some bidders page through the category listings, while others use the search tools to zero in on their targets. To reach both types of bidders make sure that each auction listing is searchable and in the best-fitting category. Conduct searches for comparable items and consider alternate locations or categories.

When choosing a category, you'll want to look at the competition in the various available areas before making a decision. For example, is Sunset's *Western Garden Book* better suited to the "Miscellaneous: Garden Items: Publications" category or to the "Books: Non-Fiction: Home & Garden" category? Well, there are six times as many gardening books in eBay's "Books" category as in its "Garden Items" category.

To take this a step further, I searched on the term **garden book** within each of the categories and subcategories, as shown in Table 11.7, and then I looked at closed listings to assess sales. While far more books were listed under "Books:Non-Fiction:Home & Garden," a higher percentage sold under Miscellaneous: Garden Items Publications.

I'd advise the 42 unfortunate sellers in the "Books" category to relist their books in the more successful category, "Miscellaneous: Garden Items: Publications."

CROSSOVERS

When selecting a category, you'll want to place your auction in the category that *most successfully sells* even if it results in a crossover listing. As you just saw, although there are many gardening books listed under the "Books" umbrella, these particular titles sell far better under the "Home Items" category.

Whenever you consider a category, give some thought to whether a crossover listing might be more successful. Cookbooks specifically written for use with bread machines may have better sales with appliances. Would a spy camera be more appropriate with cameras or with home security?

Crossover listings can be a bad idea in some categories—especially if the crossover results in a higher listing fee. On eBay, listings in the "Automotive" and

T A B L E 11.7

Compare and Select Categories

Category	Books	Miscellaneous
Subcategory	Non-Fiction	Garden Items
Subcategory	Home & Garden	Publications
Number of closed auctions	100	52
Auctions with bids	58	42
Auctions without bids	42	10
Percentage sold	58%	81%

"Real Estate" categories incur different fees than those in other categories. The listing fee is higher, but the total of the listing and final value fees on these high-priced items is lower. However, it's not likely to be a good idea to list your Hot Wheels miniature Corvette with the automotive listings.

DIRECTORIES AND CATEGORIES

Next you should visit each of the major auction sites and check the counts for each category that you're considering. That's an important step in determining the best placement for your product.

Amazon

Choose a category link from the Amazon auction home page (**auctions.amazon.com**). On the next page, under "Full Results," it will list how many auctions are currently in that category. If no number is stated, select a subcategory for a count. Amazon is growing quickly and can be expected to fall between eBay and Yahoo! in most categories.

Auctions.com

The Auctions.com (**www.auctions.com**) home page features the categories and the item count for each category. As you select subcategories, the category counts appear. For collectors this is an okay site, but not a stellar venue. There are *many* low-count subcategories.

CityAuction

CityAuction (**www.cityauction.com**) has a good PR team, but the auction site has little depth. Select a category from the home page, and you will encounter short lists on successive pages. My local selection, Washington, D.C., yielded only 20 auctions. A look at the baby items category listed two items—and neither was appropriate for a baby.

TIP

Shopping Bots

BotSpot.com is a good place to start if you just aren't satisfied with these multiauction search tools. Bots are agents that conduct your searches for you. Give up the thought of a micron-sized person doing your searches. Bots are specialized search engines. This site (**http://botspot.com/search/s-shop.htm**) links to four dozen Shopping bots for auctions searches and for "retail" e-commerce searches.

eBay

This blockbuster has it all. With 3 million auctions, what might be missing? There are so many packed categories that eBay (**www.ebay.com**) frequently adds new categories and subcategories. Counted among 600,000 collectibles are 1,937 lunchboxes! Delve into subcategories and get to know the powerful search tools. The search page helps users sift through the hundreds of thousands of items that are added each day.

Excite

Just as with Auctions.com, the Excite (**auctions.excite.com**) home page features the categories and the item count for each category. As you select subcategories, the category counts appear. Beanies and sports collectibles top the list here, which pales in comparison to other sites.

Yahoo!

Just like Auctions.com and Excite, the Yahoo! (**auctions.yahoo.com**) home page features the categories and the item count for each category. Forty thousand trading cards indicate that this is a good place for collectibles. Surprisingly, sports equipment and computers also have strong categories here.

Refer to Table 11.8 for a quick list to locate the category listings for the major auction sites.

RESOURCES

Newsgroups are resources for references to auctions of interest to specific groups. Through the newsgroup **misc.kids**, I found the free auction site at **mothersnature.com**.

TABLE 11.8

Auction Sites and Category Lists

Auction Site	Category List Location
Auctions.amazon.com	Home page
eBay.com	Choose the "Browse" link on the home page for an extensive list with counts for each category
CityAuction.com	Home page
Auctions.com	Home page
Auctions.yahoo.com	Home page; counts included
Auctions.excite.com	Home page; counts included

Check mailing list sites, including **www.onelist.com** and **www.egroups.com** to find lists pertinent to your interests. There are thousands of lists, pertaining to items that range from Beanie Babies to collectible books to pottery. Review these lists to learn from other sellers' experiences.

KEY POINTS

This chapter looks at six leading auction sites. We reviewed the features of each: Amazon, eBay, Excite, Auctions.com, City Auction, and Yahoo! When considering the best auction site for your bounty:

- Compare fee and free auction sites.
- Assess the advertising features at each site.
- Take advantage of multiauction search engines.
- Choose the best categories at each auction site.
- Select the particular category that is most appropriate for each of your salable items.

12

CHAPTER

WRITING YOUR AD: DESCRIPTIONS THAT SELL

Now that we've studied other ads and reviewed the best auction venues, it's time to get to work defining the elements of auction ads that sell.

The two major creative components are the *auction title* and the *auction description*. For our purposes, we'll cut to the chase and simply call them *titles* and *descriptions*.

ADDING ADJECTIVES

After searching the corners of the dining room, you can list a Silver Baby Cup, or you can draft something more generously titled: Tiffany Antique Sterling Silver Baby Cup. Bidders possess specific radar that zooms in on listings that promise not to waste their time. (The more detailed description is better, as you'll soon see.)

Good auction titles tease and entice. Searching is a task filled with boring text. Whether potential bidders are using the search engine or weeding through categories, auction titles provide their first encounters with your merchandise. As with any other first impression, those initial seconds count. Grab the bidders' attention and get them to take a look at your auction ad.

- Fuji Disposable Quicksnap Flash Cameras
- Ping Double-Strap Golf Bag w/Built-in Stand
- Baby Coupons HUGGIES~PAMPERS~FORMULA~$35

These auction titles clearly provide information. Wise auctioneers have crafted these titles so that potential bidders will know exactly whether it is worth their time to look further.

I'll look. I want to know how many Fuji cameras are up for bid. (They make great gifts for adults and kids.) There are 500 for sale in a Dutch auction. The Ping golf bag listing tells me about the important features, but I need to know if it is new or used. They got me to click on the title and look at the complete listing. (It's used but in great condition, and has a clear picture so bidders can evaluate its features.) And, for the baby coupons, I know that this batch includes coupons for the most popular and expensive baby commodities. A look at the ad shows that the coupons are clearly listed so that potential bidders can quickly tally the coupons.

KNOW WHEN TO HOLD

Sometime in your life, your mother probably told you to "hush up." That's a lesson I should have heeded when I auctioned the baby backpack. It sold for less than I had anticipated based on the research I'd done. In the description I revealed the presence of a small dent in the frame. After the sale, I asked other auction sellers for their opinions. The eBay Seller's List advised that I not call the blemish a dent, but rather "a flaw or a ding that does not affect structural integrity in any way." So, heed the warning found in my experience, and be descriptive—within reason. (The buyer ultimately gave me great feedback—she got a steal of a deal.)

CHOOSING YOUR WORDS

When preparing to place a listing, think carefully about the search items that will be used by potential buyers. Take a look at what makes other ads successful.

Run a search for antique maps of Paris. Try it a couple of different ways: **Paris charts, Paris map*, antique map.*** My search for **Paris map*** turned up 15 possibilities. Look at the listings to see what searchable terms were included that drew the most bids. Do they use terms like **antique, 18th Century, historic, preserved,** or **restored?** When I checked on eBay, I found **Paris France Early Tourist Map Eiffel Tower,** which drew seven bidders. On first glance, the wording is awkward, but it was also nicely searchable!

Power-pack titles with the most likely search terms. Crafters who do beadwork may take apart jewelry made by others. If advertising an antique jade necklace, specify the title as **Antique Jade Bead Necklace** to attract more looks. This will appear when bidders search for bead* or bead. Any additional terms in the description add power to your listing.

Load the description with related terms to:

- Attract more views
- Provide a full description

Another idea is to incorporate as many descriptive words as possible into both the title and descriptive text. There's **Green Wool Yarn,** or there's **Brown Sheep**

Green Wool Nature Spun Yarn. Study the titles and take full advantage of the number of characters available on the auction's title, as seen in Table 12.1. eBay limits titles to 45 characters, while Amazon allows 80.

BRAND NAMES AND ADJECTIVES

Savvy buyers soon learn to make specific searches to sift the wheat from the chaff. Each additional descriptive word—or keyword—that you use, returns fewer items. Make it easy on the buyers to find what they need. Knowledgeable buyers search with brand names, and brand names convey value even to a lot of auction "newbies." Use them in auction titles. Many buyers bid higher for Craftsman, Waterford, Gap, Gymboree, Cuisinart, Black & Decker, IBM, Gateway, Sony, RCA, Panasonic, Kitchen Aid, Wedgwood, Lenox, Fisher-Price, Parker Brothers, and other major brand names.

Use adjectives to enhance the titles to make them as searchable as possible. Consider descriptive titles such as these: **navy Gymboree Spectator jacket XXL, denim Gap hat size M,** and **Lismore Waterford water goblet.** Try more: **Franciscan Ivy dinner plates, pink Wedgwood cup and saucer, vintage Brooks Brothers charcoal trousers, large opal ring 14K gold, red Converse hightops, Cartier Men's Tank Watch, Donna Karan little black dress sz 6,** and **small purple Gottex bikini.** Specificity counts.

Take a look at these keyword searches from eBay, and you'll see how additional descriptive terms can help bidders find what they are seeking:

T I P

Think Like a Bidder!

Take a look at Chapter 3, "Finding the Items You Want to Buy," and try on thinking like a bidder.

T A B L E 12.1

Auction Sites and Title Character Counts

Auction Site	No. of Characters Allowed in Titles
Excite	30
AuctionUniverse	40
CityAuction	40
eBay	45
Amazon	80

Be Specific

Be as specific as possible to get a precise list. On most auction sites you can search within categories. Go to the top-level page for that category and use the search box located there.

Wallpaper 169
Waverly Wallpaper 3

Drill 64
Craftsman Drill 30
Cordless Craftsman Drill 11

Swing 722
Little Tykes (Tikes) Swing 4

Toys 2193
Discovery Toys 24
Discovery Toys Puzzle 4

Microwave 88
Microwave oven 7
GE Microwave Oven 3

Bra 629
Wonderbra 18

THE SPELLING TRAP

Spelling is a bugaboo. Did I spell that correctly? This is one area where it may not always pay to spell words—particularly brand names—correctly. Before you place an item for auction, see how other items with the same name are advertised. Buyers may not be savvy enough to consider alternate spellings; if you find a dominant spelling, go with that. Jump Start software and L.L. Bean products provide two cogent examples. On eBay, a search for **Jump Start** returned 53 current software listings, 34 of which had bids. A comparable search for **Jumpstart** (no space) yielded 47 auctions, 16 of which had bids. The comparison can be seen in Table 12.2. What does that tell

T A B L E 12.2

Spelling Counts

Spelling	Number of Auctions	Number with Bids
Jump Start	53	34
Jumpstart	47	16

you? As an auctioneer, I'd make sure to list the product as Jump Start. In the text portion, spell **jumpstart** both with and without the space to catch users who search description as well as titles.

A search for items by the Maine retailer L.L. Bean provides an example of how spacing and punctuation can impact search results (see Table 12.3). It is interesting to note that the L.L. Bean company is somewhat inconsistent in its catalog. Four of the current catalogs use both L.L. Bean and L.L.Bean. Still, it does not matter much how the name appears in the catalog. What *does* matter is what spelling and punctuation online auction buyers will employ to search and find.

MAKING YOUR AD COMPETITIVE

Print out copies of auction ads that are well-written. Keep them on hand when you draft the titles and descriptions for your merchandise. There are many talented auction sellers. Use your research skills to take advantage of their advertising copywriting skills. Make note of the keywords and descriptions. Use their text to fairly reflect, yet sell, your merchandise.

HUMOROUS DESCRIPTIONS

A seller on eBay provided this fun list of descriptive terms that are often used in auctions. Have a laugh and then write descriptions accurately and treat bidders well.

Item Description	What It Really Means
ADORABLE	Nauseating
BEAUTIFUL	Thinks rust is artistic
BRILLIANT SHINE	What I just gave it with my buffer (to make it near-mint)

TABLE 12.3

Alternate Spelling and Punctuation

Search	eBay Result
L. L. Bean	3
L.L. Bean	34
L.L.Bean	10
LL Bean	36
LLBean	8

CIVIL WAR	Made in India last week
COLLECTIBLE	I have WAY too many of these.
CUTE	Butt-ugly
DON'T MISS THIS ONE!	I'm really tired of dragging this around, somebody buy it!
EXCEPTIONAL	Has everything EXCEPT what you want
FABULOUS	Dictionary says this means Mythological, and the quality is somewhat less
FINE	Paint covers flaws, parts taped in place
GREAT CONDITION	Dents can be used as salt dips
GREAT CONDITION FOR SOMETHING THIS OLD	(see PRIMITIVE)
HARD TO FIND	Will be lost in mail after auction
I WAS TOLD THAT THIS IS . . .	No one bought this when I said what it REALLY was, so I'm gonna try calling it this.
L@@K	Please look at this item—it has no good qualities that would otherwise make you want to check it out.
MIB	Mashed In Box
MINT	Meticulously cleaned (spelling optional)
MUST SEE	Lord knows the description won't pull you in without this added.
NEAR MINT	Cleaned even harder
NICE	I'm keeping the good one, and getting rid of this piece of . . .
NO RESERVE	I used a massive beginning bid instead.
OLD	Useless
ONE OF A KIND	"I have no idea what this is."
PATINA	Rust
PERFECT	"I have no idea what this is supposed to look like."
PRIMITIVE	Unrecognizable
PRISTINE	"I thought that meant primitive."
RARE	Not able to be found at Kmart
STUNNING	Garish
UNBELIEVABLE	In the bad sense
UNIQUE	Tinkered together from parts yesterday
UNUSUAL	"Well, I've never seen one before."

VERY OLD	Very useless
VERY RARE	No longer available in mail order catalogues
VINTAGE	I was born in 1974, and it looks old to me.
WONDERFUL	You'll WONDER where the rest of it is
WONDERFUL PATINA	Deep rust with pits
WOW!!!	I'm really desperate

MAKING THE MOST OF ABBREVIATIONS

Auction abbreviations are the shorthand employed by auction sellers, and they're often used to make the most of the title space that's been allocated by the auction venue. A few of the most useful abbreviations can be found in Table 12.4. Each category, such as books, also has its own abbreviations. On the very popular eBay, spaces for only 45 characters are available in the text box. Amazon offers a generous 80 characters.

LOCATING PRODUCT DESCRIPTIONS

Use Web search engines to locate product descriptions. Selling a modem? Check the manufacturer's Web site and use their product description as the basis for yours. Selling Fiestaware? Other pottery collectors may have created Web sites dedicated to their collection. Check the terminology for use in your auction title and description.

T A B L E 12.4

Useful Abbreviations

Shorthand	Defined
HTF	Hard to find
NIB	New in box
NBP	Never been played
MIB	Mint in box
MISP	Mint in sealed package
MWMT	Mint with mint tag(s)
NMT	Near-mint
NWT	New with tag(s)
NR	No reserve
SZ	Size
PC	Piece
VHTF	Very hard to find

IMPROVING ADS

Auction selling is a two-step process. Auction titles grab views, and the descriptive text and pictures invite bids. To locate a selection of bad ads, use your knowledge of closed auction searches to find auctions that failed to attract bids. Many had poorly written ads.

Look at Figures 12.1 and 12.2. They represent an auction listing for a Radio Shack cell phone. It failed to sell. A review of the list of other cell phones suggests that the Radio Shack brand name isn't a strong selling feature, so that could be why it failed to draw bids. There's no image, so bidders must rely on the seller to accurately describe the phone. This is a very poor description, and it is poorly punctuated and abbreviated.

The possible and probable issues with this ad are:

- Failure to include image.

- It was categorized in "Photo & Electronics: Consumer Electronics: Telephone." A better choice may have been: "Photo & Electronics: Consumer Electronics: General."

- Radio Shack may not be a desirable brand.

- Poor product description.

- It's missing the battery.

FIGURE 12.1

The poor text and lack of image defeat the reasonable opening bid.

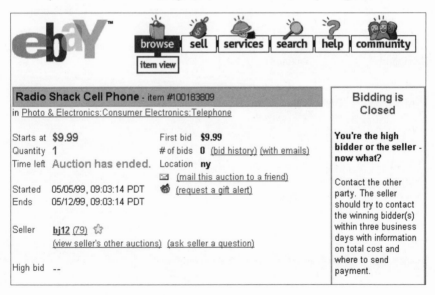

FIGURE 12.2

Make sure that your text is better than this.

Description
Radio Shack Cell Phone - plugs into cig. lighter - (no battery)- works off cig. lighter. 5. shipping. Like new. Similar to bag type phone.

- $5 shipping? Is that what 5 means?
- $5 shipping could be too high. If it doesn't have a battery it is not heavy.
- The reference to a bag-type phone indicates that it is an older model.
- There is no direct reference to the age of the phone, its condition, or the extent to which it had been used.

Let's take a look at a product from another category: teddy bears. A search for a Gund teddy bear returned this auction listing for a **1997 Zales Holiday Bear—White Gund Teddy,** as seen in Figures 12.3 and 12.4. It failed to attract bidders. Many of the other bears listed are older and far more collectible. This was a freebie or gift-with-purchase, and that may have diluted its value in the eyes of true Gund collectors. The

FIGURE 12.3

All's well except the missing picture.

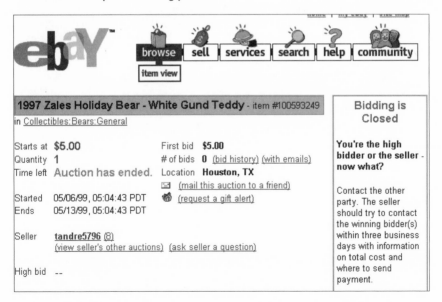

FIGURE 12.4

The description needs a copywriter's finesse.

Description
12" white Gund 1997 Edition Zales Holiday Bear - brand new - red satin ribbon on neck - holding a gold star sack- I think this was for jewelry to be placed in as a gift...(some using as a tooth fairy bear) or "gift wrapping" for small item. Buyer pays shipping of $4.50

seller failed to include a picture. Teddy bears are supposed to be appealing and huggable. Without the picture, we have no idea of its appeal. The description is not well-written. It's also important to note that the auction closed at 5:04 A.M. Pacific time, on a Thursday.

The possible and probable issues with this ad are:

- Failure to include image.

- Description poorly written.

- Even if the pouch was not for jewelry, say that it was. Make it a feature.

- Seller did not indicate shipping method.

- Shipping cost does not correlate to the highly desirable Priority Mail fees.

Clear, accurate, and appealing titles and descriptions are the seller's responsibility. Photos add visual appeal and a level of trustworthiness. In both cases presented, the sellers appear to have given little care or forethought to advertising their auction sales.

Learning Lessons

From the teddy bear and cell phone, we can draft a checklist for our sales:

- Include an image.

- Write a clear and excellent description. (Always write the description, packed with details, as if there were no picture).

- Clearly indicate shipping method and fee.

- If an element is missing (like the battery), explain how the bidder can purchase the missing item.

- Make sure that the auction closes at a day and time when buyers are awake and available.

RESOURCES

Use a shopping bot to find items like yours and refer to those product descriptions. A Web site filled with shopping and auction resources is Bot Spot, located at

botspot.com/search/s-shop.htm.

Another site for comparison pricing is E-Compare (**www.ecompare.com**).

KEY POINTS

In this chapter, we covered the critical task of writing a great ad, in the form of an auction description. To make the most of your auction ads:

- Use descriptive adjectives to attract bidders.
- Include brand names.
- Consider alternate spellings.
- Make the most of the allocated space with auction abbreviations.
- Critique poor ads to improve your ads.

13

CHAPTER

DECIDING YOUR PRICE

THE PRICE IS RIGHT

We've looked at the venues and we've found some terrific auction options. We've also reviewed the "advertising" side of auctions, and you've learned how to write ad descriptions that sell. Now it's time to return to the researching tactics, with an eye toward pricing. Savvy sellers will tell you that some of their best sales have come from taking a few minutes to research the sales of comparable items.

It's imperative that you uncover the auction market value for each item that you plan to sell. Wise sellers know the current retail market value in addition to recent auction sales. If an item has a collectible value, a speculative bidder may thrill a seller by paying more for an item at auction than through a traditional retailer.

When establishing an opening bid, don't be greedy. You'll create more future earnings by pricing well and treating your customers to great service. In turn, your feedback ratings will prosper, making other bidders more confident in dealing with you. As an example, used software purchased for your last computer just isn't worth what you paid for it. I recently auctioned six children's titles. Do I plan to buy six new titles? Heck, no. At most I expect to buy one or two new packages with the proceeds.

Amazon, Auctions.com, eBay, and CityAuction make it easy to search closed auctions from their search pages. Use those search tools to determine realistic starting bids and fair expectations for the final bids.

For a particular class of items, such as electronics, you may notice that there is an opening price level below which auctions do not attract bidders. This happens! Generate a list of closed Walkmans (or computer printers, or shoes, or answering machines) and make the appropriate selections for the list to appear in descending order by final bid price. There may be a price point, such as $10, that is the minimum level for auctions receiving bids. I noticed this phenomenon with cell phones.

If you possess a multitasking brain, open multiple browser windows. With multiple windows, you can run comparative searches across several auctions, or across several categories. Search open auctions to assess the competition. Search closed auctions to look at opening bids, reserves, final bids, and auction closing times. Array the closed auction list by date to look at day-of-the-week trends, and rearrange each list to review ascending or descending final bid lists.

Gerry Backpacks on eBay

When conducting research, I often return to eBay. With 2.8 million current auctions, it is most likely to have comparisons (or "comps") for my sales. Having once sold a baby backpack, let's take a look at the current and recent market there.

Plugging **Gerry Backpack** into the current auction search window yields four backpacks, with current bids ranging from $3.00 (no bids) to $26.99 after 13 bids. This list appears in Figure 13.1. Select the Search Completed Items link above the Search Result banner. A list of 18 closed auctions appeared. I made a selection to sort the list by bid price in descending order. The closed list appears in Figure 13.2. Closed auctions range from a high of $56.99 (after seven bids) to a low of $10. The $10 auction was the only one that failed to attract bids. (The poorly written title appears under Closed and Current auctions, indicating that the seller relisted the backpack auction without making a significant change to the title or description.) Within the listing, the backpack is described as being "in good shape but slightly dirty." The color is beige, and serious auction bidders will note that the newer backpacks are made of brightly colored fabric and have more features.

There were four open auctions with bids ranging from $3 to $26.99.

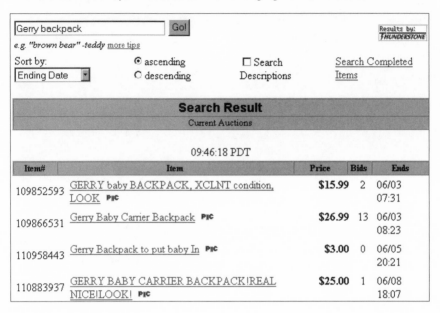

Only three of the closed auctions do not have pictures. Deluxe and Ultra Deluxe appear to be successful selling terms. The top 6 auctions make extensive use of capital letters, while auctions 7 through 14 do not. With good pricing and informative descriptions, the top 10 auctions averaged 10.7 bids each.

Of the top 10 auctions, 3 closed on Thursday (Pacific mornings) and 3 closed on Saturday (Pacific afternoon and evening), followed by 2 Sunday (afternoon and evening) closings. Maybe I am going out on a limb here, but I think I see two markets: at-home parents bidding on weekdays, and two-career couples bidding on weekends.

The highest-price backpack, with seven bids, closed at $56.99. It opened at $15 and the seller noted a reasonable reserve. (As a bidder, I'd send an email requesting the reserve.) The seller provided clear information, listed eight product features, and also included the comparative retail price of $120.

Most auction sites make it possible to view bid histories for closed items. For the first auction, the bidding history shows four bidders with a total of seven bids. Proxy bidding accounts for the multiple bids. Briefly, proxy bidding is automatic bidding. Each bidder enters his or her high bid. The auction programming increases the bids at set increments based on the proxy bids. (Later in this section, you'll have the opportunity to read more about proxy bidding.)

F I G U R E 13.2

Eighteen closed auctions provide a great research opportunity.

Item#	Item	Price	Bids	Ends
101503726	GREAT GERRY BABY BACKPACK-LIKE NEW-CREDITCARD ᴾᴵᶜ	$56.99	7	05/18 11:27
100616927	Like NEW Gerry DELUXE baby backpack! WOW!! ᴾᴵᶜ	$53.50	16	05/13 07:28
105259030	GERRY ULTRA DELUXE BABY BACKPACK PURPLE ᴾᴵᶜ	$51.00	11	05/23 19:08
107807492	GERRY BABY BACKPACK "L@@K" ᴾᴵᶜ	$46.00	10	05/29 21:30
108464868	GERRY ULTRA DELUXE BABY BACKPACK BLUE/TEAL ᴾᴵᶜ	$42.00	12	05/31 09:24
105019394	GERRY TRAILTECH BABY BACKPACK ᴾᴵᶜ	$42.00	12	05/23 12:26
100673259	NIB Gerry Trailtech Baby Backpack/Carrier ᴾᴵᶜ	$42.00	14	05/13 10:49
104660132	Gerry baby backpack carrier	$36.50	13	05/22 15:20
107812072	GERRY Ultra Deluxe Backpack Carrier LIKE NEW! ᴾᴵᶜ	$33.00	5	05/27 21:42
101774560	Gerry Child Backpack Carrier ᴾᴵᶜ	$28.80	7	05/15 20:49
103781996	Gerry Child Backpack Carrier ᴾᴵᶜ	$26.00	8	05/20 11:57
108489985	Gerry child backpack carrier *deluxe ᴾᴵᶜ	$22.00	9	05/29 10:42
101929770	Gerry Baby Backpack - Kiddie Cruiser ᴾᴵᶜ	$21.50	7	05/16 11:04
104730941	DELUXE Khaki Gerry backpack w. back support! ᴾᴵᶜ	$19.50	6	05/22 17:57
102638839	GERRY BACKPACK FOR BABY Great condition! ᴾᴵᶜ	$17.05	7	05/17 19:40
107639775	Gerry child carrier backpack	$15.50	9	05/27 16:24
107982690	GERRY BACKPACK WITH METAL FRAME	$10.50	5	05/31 11:56
109706570	Gerry Backpack to put baby In ᴾᴵᶜ	$10.00	0	05/29 19:37

The second-highest-price backpack closed at $53.50 after 16 bids from 6 bidders. This auction had no reserve, and the opening bid was established at $16.95. The description is clearly written by a seller with hundreds of feedbacks, indicating a high level of experience. The third-highest-price auction opened at $20 without a reserve and closed at $51. There were 11 bids from 9 bidders, and it had a Sunday closing. The seller's description included many product details.

Let's look at the attributes of these successful auction titles and listings and build upon what you've learned in the backpack auctions:

- Titles are clearly written to attract bids.
- Images are included and are clear.
- Set fair opening bids. The research shows $15 to $20 to be a good starting point.
- Set reasonable reserves.
- Close on days and at times when bidders can participate.
- Write searchable titles.
- Use appropriate capital letters and attention-getters.
- Properly categorize (in this case: "Miscellaneous: Baby Items").
- Set fair and comparable shipping fees.

Value Guides

Many online auction sellers check the Kelly Blue Book (**www.kbb.com**) before selling a used car. Consider using data from similar price guides to set opening bids (and to adjust expectations) for your sales of collectibles. Search for comparable guides (see Table 13.1 for examples) with your favorite Web search engine.

When true value guides are not available, conduct a search for price lists. For example, there's a healthy market (once dominated by mail order) for replacement

T A B L E 13.1

Price Guides for Collectibles

Category	Web Address
Antiques & collectibles	**www.tias.com/stores/kovels/**
Barbie guide	**www.dolliedish.com/barbie/**
China	**www.discontinuedchina.com**
Sports cards and collectibles	**www.beckett.com/**

china patterns. The retail prices offered by such companies should be regarded as the top prices that you can expect to get. Price that Lenox meat platter accordingly.

TIP

Shopping Agents

BotSpot.com
(botspot.com/search/
s-shop.htm) is a good
place to start when
searching auctions
and e-commerce
sites. Bots are agents
(specialized search
engines) that conduct
searches for you.
Give up the thought
of a micron-sized
person running the
searches. This site
links to four dozen
shopping bots for
auctions searches
and for "retail"
e-commerce
searches.

Shipping Terms

As you review closed auctions for opening and final bid levels, also look at the shipping terms offered to buyers. When you list the auction, you'll need to be ready with your shipping terms, too. If the other sellers are shipping by Priority Mail, there's good reason for you to do the same.

Within a particular category, it may be common for the seller to add handling charges. Handling charges won't hurt your auctions if others are charging them on comparable goods. Such charges are common for breakables and large items, but may be unnecessary, unwarranted, and unwelcome for single items that can be slipped into an envelope or Priority Mail box.

Large, bulky items tend to have shipping terms labeled "buyer pays actual shipping charges." This is fair, but you may be thinking of UPS charges, while the buyer is envisioning parcel post. Be clear if your intentions are to only ship through one carrier. State the shipping details as, "Buyer to pay actual UPS shipping charges."

Bidders take shipping charges into account when bidding. If you add high handling charges to your listing, expect lower bids.

More on shipping will be covered in Chapter 21, "Shipping."

BIDDING SYSTEMS

Online, as in any estate auction, sellers set opening prices and reserves. The sites set the bid increments, graduated according to price levels. The higher the price, the greater the bidding increment. Amazon's bid increments, as shown in Table 13.2, are typical.

When the bidding for Elvis' "used once" toothbrush surpasses $24.99, bids will jump $1 at a time. Well, that's in a perfect world. Next up, proxy bidding.

T A B L E 13.2

Opening Bids and Bid Increments

Current High Bid $	Minimum Bid Increment $
$0.01–$0.99	$0.05
1.00–9.99	0.25
10.00–24.99	0.50
25.00–99.99	1.00
100.00–249.99	2.50
250.00–499.99	5.00
500.00–999.99	10.00
1,000.00–2,499.99	25.00
2,500.00–4,999.99	50.00
5,000.00 and up	100.00

What You Need to Know About Proxy Bidding

Proxy bidding puts technology to use and helps us all to deal with this 24-hour world-wide marketplace. I know that I've focused on setting selling times to meet U.S. closing hours, but in the future that focus may change.

Proxy bidding opens auctions to all, without regard to time zones. Bidders can enter their maximum bids, which are only revealed when exceeded by another bidder.

Dutch Auctions

Dutch auctions are auctions that sell one type of merchandise in quantity. They are a great way for sellers to auction duplicate items quickly and with only one listing.

Let's say that I have a dozen identical disposable cameras to auction. I place one auction for 12 cameras with opening bids of $3 each. (The listing fee is 12 times the insertion fee for a single $3 item). At the close of bidding, the high bidder, Tom, has placed a bid for six cameras at $3.50 each, and the next in line, Linda, has bid for three at $3.25. The next four bidders (Moe, Curly, Larry, and Harry) bid for single cameras at $3.05.

- Tom, the high bidder, gets his fill, six at $3.50.
- The next bidder, Linda, gets her fill, three at $3.25.
- There are three cameras remaining, with four bidders. Of that group, the first three bidders (i.e., Moe, Curly, and Larry) will win the cameras at $3.05 each. The fourth bidder, Harry, will not get a camera.

Final value fees will be calculated for each price point. Before placing a Dutch auction, check the auction site's rules to see if it has a minimum quantity requirement.

Reserves

Sellers are of two minds about reserves. The first camp thinks that reserves are a deterrent to bidders, while the other camp thinks of reserves merely as a small insurance policy.

Buyers often contact sellers by email to ask about reserves. While sellers are not required to reveal reserves, many bidders won't get into the action without that information. A considerable number of auction participants regard it as good etiquette for a seller to reveal the reserve. Other sellers take reserves to the next level and list them in the text description. If a bidder knows the reserve, he or she can best assess whether it is worth jumping the bidding to that level. Bidders love to get in on the bidding, and the excitement carries some beyond their intended pocketbooks. Some bidders will immediately make a bid to get to the reserve, while others may wait to snipe at the closing bell.

Other sellers set a low introductory price to encourage bidding, and view the reserve as a safety net. Another option is to place an item up for auction at the lowest price you are willing to receive, rather than set a reserve. Reserves may be more appropriate or acceptable for certain price points and categories than for others. A $1500 Cartier watch, $500 Waterford bowl, and a mint Mickey Mantle rookie card are among the auctions where I would expect to see reserves.

For your Nikon, keep eBay's reserve requirement in mind. eBay has a reserve auction fee that is added to all reserve auctions. For auctions with opening bids less than $25, the fee is 50 cents. Above that, the fee is $1.00. Once the auction bidding exceeds the reserve, the fee is refunded. What's the purpose? This prevents sellers from posting unrealistic auctions for $1 with a reserve of $100. In the past (and at other sites) those auctions frustrated legions of bidders.

Don't forget: Auction insertion fees are based upon the reserve price, and not the initial bid, in reserve price auctions.

Footing the Bill

You'll have to register at any auction where you plan to sell. If the auction collects fees from sellers, the auction site will generally offer a small amount of credit ($10) so that you can place your first listings. That's an advance, not a freebie. As a security measure, most sites now require a credit card with registration.

A credit card also provides a pain-free option for automatic billing. At any point in time you can get an up-to-date statement of your account and you'll always be able to anticipate those credit card charges—at least the ones for auction fees.

Depending on the site, other options may include accessing and printing a monthly payment coupon. This requires mailing a check or credit card information, along with the payment coupon each month.

Resources

Check these sites for comparative pricing:

BidFind	**www.bidfind.com**
Bottom Dollar	**www.bottomdollar.com**
PriceScan	**www.pricescan.com**
AuctionWatch	**dbmeta.auctionwatch.com/meta**

Before estimating postage costs, start with these links:

USPS Postage Rate Calculator	**postcalc.usps.gov**
iShip.com (pricing, shipping, tracking)	**www.iship.com**

KEY POINTS

This chapter focuses on the research related to getting the very best price. Use the tips found here to:

- Investigate the closing bids for similar items
- Find a good opening bid
- Determine an appropriate reserve
- Use value guides
- Consider the impact of shipping terms on pricing and bidding
- Be aware of bidding increments and their impact on the bidding process
- Know the site's payment terms

14 CHAPTER

PREPARING A GREAT AD

THE VALUE OF AN IMAGE

One day, I searched for Gymboree blankets from the Spring in Bloom line—and I used my favorite search string to search for auctions that had closed in the prior 14 days: **Gymboree spring bloom blanket (new,nwt,tags)–like**.

In English, that means Spring in Bloom Blanket from the mall store, Gymboree, noted as *new,* or specifying the abbreviation for *new with tags,* or *tags.* In addition, the use of the minus sign before like (–like) signifies the exclusion of any listing with "like new" in the title. The search was conducted on only the titles, not the descriptions.

Seven auctions met the stated criteria. Six auctions possessed eBay's PIC logo denoting the presence of a picture. One seller did not include a picture. In this admittedly less-than-scientific survey, pictures added $5 to the sales price—that's a 25 percent *increase.* Auctions with pictures ranged in closing price from $20 to $28, and attracted 3 to 10 bids. Without a photo, the advertised blanket attracted 7 bids and closed at $20. Certainly this seller also benefited from the other auctions running, as potential buyers could look at their images. Additionally, the $20 picture-less seller had an excellent description and followed the guideline of describing the blanket *as if he or she had no picture.*

TIP

Great Descriptions

Write the description as if you had no picture, even if you do.

151

CAPTURING IMAGES

Auction images can be captured on a "regular" 35mm camera, disposable camera, digital camera, video camera, or with a scanner. However you grab the images, the images must be digitized for online hosting and display.

Images from Film

If you shoot regular 35mm color film—even with a disposable camera—you can request that the images be stored on disk for use in an online auction. Your photos-in-an-hour place may need to send the roll out to Kodak (**kodak.photonet.com**) to provide electronic images. When you place the order for the prints, take a good look at the order envelope. You can order photos on floppy disk, photos on CD, or photos over the Internet. Those options will give you the digital images you need for online auctions.

Hand-deliver the film to Ritz Camera (**www.ritzcamera.com**) and your prints will be ready in an hour. They'll send an email when the images are at the Web site. You can also drop film at Fuji Film (**www.fujifilm.net**) for these services.

Seattle Filmworks (**www.filmworks.com**) and Mystic Color Lab (**www. mysticcolorlab.com**) are two places where you can mail film for processing. Compare the offers and services at these sites to get the best competitive deal. Look for these photo services to announce alliances with auction sites. Auction sellers will be able to view and choose images to be automatically attached to auctions. That will make your image posting even easier.

With the disk and CD options, you'll have the advantages of reproducible media. CD and Internet options provide the best-quality images. Photos on the Internet are only stored for a certain period of time—generally 30 days. After that you'll need to pay a "storage" fee, or the images will be deleted. Following the initial display period, Kodak PhotoNet's storage fee is $5.99 for 36 images for 30 days. That's 20 cents per picture. Of course, you can download them to your hard drive at any time. The CD option costs more than images on "floppy" 3.5-inch disks. Photos on disk, as well as photos over the Internet, add about $5 to the processing cost for a typical roll of film. To make the most of this option, shoot an entire roll of auctionable items. Then ask the film processor if you can just pay for the digitized images without obtaining prints. It takes about a week for photos to be returned to you on disk or CD. The media options appear in Table 14.1. With any of these three image options, the auction photos will need to be uploaded to an image hosting site.

WHY WE NEED JPGs

Whether your image is captured by a digital camera or delivered through an Internet photo service, make sure that it is saved in the JPG (.jpg) file format. GIF (.gif), a Macintosh format, is acceptable on some sites, but the universally accepted JPG format is strongly recommended. Use the one that works at all image hosts and auction sites! The files should be named, ending in dot (.) followed by jpg. An example of this file name is **myphoto.jpg**.

Image Media and Timing

Media	Images Available Within . . .	Advantage
Photos on disk	1 week	The disk is yours; resolution okay for auctions
Photos on CD	1 week	CD is yours; images are higher-resolution, since the CD has more space
Internet photos	24 hours after receipt by processor; notification by email	No uploading from media to computer; images are high-resolution like CD since space is not an issue

SCANNED IMAGES

Photos of three-dimensional items and flat documents can be scanned and digitized. If you don't have a scanner at your fingertips, office service centers like Kinko's (**www.kinkos.com**) are the place to turn. At Kinko's you can rent scanner time or pay a bit more for their services. Scanners are best for autographs, posters, sports cards, documents, advertisements, and other flat items ready for auction. Almost-flat items like jewelry may also be scanned. Scanning can be performed in a very short period of time and will most likely be done the same day or the next day. If you do it yourself it is as fast as using a digital camera.

Ritz Camera (**www.ritzcamera.com**) locations will scan photos for $3.99 each. Kinko's do-it-yourself scanning is 40 cents per minute.

Scanners: $100 and up

Scanning Fees: $3.99 and up, per image

Video Cameras

Video cameras, in combination with a video capture card, can be utilized to take "stills" for use in auction sales. Similarly, the type of PC camera used for video conferencing can also be used.

Snappy (**www.play.com/products/snappy**) is a super gadget for grabbing video images for auction use. Just plug Snappy hardware module into your PC or laptop parallel port. Then connect a camcorder, VCR, or TV with the cable provided. View images on your PC screen and snap to capture the images. Snappy is available for about $100.

Costs: $100 and up

Digital Camera

Digital cameras can now be purchased online for less than $200. If you've been wanting one, your auction-selling plans may be the perfect excuse. Be sure to check online auctions and comparison shopping sources to find good deals. Refer to Chapter 13 for links to comparison pricing sources.

Images captured by digital cameras can be uploaded directly to your computer's hard drive. A digital camera is the most expensive—and most efficient—of the image-capturing options. The main benefit is the speed with which you can put an image online. It takes only minutes to shoot the photo, upload the image, and post the auction. Borrow a friend's and you'll be permanently hooked.

Costs: $200 and up

Image Editing

For any digital image, you'll need to check whether the photos are in JPG format. With an image editor you can crop and enhance the images—and, if necessary, save them as JPGs. Images, which provide the best visual display, are most likely to attract bidders to your auctions.

Image editing programs, such as Paint Shop Pro (**www.jasc.com**), Lview Pro (**www.lview.com**), or Microsoft Picture-It, are available free or at reasonable prices. Go to a shareware-downloading site (like **shareware.cnet.com**) to obtain a trial version. Search for Photo Editor, Image Editor, or Image Viewer. You may already have Microsoft Picture-It, which comes with many new PCs. See the Resources section at the end of this chapter for more shareware sites.

Large files take a long time for buyers to download over the Web. Busy potential bidders "kill" large image downloads that take longer than a few seconds. Image editing software, like the software that came with your digital camera, scanner, or other video capture tool, can reduce image files to a workable size. Several of the image hosts "evaluate" your image and make it possible for you to view it, as an auction bidder will. With the combination of image viewing software and the image hosts' tools, you'll be able to maintain image quality. To speed viewing

---

T I P

Cheater's Method

The cheater's method, not endorsed here, is to grab an image from another auction or from a commercial Web site. I've seen this done with toys, modems, and phones. In the early days of the auctions, this was done more often. Find two auctions with the same image and you'll have a good indication that someone cheated—and copied.

---

for potential bidders, reduce your image's size to less than 50K. Image file sizes compressed to 10 to 25K are an even better goal.

Image Tips Checklist

- Use "File|Save As" to make sure it is a .jpg.
- Crop extraneous matter from the image.
- Resize so that the larger of the height and width pixels is less than 300.
- Keep the data size to less than 50K. When you use a site like AuctionWatch, you'll get a smiley or frowning face as it evaluates the image size and download time.
- Check compression, which you'll often find in the Save As window. Typically you'll want to move the slider to the far right, where the Quality percent is noted at 100 percent.

T I P

Downloads on AOL

Check AOL's downloads area for image editors. Begin at keyword: "Computing."

Scanned Image Tips

Scanner users are advised to capture George Washington's autograph at a resolution of 150 dpi (dots per inch) or less. Evaluate the image make sure that it is relatively small (less than 50K), and upload it for a test view. To improve clarity, scan only the most important part of the image. If necessary, increase the dpi setting, but be aware that your image will require a longer download time.

- Keep the file size small.
- Scan at 150 dpi or less.
- Set scanner to high compression.

IMAGE HOSTS AND HOSTING

Some auctions host images and others do not (see Table 14.2). A few images on your hard disk may take minimal space. Just try to imagine the server capacity that would be required if eBay hosted the close to 2.5 million images needed for the current number of auctions!

Most auction sites do not host their own images. The images you see are linked. The pictures of coffeepots, canisters, and Cuisinarts reside someplace else, and the HTML code in the ad tells viewing browsers to grab the image from the image-hosting site.

Like many Internet users, I have space available through my online service account (thanks, America Online) and also through my ISP, Earthlink. Since others

TABLE 14.2

Auction Site Image Hosting

Image-Hosting Auctions	No-Host Auctions
Yahoo!	eBay
Excite	Amazon
	Auctions.com
	CityAuction

offer space for free, I've tried AuctionWatch (**www.auctionwatch.com**), Picturebay (**www.pBay.com**), and another that's not worth mentioning. AuctionWatch and Picturebay are very easy to use. They make it simple to upload images and offer more space than I can imagine needing. Most of the free places (as seen in Table 14.3) are so easy to use that I've stopped using my Web space for auction tasks. There's nothing stopping you from using more than one location.

AuctionWatch rates each image based on the amount of time each takes to be displayed. The total storage space is 20 Mbytes. At 50K per image, that's room for 400 auction images! If you need more space, use another site, too.

Pixhost.com (**www.pixhost.com**) charges a small fee for hosting images. Whether you choose that host or not, be sure to take a look at its top-notch image tutorial (**www.pixhost.com/tutorial**). For each image uploaded, pay a fee of 50 cents for the upload and 30 days' storage time. As an incentive to keep images small, images larger than 32K incur a higher fee.

TABLE 14.3

Free Image Hosts

Image Hosting Site	Fee
www.angelfire.com	free
www.auctionwatch.com	free
www.bay-town.com	free
geocities.yahoo.com	free
www.maxpages.com	free
www.pBay.com	free
www.photopoint.com	free
www.pixhost.com	free trial

Loading an Image

Let's try uploading a couple of images. Our first site will be Picturebay (**www.picturebay.com**). Once registered, enter your email address and password. Then, from the home page, as seen in Figure 14.1, add pictures.

Select "+Add Pictures." Click the large, blank photo box to begin the process of selecting the picture for uploads. A directory or folder will open. Select from the JPG images on your hard drive, CD, or floppy disk. You may note that Picturebay also accepts GIF files. To ensure that all bidders will be able to see your image, use JPG as the preferred image format.

I've selected a file that I named **bop1.jpg**. The image of the Boppy pillow (it looks like a doughnut) appears in the Picturebay window (Figure 14.2). It now fills the once-blank photo box. Select Send Photo to upload the image to Picturebay. The image will be compressed by Picturebay for expeditious display in auctions.

As the next window appears, Picturebay confirms that the picture has been uploaded. The image's URL is displayed for you to copy and paste directly into an auction form. (More on completing the auction form in the next chapter.)

If you are not ready to attach the image to an auction, you can do so at a later time. Picturebay keeps images for 30 days. Just make sure that your auction ends before your picture vanishes.

Whenever you return to Picturebay, select My Pictures to view the pictures you have stored there. As seen in Figure 14.3, the Boppy and its URL now appear at the top of my list. I can copy and paste the URL when I'm ready to post an auction. The URL for the Boppy image is:

```
http://www.picturebay.com/myimage/8/130047609-827567816-1.jpg
```

From this, we know that the image is at Picturebay. The beginning of the address, **www.pBay.com**, signifies the host. The image is in a host-defined area known as **myimage**. The next series of digits somehow means "me" and the second series of digits indicates **bop1.jpg**.

Let's try this on another site. I'll venture to AuctionWatch (**www.auctionwatch. com**). If you are not registered, be sure to do so. From the home page, seen in Figure 14.4, select the link for "Image Hosting." It's in the left column.

FIGURE 14.1

From pBay's home page, it's easy to get started.

© 1999 PictureWorks Technology, Inc. All Rights Reserved. Picturebay is a trademark of PictureWorks Technology, Inc.
PictureWorks Technology's Picturebay service is neither endorsed by nor affiliated with eBay Inc.

TIP

Passwords

In this online world I have far too many passwords. To keep it simple, I have started using the same password for all auction-related sites. And, no, I won't tell you what it is!

Log into the image hosting area with your ID and password. Use the Upload Images button to locate and add images. Select the Browse button and choose an image. Repeat for each browse button. Adding three or more simultaneously works best at off-peak Internet use times.

For our purposes, I'll just add the Boppy image here just as I did at Picturebay. Once the file has been selected, the address (from my hard drive) appears in the text box, like this:

`C:\My Photos\ebay pics\bop1.jpg`

It's on the C drive, in the folder named My Photos, in the subfolder named eBay Pics, and the image is named **bop1.jpg**. Select the button Upload These Images. A confirmation appears, with a copy of the image. The image file **bop1.jpg** is listed in Figure 4.5 with other images I have uploaded. It's a

FIGURE 14.2

The Boppy pillow fills the Picturebay window in the first uploading step.

FIGURE 14.3

The Boppy pillow image appears at the top of the list.

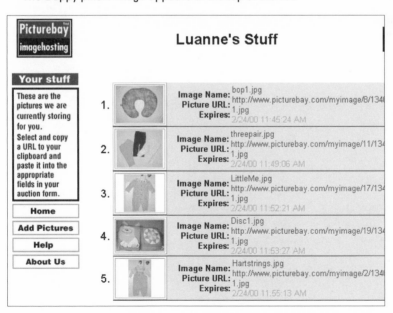

Welcome to the AuctionWatch home page.

24K file, and it was awarded the smiley face. It only takes 8 seconds for the average user to view this image.

To add this to an auction (now or later), place a check in the box at the beginning of the line. Then select the Attach To Auction button that appears below the image list.

This is an example of the cut-and-paste code issued by AuctionWatch:

```
<br><br>
<table width="100%" border="0" cellspacing="4" cellpadding="4">
<tr>
<td>
<center>
<img src="http://www.auctionwatch.com/members/lu/luanneo/bop1.jpg">
<img src="http://www.auctionwatch.com/cgi-
bin/newcount.cgi?luanneo/.bop1.jpg">
</center>
<br>
</td>
</tr>
```

```
<tr>
<td>
<center>
<a href="http://www.auctionwatch.com"><img
src="http://www.auctionwatch.com/members/
  hostedby.jpg"
border="0"></a></center>.
</td>
</tr>
</table>
<br>
```

Be sure to follow the image site's directions to the letter. Not only did you agree to the site's terms of service, you'll also want to be sure that your image remains hosted for the duration of your auction. Since these sites offer you free image space, they attach a banner or logo to the image. That's a small bit of advertising in exchange for a great and valuable service.

IMAGE POSTING CHECKLIST

- Take picture or scan.
- Save image as jpg.
- Locate image host.
- Upload image to host.
- Open another browser window.
- In the second browser window, go to the designated page for submitting new auctions.
- Follow image host's instructions for adding images to auctions.

A LITTLE HTML

Hypertext Markup Language (HTML) can be used to graphically enhance your auction ad and to include images and counters. A *little* HTML can be a good thing. Graphically fancy ads are a mixed bag. They may look good and make your items stand out from the crowd, but they can also annoy potential bidders. The more you pack into the auc-

---

T I P

Quick Compression Trial

Compress images, test sites/links, and reduce bloat at **www.raspberryhill. com.** Select the GIF Wizard link and reduce graphics based on color reduction rather than size dimensions. There are free trials at the site. Try before you buy.

T I P

Where's That Image?

If you are curious about where an auction image is stored, right-click on the image and select Properties.

The Boppy image link appears at the bottom of the list.

select	name	size	view time	last modified	last viewed	count
☐	GapDress2.jpg	27 K	☺ 9 seconds	May 29, 1999 12:37	May 30, 1999 14:21	75
☐	Oshkosh.jpg	37 K	☹ 12 seconds	May 15, 1999 08:00	May 30, 1999 14:21	0
☐	Sleepers.jpg	40 K	☹ 13 seconds	May 15, 1999 08:00	May 30, 1999 14:21	0
☐	Sleepsht.jpg	35 K	☹ 12 seconds	May 15, 1999 08:01	May 30, 1999 14:21	0
☐	bop1.jpg	24 K	☺ 8 seconds	Jun 06, 1999 10:32	Jun 05, 1999 19:19	0

tion listing, the longer it takes to download. Some bidders will immediately use the Back or Stop buttons when they encounter fancy backgrounds or annoying music.

Look at Figure 14.6 for a well-done auction ad for Jumpstart Kindergarten software. (Nope, it's not my auction.) There's a moderate variety of font sizes and colors. It's clear and direct. Okay, it does have a couple of typos. Can you find them?

You can make your own ad using graphics, and saving it as a document. Then just copy that text into the description box. Many sellers compose such ads in Word or Notepad so that they have them for future use. (Amazon even provides a basic HTML template that anyone can use as a guide. You can find this on the Sell an Item form. Select HTML Guidelines, and the link will appear on the next page in the first paragraph.) If you see an auction ad that you find particularly appealing, right-click on it to view the source code and save it in a text file. Both Internet Explorer and Netscape Navigator can do this. Keep the tags and substitute your text. In the next chapter, we'll show how to include the text in the description.

T I P

Help Needed!
Go to the Pongo
tutorials (**www.
pongo.com/howto/
quickhelp**) for great
guides on creating
Web pages and
working with images.

Now view the source code used in the "text portion" of the Jumpstart Kindergarten ad on eBay:

```
<td valign="top"><p align="center"><font color="Red" size="+1"><b>JumpStart
Kindergarten
    NEW CD Only (DOS). Still shrinkwrapped!!</b></font> </p>
    <p>Children tell time, identify upper and lower case letters, ryhme
words, match shapes,
    sort objects and more. </p>
```

With the image to the left and the text to the right, this seller has clearly positioned the software.

Description

JumpStart Kindergarten NEW CD Only (DOS). Still shrinkwrapped!!

Children tell time, identify upper and lower case letters, ryhme words, match shapes, sort objects and more.

by Knowledge Adventure includes quick reference guide

Buyer pays shipping & handling of $2.95 (Cont. U.S.), international rates will be slighltly higher. Payment by Prepay Check or Money Order, no international orders.

```
    <p><font color="#FF0000">by Knowledge
Adventure</font> includes quick
reference guide</p>
    <p><small><font color="navy"><b>Buyer pays
shipping & handling of $2.95 (Cont. U.S.),
international rates will be slighltly higher.
    Payment by Prepay Check or Money Order, no
international orders.</b></font></small></td>
    </tr>
```

When you find an ad that you like, carefully extract the HTML you need and use that as the basis for your ad.

Table 14.4 includes a few of the most useful HTML tags:

Certain HTML tags are not advised, as they can cause conflicts with Netscape browsers: <HTML>, </HTML>, <TITLE>, </TITLE>, </BODY>, <HEAD>, </HEAD>. Be sure that any <CENTER> tags are properly closed. HTML failures can be pretty ugly. That's another good reason to copy code—and to use code that works!

Musical Annoyances

Sound and images make your auction ad's file larger—and increase the downloading time. Don't

---

T I P

Don't Cheat

When you use one of the terrific image hosting sites, pay careful attention to the agreement terms. Use the buttons provided so that the auction image is posted correctly. This ensures that the host receives the advertising benefit it deserves when your image is displayed.

T A B L E 14.4

HTML Tags for Enhancing Ads

Tag	Effect on Text
<p>	Places one line of space between lines of text
 	Breaks text so next text begins on new line
<hr>	Breaks text and inserts a line in the space
<big></big>	Opens and closes areas of text to be displayed in larger font sizes
<small></small>	Opens and closes areas of text to be displayed in smaller font sizes
<center></center>	Opens and closes areas of text to be centered
<b></b>	Opens and closes areas of text to be **bolded**
<i></i>	Opens and closes areas of text to be *italicized*
<u></u>	Opens and closes areas of text to be underlined

annoy prospective buyers with backgrounds, movies, and sound files. Simply treat them to an excellent, clear, and fast-loading image.

Counting the Hits

I like to add counters by Honesty Communications (**www.honesty.com**), Auction-Watch (**www.auctionwatch.com**) or BeSeen (**www.beseen.com**) to my auctions so that I can tell just how many hits my potential sales are getting. As an option, you can select a hidden counter so that bidders aren't influenced by low counts. Just as you can get free image hosting, you can also take advantage of free counters.

I keep Honesty open in a separate browser window when preparing to add an auction. If the counter is being added to an eBay auction, Honesty can add it as you are posting the auction, or after, as a revision. When adding a counter to other sites, Honesty provides cut-and-paste text. You can post your ad, image, and counter through AuctionWatch. At BeSeen, the process works differently. They send an email with the HTML to be added to your auction through cut-and-paste.

So why do you need a counter? It's good to know if your auction advertisement is drawing viewers. If competing auctions also have counters, you can use them to compare your audiences and assess the effectiveness of your auction title.

RESOURCES

Auction facilitators abound. Free image hosting, free counters, and free advice can be had. Check these sites for image and HTML tutorials:

- **pongo.com**
- **www.pixhost.com/tutorial**
- For AOL members, **www.twaze.com/aolpix**

For image editing software, try these sites:

- **www.tucows.com**
- **shareware.cnet.com**
- On AOL, the keyword is "Computing"

KEY POINTS

This chapter covers the items that add jazz and pizzazz to any auction listing: photographic images, HTML coding, and hit counters. Let's review:

- Use images to add value and boost final bids.
- Capture images on film and obtain images on disk, CD, or via the Internet.
- Try a scanner.
- Use a video camera.
- Capture images with a digital camera.
- Become familiar with image editing.
- Store images with an image host.
- Add HTML to graphically enhance auction listings.
- Employ a hit counter.

15

CHAPTER

POSTING YOUR AD

CHECKLIST FOR POSTING AN AUCTION

Organization is the key to many accomplishments. Just ask any business maven or military strategist. When auctioning one item at a time, only a modicum of organization is needed. But if you load four or five auctions on the same day, it requires some organization.

Before beginning any auction, I consult my checklist so that I don't forget the details. For the auctions in this book, I've complicated matters with tests of multiple auction sites, several image hosts, various "hit" counters, and a couple of escrow companies. Most users will use *one* favorite auction site, *one* image host, *one* hit counter, and *one* escrow company.

Just before each auction, I scratch out a quick auction checklist. An auction checklist is crucial. Because of the details involved in obtaining the image, storing the image, creating the auction ad, attaching the image to the auction, adding a counter, and verifying the auction, I need to make sure that I haven't missed a step. If anything goes awry, the auction listings must be modified or cancelled, causing more detail-minded work. With the guidance of a checklist, my auctions are posted correctly. Refer to the checklist in the accompanying sidebar as we proceed through this chapter.

I'll cover more organization tips in Chapter 19, "Organizing Tips for Better Selling."

- Select the auction site.
- Prepare text of ad in word processor.
- Open browser windows for auction site, image host, and counter host.
- Upload image to image host.
- Set price and shipping terms.
- Copy and paste ad text into auction form.
- Add image.
- Add counter.
- Verify and confirm.

LISTING AN AUCTION

Among eBay, Amazon, Auctions.com, CityAuction, Yahoo!, and Excite, there are two distinct formats for adding an auction. In the method utilized by Amazon, eBay, and CityAuction, all information is entered on one form. With Auctions.com, Excite, and Yahoo!, you'll select the auction category and then proceed to the auction form.

Some sample forms to sell or submit an item are featured in Figures 15.1 and 15.2.

Similarities and Differences

Most entries are the same across all auction sites. The number of allocated spaces might be different, but the basic sales points are identical. Those are: Title, description, reserve price, Dutch auction, initial bid, auction duration, payment methods, shipping terms, and picture URLs.

Now let's take a look at what's different across the big six:

- *Categories.*   Each site has its own category list. For those forms that require a category selection *first,* for the purposes of illustration, a selection was made in the Art category.

- *Private auctions.*   Only Amazon and eBay have private auctions. In private auctions, the identity of each bidder is hidden. These are most often used for auctions of very-high-priced merchandise or celebrity memorabilia auctions. They are used to protect bidders' identities.

- *Closing early.*   Most sites allow an auction to be closed if it has no bids. Amazon, Auctions.com, eBay, and Yahoo! allow an auction to be closed early, making the high bidder at closing the winner. CityAuction does not allow early closes, and Yahoo! only allows early closes if the seller selected that option on the auction listing form.

- *Duration.*   Auction timing varies with each auction site. Sellers on Amazon and eBay choose the number of days the auction will run. The two

F I G U R E   15.1

---

ebay™

| Browse | **Sell** | Services | Search | Help | Community |

sell your item form

▶ Subscribe now! Get your charter subscription to eBay magazine.
▶ Noticed something different? Read about what's changed.

[   ] Search tips

☐ Search titles and descriptions

Tell us what you think of this sell your item page.

Sell Your Item

Related • New to Selling? • Seller Tips • Fees • Registration
Links: • Free Shipping Estimates from iShip.com

Registration required. You must be a registered eBay user to sell your item.

| **Title** required | [   ] |
| | (45 characters max; no HTML tags, asterisks, or quotes, as they interfere with Search) see tips |

If you prefer to use the old-style method of choosing a category, click here.

Category required   You have chosen category # [   ]

Just click in the boxes below from left to right until you have found the appropriate category for your item.
The chosen category number will appear in the small box to indicate that you have made a valid selection.

Antiques ->			
Books, Movies, Music ->			
Coins & Stamps ->			
Collectibles ->			
Computers ->			
Dolls, Figures ->			
Jewelry, Gemstones ->			
Photo & Electronics ->			
Pottery & Glass ->			
Sports Memorabilia ->			
Toys & Beanies Plush ->			
Miscellaneous ->			

Posting Your Ad

(Continued)

Description required	
	You can use basic HTML tags to spruce up your listing. see tips You can add links to additional photos, but enter your primary photo in the Picture URL below. If you want more than one photo for your item, insert its URL in the Description section in the following format: \<img src=http://www.anywhere.com/mypicture.jpg>
Picture URL optional	http:// ◻ It's easy! Learn the basics in the tutorial, and enter your URL here.

The Gallery Don't get left out! Items in the Gallery get more bids! learn more	⦿ Do not include my item in the Gallery ○ Add my item to the Gallery (only **$0.25!**) ○ Feature my item in the Gallery (Featured fee of $19.95) http:// If you leave the Gallery URL empty, your Pic URL will be used as your Gallery URL. (Only jpg, bmp, or tif files can be used in the Gallery. Please note that **gif** files will **not** appear in the Gallery!)
	Make your item stand out and get more bids! Try these winning options.
Boldface Title?	◻ $2.00 charge
Featured?	◻ $99.95 charge learn more
Featured in Category?	◻ $14.95 charge learn more
Great Gift icon?	Not Selected ▾ $1.00 charge learn more

(Continued)

Item location required	
	City, Region (e.g., San Jose, CA)
	Zip or postal code (e.g., 95125)
	United States ▾
	Country

Payment Methods Choose all that you will accept	☐ Money Order/Cashiers Check	☐ Personal Check	☐ Visa/MasterCard
	☐ COD (collect on delivery)	☐ On-line Escrow	☐ American Express
	☑ See Item Description	☐ Other	☐ Discover

Where will you ship?	⦿ Ship to Seller's Country Only see tips	◯ Will Ship Internationally

Who pays for shipping?	☐ Seller Pays Shipping	☐ Buyer Pays Fixed Amount
	☐ Buyer Pays Actual Shipping Cost	☑ See Item Description

Quantity required	1
	If quantity is more than one, then you will have a Dutch auction. see tips

Minimum bid required	per item see tips
	(e.g., 2.00 -- Please do not include commas or currency symbols, such as $.)

Duration required	7 ▾ days

Reserve Price optional	see tips
	(e.g., 15.00 -- Please do not include commas or currency symbols, such as $.)

Private Auction? optional	☐ Please don't use this unless you have a specific reason. learn more

UserID / Password required		
	User ID or E-mail address	Password (forgotten it?)

FIGURE 15.2

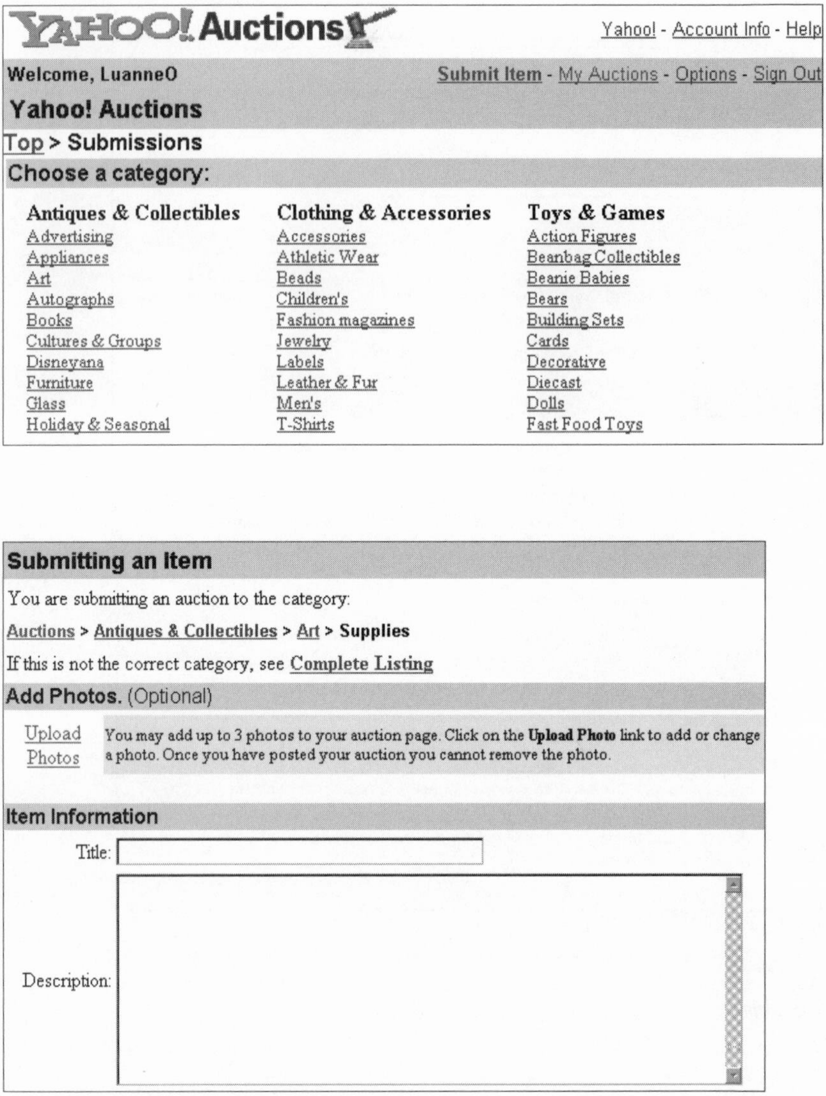

FIGURE 15.2

YAHOO! Auctions

Yahoo! - Account Info - Help

Welcome, LuanneO

Submit Item - My Auctions - Options - Sign Out

Yahoo! Auctions

Top > Submissions

Choose a category:

Antiques & Collectibles	Clothing & Accessories	Toys & Games
Advertising	Accessories	Action Figures
Appliances	Athletic Wear	Beanbag Collectibles
Art	Beads	Beanie Babies
Autographs	Children's	Bears
Books	Fashion magazines	Building Sets
Cultures & Groups	Jewelry	Cards
Disneyana	Labels	Decorative
Furniture	Leather & Fur	Diecast
Glass	Men's	Dolls
Holiday & Seasonal	T-Shirts	Fast Food Toys

Submitting an Item

You are submitting an auction to the category:

Auctions > Antiques & Collectibles > Art > Supplies

If this is not the correct category, see Complete Listing

Add Photos. (Optional)

Upload Photos You may add up to 3 photos to your auction page. Click on the **Upload Photo** link to add or change a photo. Once you have posted your auction you cannot remove the photo.

Item Information

Title: [   ]

Description: [   ]

FIGURE 15.2

(Continued)

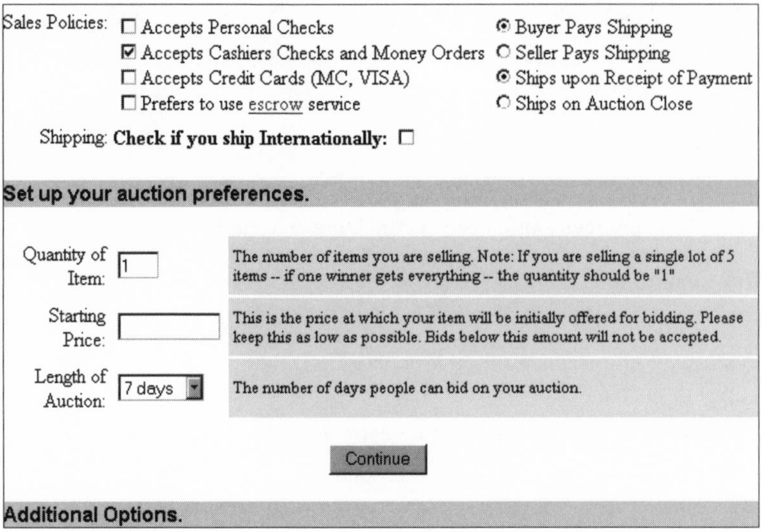

Sales Policies: ☐ Accepts Personal Checks   ◉ Buyer Pays Shipping
☑ Accepts Cashiers Checks and Money Orders ○ Seller Pays Shipping
☐ Accepts Credit Cards (MC, VISA)   ◉ Ships upon Receipt of Payment
☐ Prefers to use escrow service   ○ Ships on Auction Close

Shipping: **Check if you ship Internationally:** ☐

Set up your auction preferences.

Quantity of Item:	`1`	The number of items you are selling. Note: If you are selling a single lot of 5 items -- if one winner gets everything -- the quantity should be "1"
Starting Price:		This is the price at which your item will be initially offered for bidding. Please keep this as low as possible. Bids below this amount will not be accepted.
Length of Auction:	`7 days ▾`	The number of days people can bid on your auction.

[Continue]

Additional Options.

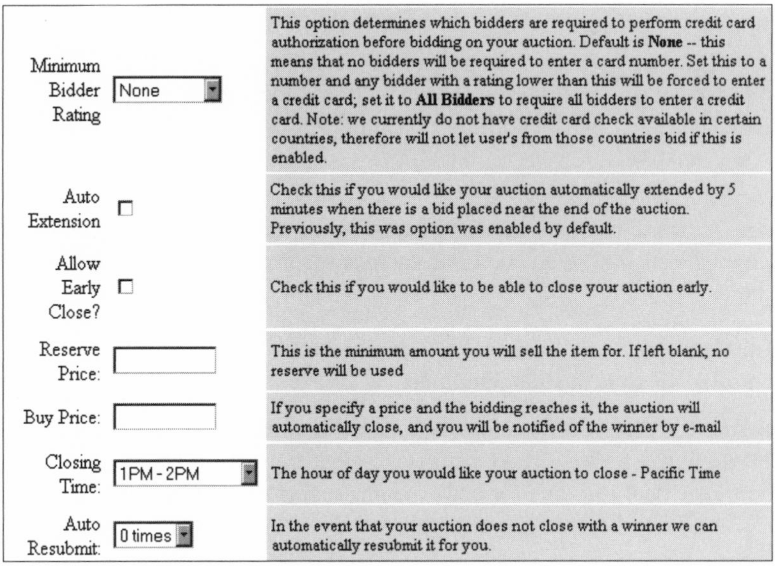

Minimum Bidder Rating	`None ▾`	This option determines which bidders are required to perform credit card authorization before bidding on your auction. Default is **None** -- this means that no bidders will be required to enter a card number. Set this to a number and any bidder with a rating lower than this will be forced to enter a credit card; set it to **All Bidders** to require all bidders to enter a credit card. Note: we currently do not have credit card check available in certain countries, therefore will not let user's from those countries bid if this is enabled.
Auto Extension	☐	Check this if you would like your auction automatically extended by 5 minutes when there is a bid placed near the end of the auction. Previously, this was option was enabled by default.
Allow Early Close?	☐	Check this if you would like to be able to close your auction early.
Reserve Price:		This is the minimum amount you will sell the item for. If left blank, no reserve will be used
Buy Price:		If you specify a price and the bidding reaches it, the auction will automatically close, and you will be notified of the winner by e-mail
Closing Time:	`1PM - 2PM ▾`	The hour of day you would like your auction to close - Pacific Time
Auto Resubmit:	`0 times ▾`	In the event that your auction does not close with a winner we can automatically resubmit it for you.

sites offer different, but overlapping, durations. A seven-day auction is most common. Barring site server problems, auctions that start at 10:06 A.M. will close at 10:06 A.M., seven days later. Read ahead. You'll find more on auction timing and duration in the Chapter 16, "Timing Your Auction."

Beyond these somewhat in-common features, there are some significant differences among the big-six sites.

Advantage Amazon
Amazon offers few unique features on the sales form.

- Amazon's 80 character title space is the largest around.

Uniquely Auctions.com
Auctions.com has a nice selection of goodies on its sellers form.

- *Web sites.*   Sellers can list their Web site URL (not the same as image hosting) in the auction listing for $1.
- *Flat listing fee.*   Any auction can be listed for only 25 cents.
- *Second category listing.*   Choose a second category for display, only 25 cents.
- *Specific shipping method.*   Unlike other auction sites, Auctions.com asks sellers to be very specific in naming a shipping method. There's an extensive drop-box with selections for UPS, USPS, FedEx, and Airborne shipping terms.
- *Second-chance listings.*   An automatic second try, called Auto Relist, is offered from the start. The birdhouse will be automatically relisted for a second chance if the auction closes without a high bidder. Second-chance listings are free.
- *Start date, closing date, duration.*   It's unusual to be able to select the starting date. It presents great advantages to savvy sellers. Only have time to load the auction on Sunday, but you want it to start on Wednesday? List it here.

Solely at CityAuction
CityAuction offers flexible auction durations:

- *Duration.*   CityAuction offers the longest timeline for auction durations. Sellers with patience can set auctions to close four weeks hence. You can choose the date and time for both opening and closing the auction.

eBay Extras
eBay offers few extras. They often add new marketing ideas to help sellers sell well.

- *Gallery features.*   Available to all categories. For 25 cents an auction can be added to The Gallery, a catalog-style category sales page.

- *Gift icons.*   Popular with eBay sellers—and bidders, too. eBay's gift icons are available for more than a dozen holidays and important events.

Exceptional Excite

Excite's hidden feature is uniquely helpful:

- *Image host.*   It's a hidden feature, but Excite will host images for you. Upload the images through your "My Account" page.

Yippee Yahoo!

Yahoo! offers a great selection of features at its free auction site:

- *Photos.*   Like Excite, Yahoo! hosts images. Unlike any other site, you can upload one, two, or three photos, not to exceed 1.5 Mbytes. HTML is accepted in the description window, so you can link in a photo. Yahoo! recommends that each photo be smaller than 7K!

- *Text description.*   HTML is okay to use, even though it is not mentioned on the form.

- *Shipping terms include options.* Glaringly, there's no option for sellers who hold checks for 10 days. This calls for sellers to be explicit in the description.

- *Autoextension.*   Auction closes only if five minutes have elapsed without a bid; bids within the five-minute window extend the duration of the auction. This policy is also found at Amazon and Yahoo!. Here's the example: If an auction is supposed to close at 7:00 P.M. and there's a bid at 6:59 P.M., the closing time will be pushed forward to 7:04 P.M. As long as there are no bids between 6:59 P.M. and 7:04 P.M., the auction will close on the new schedule at 7:04 P.M.

- *Closing time.*   Within the time frame of an hour, Yahoo! allows you to select a closing time for your auction. My preference is 6 to 7 P.M., Pacific time. That's 9 to 10 P.M., Eastern time. The window includes the

TIP

Don't Crash

Write your auction ads in a word processor and copy-and-paste the ad into the auction form. This saves critical time if a snag is hit. Is this advance planning worth it? Imagine how you'd feel if your computer crashed, your Internet connection was lost, or the auction site's server went down just as you were uploading the ad.

Custom Appearance

To stand out among millions of listings, some volume sellers develop HTML templates that give their ads an easy-to-identify custom appearance. All ads use the same colors, backgrounds, and formats so that bidders will recognize them.

TIP

Include Insurance

In the listing description, include the phrase, "Insurance additional upon request." Buyer beware, caveat emptor, and watch out!

U.S. population targeted by many sellers. Select the number of days and pick the closing time period of your choice.

- *Allow early close.* Closing early may cause you to lose out on bidders who love to snipe. Keep this option available in case you need to leave town in a hurry. eBay and Amazon also allow early closes; sellers do not need to make a selection when they post an auction.

- *Autoresubmit.* In the event your auction fails to attract bidders, you can select to automatically resubmit it up to 5 times. You can also elect not to resubmit the auction. That's called resubmitting it zero times. The resubmission is free, because all listings are free here.

COMPLETE THE FORM (DETAILS, DETAILS . . .)

Your first auction is the most challenging one you will face. If your house is like mine, there's a lot that can zing by while posting an auction. ("Mom, what's for dinner?") I need to refer to my checklist to ensure that I don't skip any details.

You can draft your auction in the listing form, but we don't advise it. Open your word processor, and create the text of your ad there. You can even make your own ad using HTML and saving it as a document. Customize it for each auction and paste the text into the description box. By creating the ad in your word processor, you can take advantage of the spell-checker. (Don't forget to use it!) You'll also have the auction details in a safe place. There's nothing worse than losing your Internet connection or experiencing an auction site crash just as you are loading your auction.

Let's begin with posting an auction at Amazon. Once registered, select Sell Your Item Now. It appears in the banner at the top of the "Auctions" home page. For reference, print the auction form by selecting File/Print in the browser window.

We'll use the Amazon's HTML template, mentioned in the last chapter. It's accessible through a link on the "Sell an Item" form. Choose HTML Guidelines adjacent to the title description. In the first paragraph choose the Click Here link to access the template. Copy and paste the template into your word processor. It looks like this:

```
<center> <b> <h4>
Your Title
</h4> </b> </center >
<p>
Your Text, Paragraph 1.
<p>
Your Text, Paragraph 2.
<p>
<p>
<center>
<img src="YourImageURL">
<p>
Your Image Caption.
</center>
```

Amazon: Listing the Video

Now let's use that same template to create an ad in the word processor. From my stash of exercise videos, let's list *Warm-Up to Fitness.*

```
<center> <b> <h4>
Warm-Up to Fitness Exercise Video
</h4> </b> </center >
<p>
Warm-up to Fitness is a great exercise video.
This instructional video is designed to improve
your body, increase your stamina, and help to
reduce stress. Led by Libby Roberts, one of
England's top fitness instructors. Full color,
33 minutes running time.
<p>
No reserve. Buyer to pay $3.20 for Priority
Mail. Insurance optional at buyer's risk and
expense. Seller accepts money orders and per-
sonal checks (and reserves the right to hold
personal checks for 7 days). No international
sales.
```

T I P

Print the Auction Listing Form

Keep a copy of the auction listing form at hand to refer to when creating auction listings in your word processor. That way you'll have all the information you need at your fingertips.

T I P

Count the Spaces

Know how many characters and spaces are available in the auction title. Write the title to make the best use of that space. Fill it up with keywords.

```
<p>
<p>
<center>
<p>
The First Step to a Beautiful Body</center>
```

Let's review what we did here. This HTML code is to be cut and pasted into Amazon's Describe Your Item text box. It's limited to 4,000 characters, including spaces. I can't imagine using 4,000 characters. What's the comparison? A full page of 10-point text is about 3,900 characters.

I've removed the image tag `<img src="YourImageURL">` from the template. When there is only one image to include in an auction, just include the image URL in the form's designated space. This will assure that the auction gets the site's PIC logo or icon.

With two images, you can include one in the text description, using the `<img scr>` tag shown above, and the other in the form's image URL space. As demonstrated in the template, the image included in the description area will appear above the image listed in the image URL space.

In the Word file, list the title, another picture URL, opening bid, and reserve price (if you are using one). Any special reminders should be listed here. Those might include the length of the auction or payment terms.

```
Title: Warm-Up to Fitness Exercise Video
Picture URL: http://www.pbay.com/myimage/95919455~417727487~1.JPG
Opening Bid: $3.00
No reserve.
```

The completed form appears in Figure 15.3. After completing the form, you will select a category and will then see a Preview Your Auction button.

The auction confirmation appears in Figure 15.4. It looks ready to go. To proceed from this page, select Click Here to Submit Your Auction. Wait! Read on . . .

Yahoo!: Listing the Video

Now, let's try something from the free side of the street. Surf over to Yahoo! and get registered. Select Submit Auctions to access the auction submission form. Don't forget to print the form.

Let's give this tired video another try. Start by selecting a category from the list appearing in Figure 15.2. There's no category for fitness videos! First I tried "Electronics & Cameras," but that only led to "Video Players (VCRs)." Other fitness videos are in "Sports & Recreation, Sporting Goods, Tents"! Awkwardly, I've selected "Arts & Entertainment, Movies, Videotape, and Other." If you can't get a good category fit, consider changing to another auction site. In the meantime, I'll continue with the example.

The first step is to select a category. Your choices will look something like the list on the bottom of page 180:

The completed auction form.

Here's where you create your listing--where your words and
images combine to entice bidders. Just fill out the form below. It's
fun and easy!

Item Title:
Limit 80 characters

Warm-Up to Fitness Exercise Video

Describe your item:
Limit 4,000 characters
(spaces count). Feel free to
use basic HTML in your
description.
HTML guidelines.

```
<center> <b> <h4>
Warm-Up to Fitness Exercise Video
</h4> </b> </center >
<p>
Warm-up to Fitness is a great exercise
video. This instructional video is
designed to improve your body, increase
```

Add a picture (optional):
Image tips and tricks.

bay.com/myimage/95919455~417727487~1.JPG

Example: http://yoursite.com/image.gif

Bidding starts at: $ 3.00   US Dollars

Reserve price: ⊙ No ○ Yes [   ] US Dollars
What is a reserve price and
why we discourage it.

Type of auction: ⊙ Standard
What is a Dutch auction? ○ Dutch [   ] Quantity

Private auction: ⊙ No ○ Yes
What is a private auction?

Duration of auction: [7 days ▼]

Where will this item be
shipped from?

Virginia

Example: El Paso, TX

Shipping terms: ⊙ Buyer pays shipping costs
How to calculate shipping Please specify the amount in the item description.
costs. ○ Seller pays shipping costs
☐ Will ship internationally

Accepted payment ☑ Money order/Cashier's check
methods: ☑ Personal check
☐ C.O.D.
☐ Visa/Master Card
☐ American Express

I will work with online ☑ Yes
escrow:

FIGURE 15.4

The Amazon ad is ready for final approval.

 Sell an Item

10:51:26 PST

Review and Submit your Auction

Click here to submit your auction.

(You can always add information later.)

Auction Title: Warm-Up to Fitness Exercise Video

Picture: http://www.pbay.com/myimage/95919455~417727487~1.JPG

Category: Movies & Video / VHS / Fitness

Auction type: Standard

Duration: 7 days

Minimum Bid: $ 3.00

Location: Virginia

Accepted Payment Methods: Escrow
Money Order/Cashier's Check
Personal Check

Shipping Terms: Buyer Pays
Will not ship internationally

Optional Features: No Features Selected

Description and Picture:

Warm-Up to Fitness Exercise Video

Warm-up to Fitness is a great exercise video. This instructional video is designed to improve your body, increase your stamina, and help to reduce stress. Led by Libby Roberts, one of England's top fitness instructors. Full color, 33 minutes running time.

No reserve. Buyer to pay $3.20 for Priority Mail. Insurance optional at buyer's risk and expense. Seller accepts money orders and personal checks (and reserves the right to hold personal checks for 7 days). No international sales.

The First Step to a Beautiful Body

Arts & Entertainment

Books

Magazines

Memorabilia

Movies

FIGURE 15.4

(Continued)

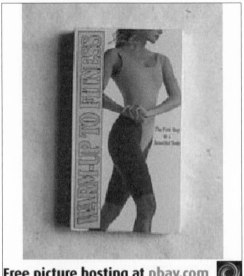

Music

Musical Instruments

Services

Tickets

Art

Video Games

Begin to complete the form as seen in Figure 15.5.

Note that Yahoo!'s photo entry is different from what we've seen at Amazon. Select the Add Photos link as seen in Figure 15.6.

Yahoo! hosts up to three images for each auction—up to a total of 1.5 Mbytes per auction. It's an easy upload and there's no tricky linking. The seller's preferences are in Figure 15.7.

Pay particular attention to Yahoo!'s options, which are quite different from those at Amazon (and eBay). Those options are seen in Figure 15.8. Review the disclaimer (not shown here) and select Continue to proceed to the next step.

The listing confirmation appears for review in Figure 15.9. If you're ready to go, scroll to the bottom and click the Submit Auction button.

FIGURE 15.5

Verify the category placement and select the link to add photos.

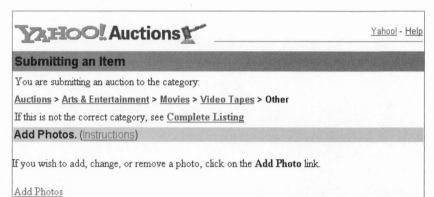

ADD AN IMAGE

Like many things in life, the process of adding an image can be difficult and confusing to auction newbies. However, by providing the right guidance, we can make the first time easy.

Amazon, Auctions.com, eBay, and CityAuction include picture or image URL boxes in the "Sell an Item" form. Excite and Yahoo! host images, and image handling works differently with them. Excite accepts images by email, snail mail, or direct upload. Yahoo! accepts direct uploads.

When an image URL is placed in the image URL box, an icon denoting an image is attached to the auction title. The image icon will be seen by bidders paging through the category or viewing search results. Image URLs in the descriptive text box don't trigger the attachment of the image icon.

The correct format for image URLs is: **http://www.mydomain.com/userid/picture1.jpg**.

Your URL may be longer or shorter than this, but it must be correct. Just *one* errant character and the framed *New Yorker* print will be nowhere to be found. Image hosting sites work hard to provide inviolable image URLs. See the Picturebay example in Chapter 14, "Preparing a Great Ad," for an example of image URLs.

> **TIP**
>
> **Never Count on the Back Button.**
>
> The form data is rarely saved by the site or browser. The Back button often reveals a blank form. Create your ads in a word processor so you can cut and paste into the auction form.

FIGURE 15.6

Use the browse button to locate the image.

When posting from AuctionWatch or a similar site, follow the on-screen directions to the letter. Most auction hosts include a logo or banner ad with your image. You agreed to that in the terms and conditions. Follow each site's posting procedures to ensure that you stay in compliance with the host's terms.

Let's review the importance of images and image URLs:

- Images sell.
- URLs must be precisely and uncompromisingly correct.
- Copy and paste for accuracy.
- URLs must be in the right place to get the all-important PIC logo.
- Image URLs end in **.jpg**.
- Make sure that **http://** is not duplicated within the image entry box.

Posting from AuctionWatch

Work with several open browser windows when listing auctions. Open one for eBay, another for the image host, and a third for the counter host.

Let's go through the process of posting an auction and adding an image from AuctionWatch. When posting an auction from AuctionWatch, you can even omit the eBay browser window.

Complete the form and note your preferences.

Item Information

Title: | Warm-Up to Fitness Exercise Video |

Description:
```
increase your stamina, and help to reduce stress. Led by
Libby Roberts, one of England's top fitness instructors.
Full color, 33 minutes running time.
<br>
No reserve. Buyer to pay $3.20 for Priority Mail. Insurance
optional at buyer's risk and expense. Seller accepts money
orders and personal checks (and reserves the right to hold
personal checks for 7 days). No international sales.
<br>
```

Sales Policies:
- ☑ Accepts Personal Checks
- ☑ Accepts Cashiers Checks and Money Orders
- ☐ Accepts Credit Cards (MC, VISA)
- ☐ Prefers to use escrow service

- ◉ Buyer Pays Shipping
- ○ Seller Pays Shipping
- ◉ Ships upon Receipt of Payment
- ○ Ships on Auction Close

Shipping: **Check if you ship Internationally:** ☐

Set up your auction preferences.

Quantity of Item: | 1 | The number of items you are selling. Note: If you are selling a single lot of 5 items -- if one winner gets everything -- the quantity should be "1"

Starting Price: | 3.00 | This is the price at which your item will be initially offered for bidding. Please keep this as low as possible. Bids below this amount will not be accepted.

Length of Auction: | 7 days ▾ | The number of days people can bid on your auction.

Log into AuctionWatch with your name and password. Navigate to your images and click to select the desired image. We'll use the image uploaded in Chapter 14. Place a check mark before the image, as seen in Figure 15.10. Next, choose the Attach Image button.

The resulting page confirms the image selection, as seen in Figure 15.11. Using the drop box, select the Amazon, eBay, or Other Auction site. Then click the buttons for New Auction and Add These Images.

A selection of New Auction with Amazon, eBay, or another named site will result in the site's auction submission form appearing on the next screen. Let's select eBay. An eBay form will open and you will complete it just as if you had logged into eBay. AuctionWatch creates the form and, once completed, the data is transmitted to eBay. Take a close look and you'll see that AuctionWatch has added the necessary code for linking your AuctionWatch image. If the code is not immediately apparent, use the scroll button on the Description box and look for HTML code like this:

FIGURE 15.8

Make the final selections here.

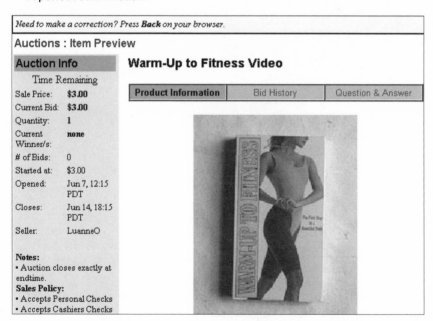

Additional Options.

Auto Extension	☐	Check this if you would like your auction automatically extended by 5 minutes when there is a bid placed near the end of the auction. Previously, this was option was enabled by default
Allow Early Close?	☐	Check this if you would like to be able to close your auction early.
Reserve Price:		This is the minimum amount you will sell the item for. If left blank, no reserve will be used
Sell Price:	3.00	If you specify a price and the bidding reaches it, the auction will automatically close, and you will be notified of the winner by e-mail
Closing Time:	6PM - 7PM ▾	The hour of day you would like your auction to close - Pacific Time
Auto Resubmit:	1 times ▾	In the event that your auction does not close with a winner we can automatically resubmit it for you.

FIGURE 15.9

A perfect confirmation.

*Need to make a correction? Press **Back** on your browser.*

Auctions : Item Preview

Auction Info

Time Remaining

Sale Price:	**$3.00**
Current Bid:	**$3.00**
Quantity:	1
Current Winner/s:	**none**
# of Bids:	0
Started at:	$3.00
Opened:	Jun 7, 12:15 PDT
Closes:	Jun 14, 18:15 PDT
Seller:	LuanneO

Notes:
• Auction closes exactly at endtime.
Sales Policy:
• Accepts Personal Checks
• Accepts Cashiers Checks

Warm-Up to Fitness Video

Product Information	Bid History	Question & Answer

FIGURE 15.10

Select the image by placing a check in the box.

select	name	size	view time	last modified	last viewed	count
☑	bop1.jpg	24 K	☺ 8 seconds	Jun 06, 1999 10:32	Jun 07, 1999 3:00	0

```
<p><center><img
src="http://216.32.245.142/imageserver/00002053/luanneo/bop1.jpg"></center>
     <br>
<br><center>
<A HREF="http://www.auctionwatch.com">
<IMG SRC="http://216.32.245.142/images/hostedby.jpg" BORDER="0"></A>
</CENTER><BR>
```

Enter your description above this code in the text box and proceed with listing the auction.

FIGURE 15.11

Confirm the image and select the auction site.

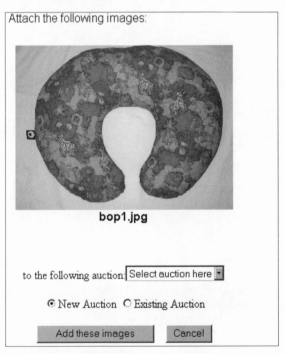

Attach the following images:

bop1.jpg

to the following auction: Select auction here ▾

⊙ New Auction ○ Existing Auction

Add these images   Cancel

AuctionWatch Method No. 2

AuctionWatch provides a different method for including images when working with a site other than AuctionWatch's preferred sites. This alternative method is similar to what you'll find at other image hosts. To try this, choose Other Auction Site, followed by New Auction (or Existing Auction) and Add These Images. AuctionWatch provides HTML code to be copied and pasted into the description and image sections of auction listing form, as seen in Figure 15.12.

The complete code group must be inserted as is to ensure that the AuctionWatch banner is displayed in the ad. Copy and paste into the auction's description form. Then, the single line of code

```
http://www.auctionwatch.com/images/cleardot.gif
```

can be copied into the image URL box. It acts as a placeholder. With the **cleardot.gif** in the picture URL box, the auction will get the important PIC icon denoting an attached picture.

T I P

What's the Image URL?

Storing images on your own Web space? Right-click on any image to obtain the image URL. It's listed in the Properties dialog box. Copy and paste it into the box.

F I G U R E 15.12

Obtain the text to be copied and pasted into the text area of the auction form.

> To put your image(s) into your auction, simply copy and paste the information below into it. Please note that an auction site must be registered with us first in order for this code to work. The authorized list can be found on the main menu. If you've got a favorite auction and would like to get them authorized send us an email and let us know.
>
> If the auction you're using has a picture URL box, you should place the following line into it if you can:
>
> http://www.auctionwatch.com/images/cleardot.gif
>
> The code below MUST be inserted as-is. Users bypassing the code below risk image and account deletion without notification.
>
> COPY AND PASTE ALL INFORMATION BELOW:

```
<p><center><img
src="http://216.32.245.142/imageserver/00002053/luanneo/
bop1.jpg"></center><br>
<br><center>
<A HREF="http://www.auctionwatch.com">
<IMG SRC="http://216.32.245.142/images/hostedby.jpg"
BORDER="0"></A>
</CENTER><BR>
```

Picturebay

In the previous chapter, "Preparing a Great Ad," we also uploaded an image to Picturebay (**www.pbay.com**). Picturebay provides users with a single-image URL to be pasted into the auction's image URL box. That single line directs visitors' browsers to the image and Picturebay banner. That single line of code acts as an alternative to the several lines of code copied by AuctionWatch users. Both methods provide excellent images and are easy to work with.

MULTIPLE PHOTOS

To add multiple photos in an auction listing, you'll want to put one in the Picture URL text box and the others in the body of the descriptive text. By placing the first in the Picture URL box, the listing will carry the green PIC icon (or whatever icon is used at the site). You can have multiple images of an antique rocking chair in your auction ad, but to get the icon you must have one in the image URL box. At most sites, there's only one chance to get that all-important icon.

To embed pictures in your descriptive text, enclose the URL(s) in the HTML image tag. To enhance the photos, it is a good idea to add a line break between them. Using the prior example as a basis, here's the sample HTML:

```
<HR>
<IMGSCR=http://www.mydomain.com/userid/image1.
     jpg>
<p>
<IMGSCR=http://www.mydomain.com/userid/image2.
     jpg>
<HR>
```

The <HR> was added to keep the descriptive text from bleeding into the image. The second tag was added to keep the images from running into a counter or any text that might appear after the images.

ADD COUNTER

Place an ad and you'll want to add a counter to keep track of your auction's popularity. But, what type of counter should you choose? Counters can count every refresh and reload, or only new visits.

Traditional counters, like that added from Honesty Communications (**www.honesty.com**), count only new visitors. They do not count repeti-

---

T I P

Sneaky Pics

Following the AuctionWatch description, put an URL for a one-pixel-by-one-pixel GIF or JPG image in the image URL box. When you add images in the description box you'll still get the icon.

---

tive or reloaded views by the same user. Honesty's "Page View" counter sums all views, including reloads. Sit at your computer, hit the browser's reload button, and watch the count climb.

The counters at AuctionWatch (**www.auctionwatch.com**) perform the same functions under different names. Simple counters tally every page hit, while smart counters ignore back-to-back hits from the same visitor. In the prior chapter we looked at the counters offered by AuctionWatch, Honesty, and BeSeen (**www.beseen.com**). With your email address, eBay password, and eBay auction number, Honesty will add a counter for you. Honesty works with several big-name sites, but we'll use eBay for our example.

When working with eBay and Honesty, keep a browser window open and complete all information with the exception of the auction number. As soon as the auction has been posted and confirmed, copy the auction number into the space on Honesty's form. Click the Add Counter button, and the auction will be *revised* with the counter added.

If your auction is on a site other than those on Honesty's list, select Honesty's "Generic Counter" option. Enter your email address and Honesty password. Select among the dozens of digit styles, choose Hidden or not, a border (or not), and lastly choose Traditional or Page View counting method. Click the Add Counter button and the counter code will appear on the subsequent page, as seen in Figure 15.13. Copy and paste the counter code into the auction ad's text description. For the best appearance of your counter, place the code at the bottom of the text description box.

Honesty and BeSeen utilize different processes for attaching counters to ads. BeSeen's HTML code is sent in an email to be cut and pasted into the auction text box. It's easiest to do this while you are preparing the listing.

Visit BeSeen (**www.beseen.com**) and select the Hit Counter link. On the next page, choose the Counter Style. Enter your email address, create and enter a name for this counter, and choose a category. This is also called a site subject. (The site subject helps BeSeen to keep track of where counters are used.) Select the starting count for your auction and Click Here to Submit this Form.

A confirmation page will appear, telling you that your counter code is being sent to you via email. Check your email for new messages. The text of the email includes the copy and paste code as seen in Figure 15.14.

- Request the counter.

- Receive counter by email.

- Cut and paste into auction text, at the end of the description.

Copy and paste the code into the auction text box while you are preparing the listing form. Pay close attention to where the code is inserted. If you place it at the beginning of the listing, bidders will see the counter before the descriptive text. Don't do that! Place it at the end of the text description.

FIGURE 15.13

The counter code is ready for copy-and-paste.

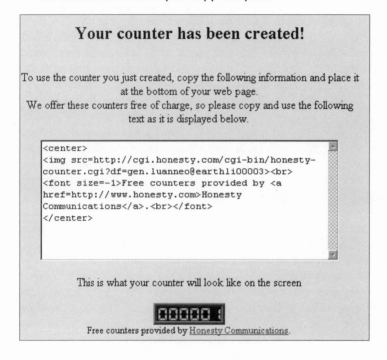

Your counter has been created!

To use the counter you just created, copy the following information and place it at the bottom of your web page.
We offer these counters free of charge, so please copy and use the following text as it is displayed below.

```
<center>
<img src=http://cgi.honesty.com/cgi-bin/honesty-
counter.cgi?df=gen.luanneo@earthli00003><br>
<font size=-1>Free counters provided by <a
href=http://www.honesty.com>Honesty
Communications</a>.<br></font>
</center>
```

This is what your counter will look like on the screen

Free counters provided by Honesty Communications.

VERIFY THE AUCTION LISTING

Upon the completion of each auction form, take a deep breath before hitting the Submit Auction button. Get out of your chair and stretch a bit before you sit back down to review the verification. Utilize the proofreader's technique of reading it aloud. This simple action makes you slow down and carefully read the words you have put to pixels.

Are the title, price, and category correct? Is the description accurate? Have the shipping terms been clearly described? Does the image appear? If so, click one more button. It's showtime!

Auction Confirmation

Within minutes after the last click of the mouse, an email will be sent to your account. This confirms the basic auction details and includes a link to the auction. Use this link to make one more check. Now is the time to cancel or revise. If cancellation or revision is necessary, it's much easier to do so before bids are received.

Copy the code from the email and paste it into the auction form.

```
Hello,

Welcome to Beseen - a Looksmart service, the leading category-based
Web directory. Your Beseen Hit counter has been set up and is
ready to use.

Here is the HTML code for your Hit counter. Copy this and insert it
into the source of your web page:

<!-- Begin Beseen Hit counter -->
<A HREF="http://www.beseen.com/hc-index.html">
<IMG SRC= "http://pluto.beseen.com/hit.counter?account=LuanneO@earthlink.net-test&font=&base=0"
BORDER=0></A>

<!-- End Beseen Hit counter -->
```

Your attention to detail results in the perfect seller's auction—congratulations! Sit back, relax, and wait for tomorrow morning's auction status email. The daily auction status message tells sellers how the bidding is going. It can make my day, and hopefully, it will brighten yours too.

TROUBLESHOOTING

You can do everything perfectly—and an occasional auction glitch will still occur. You've relied on your ISP or online service for access to the auction site, image host, and counter host. Like all sellers, you also rely on the auction site's servers and services. Add in image hosts and counter hosts, and you've got a whole team relying on each other.

Ad Trouble

In the first few hours after posting, your auction won't be available through auction search engines. Only users looking at new listings will have a chance of finding it. You'll be able to locate it with the auction number or through the link in the confirmation email. If you want friends to see it right away, send the link.

Auction sites have been known to encounter server problems during periods of rapid growth. New features and directory updates can cause glitches and temporary outages. If you suspect that the problem is with the site, check the site map for a link to System Status Updates. On eBay, choose the Community link in the banner, followed by a selection for Announcements.

Auction sites extend all auctions closing within a designated time period after serious system outages. These can be annoying for most auctioneers. Some sellers are convinced that outages and delayed closing times impact their auction profits. Outages are enough to convince me to stay away from short auctions like three-day auctions. With a seven-day auction, auction downtime has less impact.

TABLE 15.1

Image Problems and Solutions

Problem	Try This
Web server hosting the images is temporarily down.	Verify by going to the image host's site. Check system status and try to review images.
URL is invalid or misspelled.	Correct the URL. If the auction ad has been posted, it may be necessary to cancel the ad.
Viewer's Web browser is not configured correctly for viewing images.	Check the Web browser's help files to ensure that it is configured correctly.
Image has been moved, resulting image address is incorrect, or URL points to a nonexistent .jpg.	If bop1.jpg is no longer at AuctionWatch, the URL won't be accurate. Check the image at the host and verify the image URL by right-clicking and selecting properties.
Image is in a format not supported by all Web browsers (.art, .bmp, .pcx) rather than the "correct" .jpg or .gif formats.	Go back to your image viewing software and resave it as a JPG, or if you must, a GIF. Reload image to site or host.
Image URL points to a web page (ends in .html) rather than an image.	Right click on the image, select properties, and check the image URL. It should end in .jpg.
Quotes were used in HTML code.	Please, no quotes!

Image Issues

If you've added an image to your auction, but it doesn't appear, you'll need to check the troubleshooting list in Table 15.1. First, make sure the image host is online. Surf to the host and check your images. If the images appear correctly at the image host, then the problem lies with the image URL.

Images posted through Image Hosts present a specific group of challenges. Auctions posted at Amazon, Auctions.com, eBay, Excite, and CityAuction link images from other sites. AuctionWatch has added a system status board, and the link is available from the home page.

Sites that host images simplify auction image issues. Auctions posted at Excite and Yahoo! yield another line of image corrections, as shown in Table 15.2.

Counter Crunches

It's rare for counters to fail. A counter site may go down, but I haven't seen it happen to my auctions. If you can't get into a counter's site, go to an auction site's help mes-

T A B L E 15.2

Image Problems and Solutions (Excite and Yahoo!)

Problem	Try This
Auction host is temporarily down.	Confirm through system status or through an email group or newsgroup.
Viewer's Web browser is not configured correctly for viewing images.	Check the Web browser's help files to ensure that it is configured correctly.
Image is in a format not supported by all Web browsers (.art, .bmp, .pcx) rather than the "correct" .jpg or .gif formats.	Go back to your image viewing software and resave it as a JPG, or if you must, a GIF. Reload image.
Image was too large or exceeded host's standards.	Go back to image editing software. Resize or compress the image.

sage board. (eBay's HTML board is very active.) Other users may be sharing information on the same problem.

If you can access the counter site's message board and frequently asked questions (FAQs) look for comments related to system status and troubleshooting. BeSeen's Hit Counter FAQ reveals that users of *Netscape Composer* most often mistakenly use a *local file* name rather than the correct hit counter. If you run into problems like this, check with your image host for its specific list of problems and solutions.

LISTING CONFIRMATION

The listing confirmation will arrive in your email box within minutes of the auction's posting. Read it, verify it, and test the link to the auction. The auction site's search engine may not be able to "find" it until the auction files have been updated. This process is usually undertaken several times a day.

REVISING AUCTION LISTINGS

Failed to include shipping terms? Just realized you'll be away and won't be able to answer emails? On most auction sites, you can modify or revise a listing.

Check your auction site's site map or customer service links for information on revising auction listings. You may find it more expedient to cancel the auction and start over.

See Chapter 17, "During the Auction," for more information.

RESOURCES

Auction organizers and loading tools will be included in Chapter 19, "Organizing Tips for Better Selling."

Know your auction site. Check the site map for message boards offering help with the auction postings, images, and HTML.

Need another image host? Honesty has a link to several at **www.honesty. com/imagehosters.html**.

Need another counter? Try Ruby Lane (**count.rubylane.com**).

eBay Spy (**www.ebayspy.com**) is yet another provider of image hosting and counters. This site's twist: the spy-level message boards.

When troubleshooting, membership in an egroups (**www.egroups.com**) or onelist (**www.onelist.com**) mailing list can be a good thing. Members zing messages about system status and generally get answers in a few minutes. Search the sites for email groups pertaining to eBay, Amazon Auctions, or your favorite auction site.

Check with your ISP and review the lists of newsgroups. Subscribe to one related to auction sales. They're great for trustworthy troubleshooting.

KEY POINTS

Posting the ad is the critical action step in auctions. Until that ad is posted, you're not in the auction business. In this chapter, we covered the mechanics of posting the ad. This is a multitask approach, and details like computer coding must be precisely accurate:

- Use the Auction Prep Checklist.
- Complete the form (on paper first).
- Utilize an HTML template.
- Add an image.
- Post from an auction site or from an image host.
- Add the counter.
- Check and double-check your auction listing.

16
CHAPTER

TIMING YOUR AUCTION

WHEN TO START

You must consider the ending before the beginning. Convoluted? You betcha. Before starting an auction, you must decide when you want it to end.

Begin by choosing the auction site, and during the research investigate the best time to sell your matchbook, beer can, and coffee mug collections. Let your research be the guide. If Tuesday nights prove to be the best closing times, then *enter your auction* so that it concludes on a Tuesday night.

When investigating a site, learn whether the closing time is the same as the starting time. At eBay, Amazon, and CityAuction, the auction listing time determines the auction closing time for most auctions.

Starting and ending times don't match on Excite and Yahoo!. At those venues, auctions can begin at any time and close at a defined hour. Auctions.com allows even more control. They've made it possible for sellers to select both the starting and the closing times.

High-volume sellers using the special bulk listing programs at eBay and Amazon have additional options for starting auctions at a specific time. When you're ready to post hundreds of auctions, get eBay's Mister Lister or Amazon's bulk loading tool. With eBay's tool you can send batches with "up to 100" auctions. No more than 1,000 can go live in a day. With Amazon's tool, you can use a spreadsheet like Excel to prepare 10 to 100 auction listings. Is your warehouse is ready for those shipping and handling requirements?

SEASONAL STARTS

Just because you cleaned the linen closet in July, that doesn't mean that July is the right time to sell the red, green, and gold holiday tablecloth. Play follow the leader. Retailers know when to sell seasonal items, and you can follow their lead for seasonal merchandise.

Peak sales periods for online auctions match the mall selling periods for the same items. It makes sense when you think about it. Back-to-school shopping is an activity that translates to online sales. To make the most of your kids' clothes, sell them at the right season. Sell summer clothes when the stores do.

TIP

Get a Life

An AOL executive was once quoted as saying that AOL's main competition was NBC's Thursday night powerhouse lineup. Avoid closing auctions during hot prime-time events.

- Back-to-school clothes sell in the fall.
- Holiday gifts sell well in October and November.
- New-with-tag clothes sell best at the beginning of the appropriate season.
- Boxed small appliances sell well in the fall and spring.
- Add your excess wedding gifts "New! In box!" in the Spring—to meet the season of weddings.
- January is for more than just white sales. Software and books sell well in the winter (especially in January), when folks add to their computer systems or buy the things they really wanted but didn't get for Christmas.

If you are buying to sell, here's the game plan: Buy in the slow seasons, sell in the high. Buy low, sell high. It works in the stock market. It works in this market, too.

Selling in the low season? Set reserves to protect your investment. Consider designating a longer time period for your auction. With summer activities, bidders may not check in as frequently. Would *you* rather sit by the pool or by the computer on an 85° day? Your bidders must face the same wrenching decisions.

In the summer, list auctions for *at least* seven days. Many new users only look at the Current Items page. Shorter-duration auctions (three or five days) are shuffled into the chronological listings and won't appear with the new seven-day listings.

Another thought for summer: Never end an auction on a Friday, a Saturday, or a Sunday. Summer weekends are far too busy in real people's lives. Weekday evenings provide the best opportunity for reaching users with a routine.

THERE'S ALWAYS AN EXCEPTION

I'd like to say, *never let an auction close on a holiday.* That makes sense, doesn't it? For every rule, there's an exception. Mine was the batch of baby coupons. In conducting research, I found people selling "lots" of baby coupons and grocery coupons. The grocery coupons were a real grab bag. It was hard to tell whether they held any worthwhile value, when I added in the time to clip and list them. Grocery coupon sellers were getting just a few dollars for "lots" of $200 to $400 worth of coupons. Baby coupons were, somehow, more tangible. The values of the lots were smaller, and sellers were more specific about listing the coupons in each lot. I was so excited to try this that I listed a seven-day auction on a Monday without regard to the next Monday—the Memorial Day holiday! The opening bid was $3.00 and it had a great title. I did not include an image (although other current auctions had images). Everyone knows what coupons look like. Of course, I used a *little* HTML so that each coupon appeared on a separate line. The auction closed early morning, Pacific time. It attracted three bidders and eight bids. Few comparable baby coupon auctions have done as well.

AUCTION DURATIONS

Across the various auction sites, you can choose auctions as short as one day or as long as four weeks, with the most common being three-, five-, and seven-day auctions. Seven-day auctions allow a fair number of days to attract bidders. And, they attract bidders who only have time to search one day each week. With seven-day auctions, all days are covered.

Reasons to consider seven-day auctions:

- It's the standard auction duration.
- Your auction may need time to build a following.
- There's no compelling reason to extend the auction to 10 days.
- You'll get a full weekend.
- Most auctions fit this "bill": kids' clothes, toys, power tools, appliances.

Three-day auctions are perfect for items with a sure-fire popularity, such as the year's hot Christmas toy. You *know* it's going to sell, and the short duration may compel bidders to quickly get involved with the action. Hardcore shoppers check their favorite auction site every day looking for a deal or hard-to-find item, and this must-have sensation intensifies during with the Christmas season. When conducting a three-day auction, be sure to stress the urgency by including "3 day auction" or "3 days only" in the title of the ad.

Use three-day auctions when:

- You are selling a sure-fire hit.
- You are selling a gift item and time is short before a big holiday.

- You are selling a commodity (something that's always for sale like toner cartridges or fax paper).

Many sellers find that they attract the best bids when auctions close at mid-week: Tuesday, Wednesday, or Thursday. That's a perfect reason to take advantage of 10-day auctions. You may only have time to post auctions on the weekend. Auctions placed on Saturday will close at the same time on Tuesday. Auctions placed on Sunday will close at the same time on Wednesday. Caveat: The best closing days and auction durations vary by category. Research closed auctions in your category to get a feel for good closing days for your item.

During the summer months there's a reason why some sellers extend their standard seven-day auctions. These are slower times at the auction sites, and busy times in real people's lives. Extended selling periods give bidders a few more days to find the merchandise. Sellers may need this to attract looks and bidders.

One avid auctioneer told me of another reason why she likes 10-day auctions. Like me, she really prefers seven-day auctions, and she also likes to stagger her auctions so that a few are added every three days. This allows her to keep track of closings and shipping so she rarely has to deal with more than 10 in a day. Let's say that she's adding a new group of 10 teapots, but finds she has more time available that day for posting new auctions. For the next group of 10 teapots, she places 10-day auctions, and she's ahead of her own game.

Consider these reasons in support of 10-day auctions:

- The extended time allows more users to find the auction.
- Auctions can run over two weekends.
- After the first three days, auction has the same impact as a seven-day auction.
- Duration minimizes the impact of major outages.
- When a seller offers a shipping discount for multiple purchases, it also gives buyers more auctions to choose from to get the shipping discount.
- Mentions in newsgroups have more time to be seen.
- The extended time is perfect for selling rare or unusual items. Load the auctions' titles and descriptions with keywords to improve their chances of success.

Review the comparisons in Table 16.1. Use this chart to compare and select auction durations.

Isn't this fascinating? All share three-, five-, and seven-day auctions. Auctions. com goes the distance at 30 days. Amazon, Auctions.com, and CityAuction grab the one-day quickies.

CLOSING TIMES

It's critical to consider the time of day for auction closings. Select a time when your target market is available in order to get the best bidding action. There will

T A B L E 16.1

Auction Durations at Major Sites

Auction Duration	Amazon	Auctions.com	eBay	CityAuction	Excite	Yahoo!
1 day	x	x		x		
2 days		x		x		x
3 days	x	x	x	x	x	x
4 days		x		x	x	x
5 days	x	x	x	x	x	x
6 days		x		x	x	x
7 days/ 1 week	x	x	x	x	x	x
8 days		x		x	x	x
9 days		x		x	x	x
10 days		x	x	x	x	x
11 days		x		x	x	
12 days		x		x	x	
13 days		x		x	x	
14 days/ 2 weeks	x	x		x	x	
3 weeks				x		
4 weeks				x		
30 days		x				

always be exceptions, but strategic timing may be the first step in closing at a better price.

Copiers, scanners, and office supplies appear to sell best in the afternoons and evenings. Few "business" sellers list auctions with morning closing times. At-home parents may have more time to buy during the day (nap times!) than during the crazy evening times my friends call "the arsenic hours." Artists' and crafters' goods sell all day long. Take a look at dolls. On eBay, Raggedy Anns sell every few minutes.

The proxy bidding systems allow anyone to bid at any time. While proxy bidding may be important, a large percentage of bidders prefer the adrenaline rush that comes from being present at the end of the auction. Passionate bidders can drive up bids. If you'd like to make the thrill possible for those passionate bidders, set your auctions to close when they are active and bidding.

In the next chapter, "During the Auction," we'll take a look at unexpected events that can impact the timing of your auction.

RESOURCES

Bid to Buy (**www.bidtobuy.com**) reveals usage statistics at its site. Weekly and even hourly usage are shared, allowing you to get a good idea of the times bidders are available. Bid to Buy's charts also reveal where the users are from (noting popular Internet service providers and active cities). Browsers and platforms are accounted for as well.

KEY POINTS

Time. There's never enough. With auctions, time has a significant role. In this chapter we took a look at the details related to time.

- Determine when to start and when to end the auction.
- Take seasons and holidays into account.
- Assess auction durations.
- Review the duration options available at each auction site.

17 CHAPTER

DURING THE AUCTION

CHANGING THE LISTINGS

Your folk art rooster is up for auction, and suddenly you realize that you left out two major selling points. This collectible was made in Italy and is still in its original mint condition. Do you pull your auction? You may only need to revise the listing. In another scenario, you may be scrolling through a similar or clearly competitive auction. They've included details you mistakenly omitted. You can add the details to your auction so that yours is complete.

Revision policies vary, depending on the site: Here's how to amend your listing:

- On Amazon, listing changes are referred to as "altering your listing." Modifications can be made through "Your Account" link in the upper-right corner of every page. When an item has already received bids, the original information cannot be modified. Under that circumstance, Amazon only allows the addition of new information.

- Excite's auction ads can be easily changed. Access the listing and select Edit This Listing. Prior to opening, the auction's duration, description, payment, and shipping may be changed. Once open you may only add an image or change the description.

- eBay's auctions can be revised until the first bid is received. You can change the title, description, and shipping and payment terms, and replace or add images. Select the link within the ad to revise the auction. After a bid has been received, the change options are limited to additions. Go to the site map and select Add to My Item's Description.

- Just as with eBay, CityAuction allows auctions to be revised at any time prior to the first bid. Select the Account link located in the navigation bar at the top or bottom of every page. Select the Seller Info link to Edit or End an Auction.

- On Auctions.com, you can edit the listing through the Auction Management link. On the home page, it's accessible through the My auctions.com link just above the navigation bar. Before receiving bids, you can change the title, description, category, shipping terms, payment terms, opening bid, and duration. You may also add a photo and change the location of the item. As with most of the other sites, after bids are received, new info can be added, but no changes can be made to the original details.

- Yahoo! allows the addition of new information at any time. Original information may not be removed or deleted. To make changes, select the Auction Manager from your item's auction page. Often bidders ask questions that may give you the idea that information should be added to your ad to clarify it for other bidders. Updated information is labeled as such, and existing bidders will receive an email notifying them that the auction has been updated. That's great service!

CHANGING CATEGORIES

When you can't decide if the gardening book should be listed with books or with gardening, try starting with one and then switching to the other. During an auction, it is fairly common to find a better-fitting or more active category.

One auction seller told me that she changes categories to expose her decorative glass items to more bidders. They may search for the brand name or encounter the vases when scrolling through "Glass:General or Glass:Italian." If listed as a 10-day auction, some may place low bids or bookmark the page to track the auction. It doesn't get exciting until it falls within the seven-day window. The auction fees are the same, and this seller thinks the extra days give her auctions time to be found. The extra time also allows for category changes if a Venetian glass vase hasn't attracted bids in the first three or four days.

Here's how to change categories:

- On eBay, you have the option to change categories during the auction. As a matter of fact, there's no limit to the number of times you can alternate categories. If there's a difference in fees, you'll be charged the appropriate fee for the last category when the auction closes.

- At Auctions.com, your item can be listed in two categories from the start, for a small additional fee. After the auction is posted, you can make changes to the category selections before the first bids.

- At CityAuction's home page, navigate to the bottom of the page. Choose Account, and look in Sellers' Resources. There you'll find a link to Edit Your Auction. With the auction number, your ID, and password, you'll be able to make changes to the category and other auction elements.

- Yahoo! does not allow category changes after the start of the auction. Since this is a free site, consider closing the auction and starting over if no bids have been received. Here's another thought: Opt not to use the Automatic Relisting option on Yahoo! if you like to change categories. With automatic relisting, you won't have the chance to change the category before the auction is re-upped. Even without the automatic relisting, you can relist an auction that failed to attract a winning bid.

- Excite makes it easy to change the category for the auction. Follow the directions in Changing the Listings.

- Amazon allows changes to auctions—and that includes changes to categories. Access the listing and select Edit This Listing.

Help! My Auction Is All Wrong

If you make the mistake of advertising your $10,000 Saturn for only $1.00, you can get out of the deal. As soon as you notice the error, use the following set of procedures to end the auction. It is not possible to change amounts, and the safest thing to do is to end the auction and then relist it correctly.

On the auction site, consult the site map or Sellers link. Select the link named akin to End Auction Early. Follow the on-screen instructions.

In the category of "Don't Let This Happen to You," take a look at Figure 17.1. This seller either didn't check her ad or didn't know how to fix it.

What should this seller have done? She should have canceled the auction, backed up, and started over. With an error of this magnitude, it's necessary to open the image editing software, rotate the image, save it, and upload again to the image host. Then the auction should be reposted.

It's possible to straighten out the image without canceling the auction listing. If the image is stored on your own site, you may be able to substitute a correct image with the same name. This correction works when the image URL does not change.

Tidbit: Do you see the date stamp on the image? While I haven't seen many date stamps on images, this one adds credibility by implying that the goods exist.

MONITORING THE BIDDING

I'm a bit avid, even rabid, about auction sales. I wake up for the daily auction status email, and throughout the day I check my auctions. The first thing I look at is the high bid, and after that I check out the bidder.

FIGURE 17.1

Don't let this happen to your auction ad.

Test drive the new site. Check out the new Help section!
Save time! Try the new, fun way to shop -- the Gallery.

Gymboree Floral Bouquets XXS NWT 2pcs.
Item #114827901

Miscellaneous:Clothing:Children:Girls

Description

Starts at	$2.00 (reserve not yet met)	First bid	$2.00
Quantity	1	# of bids	0 (bid history) (with emails)
Time left	**6 days, 3 hours +**	Location	**WI**
Started	06/07/99, 10:57:53 PDT	✉ (mail this auction to a friend)
Ends	06/14/99, 10:57:53 PDT	🎁 (request a gift alert)

Bid!

Seller   **shamrock992** (0) 👓
            (view comments in seller's Feedback Profile) (view seller's other auctions)
            (ask seller a question)

High bid   --

Payment   See item description for payment methods accepted
Shipping   See item description for shipping charges

Update item **Seller:** If this item has received no bids, you may revise it.

Seller assumes all responsibility for listing this item. You should contact the seller to resolve any questions before bidding. Currency is dollar ($) unless otherwise noted.

Description

This is brand new with tags...From the "Floral Bouquets" line. It is an adorable little dress that is reversible! It is yellow with 11 flowers embroidered on chest part and floral trim along bottom. The other side is yellow with little flowers all over. Also included is a matching floral print yellow tee. Size XXS. Look at my other auctions, I have the matching cardigan sweater listed also. Items come from a NON SMOKING HOME. Buyer to pay shipping and insurance if desired (Highly Recommend, as I cannot be responsible for lost packages!!). Please allow time for personal check to clear or send m.o. for quick shipping. PAYMENT IS EXPECTED WITHIN 10 DAYS OF AUCTION END. Good luck bidding and THANKS !

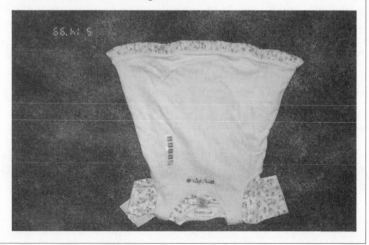

TABLE 17.1

Tracking Bidders Chart

Site	To check on bidders, do this:
Amazon	At search page, enter bidder's name. On next page, select Current Bids link.
Auctions.com	From home page, select Advanced Search, and search by bidder's email.
CityAuction	**not possible**
eBay	From search page, enter bidder's name in search box.
Excite	**not possible**
Yahoo!	Select search options link; enter bidder's name.

What can you find out about a bidder? First, check the feedback score. Don't just look at the number; take the next step and look at the comments. The feedback score is the net total of the positives and negatives (eBay) or a formula (Amazon). Take a good look at the feedbacks. Are they transaction-based? Are the comments exemplary or linguistically neutral? Beware of bidders for whom sellers have given a neutrally worded positive rating.

From the eBay search page, you can type in the name of any eBay user and find what he or she is bidding on. This is particularly helpful if you are trying to find out just how interested Joe is in the Babe Ruth autograph. Hmm, he's not much of an autograph collector. He's more often found bidding on women's shoes!

Use each site's best search page to find out what else your bidders are bidding on. (Refer back to Chapter 10, "Research Before You Sell," for tips on how to find that page.) Enter the bidder's name or ID and look up current bids, recent wins, and bidding history. Review Table 17.1 for each site's bidder tracking resources. I've been scared by new bidders with feedback ratings of zero—and 52 open bids. When I see those bidders, I hope they get feedback ratings in a hurry! And then I hope for trustworthy money orders to ensure payment.

Proxy Bids

What you don't know can't hurt you? You'll only know a bidder's proxy bid when that person is outbid by another bidder. The major auctions allow proxy bids. Consider this: My backpack is at $16.00 and the bidding increment is 50 cents. Janey is willing to pay $21 (her proxy bid). When she places the proxy bid of $21, the bid is registered at $16.50, and holds there until she is outbid. (See Table 17.2). If the auc-

TABLE 17.2

Bidding Sequence with an Uncontested Proxy Bid

Current bid	$16.00
Proxy bid	$21.00
Bid increment	$.50
Effect of proxy bid	$16.50

tion closes at $16.50, only Janey will ever know that she was willing to pay $21. As long as the bidding does not exceed $21, Janey will be the winning bidder. If Heidi exceeds Janey's $21 bid, with $21.03, Heidi will be the proud backpacker.

Take another look at proxy bidding by viewing the bidding history for a closed auction. The high bid listed is not likely to be the winning bidder's high bid. The bids listed for each runner-up bidder are the high proxy bids each placed.

Take a look at this completed auction for an Italian Decorated Rooster Pitcher, as seen in Figure 17.2. This eBay auction opened at $1.99 and closed at $26.00. Three aspiring bidders made a total of 11 bids. The first bidder who placed a proxy

FIGURE 17.2

We'll never know whether $26 was Camillea's top bid.

```
Last bid for this item:         $26.00
Date auction ends:              05/28/99, 12:03:53 PDT
Date auction started:           05/23/99, 12:03:53 PDT
Seller:                         voom (253)  ☆
First bid at:                   $1.99
Number of bids made:            11 (may include multiple bids by same bidder)


Bidding History (in order of bid amount):

camillea (26)  ☆
        Last bid at:     $26.00
        Date of bid:     05/27/99, 18:18:50 PDT

beck*kilgore (15)  ☆ 👓
        Last bid at:     $25.00
        Date of bid:     05/27/99, 07:03:53 PDT

lisarayray@aol.com (38)  ☆
        Last bid at:     $2.24
        Date of bid:     05/25/99, 21:34:51 PDT
```

bid of $2.24 entered the initial bid of $1.99. The second highest bidder placed a proxy bid of $25.00 and the winning bidder placed a bid of $26.00. The winning bidder's proxy bid may have been higher.

eBay only reveals the bid amounts after the bidding has closed. Even then, you'll never really know the winning bidder's high bid. The winning bidder's proxy bid is never revealed. Only the high bids by the second and lower bidders are uncovered.

With a 25-cent bid increment, the first bidder was only responsible for one bid. There must have been quite a bidding war between the top two bidders, as they were responsible for 10 bids.

No matter which site has your auction, select the bidding history link. It's on the auction page. Amazon lets you see the current bids—but not the proxies—during the auction. Figure 17.3 shows the bidding history for an open auction on Amazon. This "Stunning! Vintage Diamond Cut Cranberry Glass Candy Dish" opened at $9.99 with a reserve. The reserve price has been met and the current bid is $45 with 10 days remaining in the auction.

Unlike eBay, Amazon reveals the bids during the auction. But, just like its counterpart, high proxy bids remain secret.

Bidder Email

Online auctions foster a sense of community on the Internet. In the community, bidders often email sellers with questions about merchandise. Anticipate questions and be prepared for email from bidders. Check your email at least once a day during the auction period.

What types of questions do bidders ask? They ask about missing details. Some ask what reserve has been set for the chemistry set, while others ask about the insignia on the Chanel handbag. There may be a question on whether the software is on CD or floppy

FIGURE 17.3

This auction closed 10 days later at $45. We'll never know whether $45 was the bidder's highest offer. No one challenged beyond that amount.

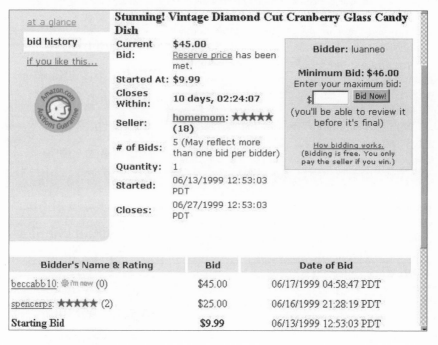

at a glance	**Stunning! Vintage Diamond Cut Cranberry Glass Candy Dish**	
bid history	Current Bid:	$45.00 Reserve price has been met.	**Bidder:** luanneo
if you like this...	Started At:	$9.99	**Minimum Bid: $46.00** Enter your maximum bid:
	Closes Within:	10 days, 02:24:07	$[ ] Bid Now!
	Seller:	homemom: ★★★★★ (18)	(you'll be able to review it before it's final)
	# of Bids:	5 (May reflect more than one bid per bidder)	How bidding works. (Bidding is free. You only pay the seller if you win.)
	Quantity:	1	
	Started:	06/13/1999 12:53:03 PDT	
	Closes:	06/27/1999 12:53:03 PDT	

Bidder's Name & Rating	Bid	Date of Bid
beccabb10: 🌱 i'm new (0)	$45.00	06/17/1999 04:58:47 PDT
spencerps: ★★★★★ (2)	$25.00	06/16/1999 21:28:19 PDT
Starting Bid	$9.99	06/13/1999 12:53:03 PDT

disk. How often was the drill used? Do you have extra bits? Why are you selling the Cuisinart? Do you have a better picture of the wallpaper? Can you send another image of the quilt? Are there any blemishes on the antique doll?

At most auctions, bidders can obtain your email address through the auction host. Email addresses may only be revealed to other registered users. At Yahoo!, bidders can leave messages, as seen in Figure 17.4. The site notifies sellers by email to visit the site to answer queries. All potential bidders (and competitive sellers) can view the questions and answers.

If you'll be away, say so in your ad. Include a note in the description area or add a comment by revising the auction. It's better to tell bidders that you'll be unable to answer questions about the garden tiller than to leave them wondering why you haven't replied.

There are doubts and fears in the Internet commerce world. To instill trust in bidders, you must be exceedingly available and answer questions promptly. To find out how bidders can contact you, see Table 17.3.

FIGURE 17.4

Question and Answer at Yahoo! Auctions.

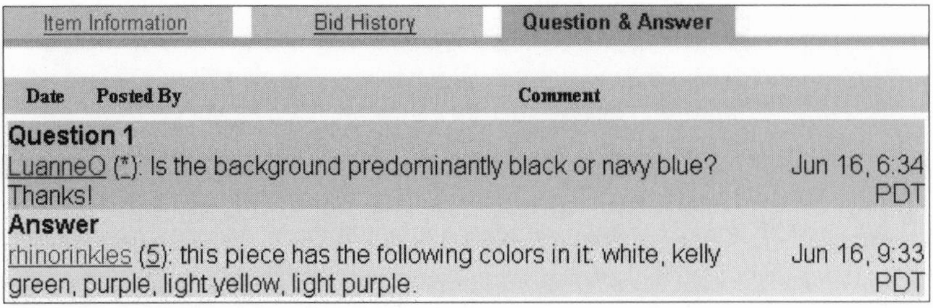

Item Information	Bid History	Question & Answer	

Date Posted By	Comment	
Question 1		
LuanneO (*): Is the background predominantly black or navy blue? Thanks!		Jun 16, 6:34 PDT
Answer		
rhinorinkles (5): this piece has the following colors in it: white, kelly green, purple, light yellow, light purple.		Jun 16, 9:33 PDT

When a Bidder Retracts

Bids are binding, and that makes a bidder's retraction an unpalatable and dicey issue. The result of retracting a bid is that it changes the order of precedence and has the potential to undermine all bidders participating in the auction. Of course, sellers detest bid retractions because auction winnings take a step backwards.

TABLE 17.3

How Bidders Contact Sellers

Auction Site	Email to Sellers
Amazon	Seller's email address is provided upon request. Link from the auction page.
Auctions.com	Within the auction, bidders choose link to Email Seller.
CityAuction	Registered users can send a message to the seller via CityAuction.
eBay	Registered users can obtain seller's email address by entering their own as verification.
Excite	Registered users can send a message to the seller via Excite.
Yahoo!	Bidders use the Question and Answer link on Auction page to submit a question. Yahoo! notifies seller that a question is waiting to be answered. Bidders may also check the seller's Yahoo! Profiles link to see if the seller has selected the option to list an email address.

Across the sites there are very few good reasons for bidders to retract a bid:

- Sellers who make substantial changes to the auction description give bidders a valid reason to retract.

- A bidder may have made a clear typographical error when placing the bid. An example is an errant bid of $45.50 when you intended $4.55. This should be retracted promptly, shortly after the bid confirmation email is received.

- When bidders are unable to contact the seller to clarify details, they may have a valid reason to retract a bid. For example, if email to a seller bounces, the bidders may have reason to doubt the veracity of the seller.

- If the seller's feedback rating has become negative since the bidder's initial bid, that's likely to be an understandable and acceptable reason for retracting a bid.

Auction sites often list bid retractions and retractors. These notations are added to auctions and to feedback pages. Bid retractions may also cause sellers to post negative feedback, which has its own penalties.

Scammers, Beware!

Scam artists have figured out a way to win online auctions in a process known as "bid shielding." It takes two people working together. The first places a low bid, and the partner in crime places a high bid that scares off other bidders. In a reverse of sniping, just before the close of the auction, the high bidder withdraws, leaving the low bidder as the winner. Sellers may never know why their items sold for such a low price. On sites like eBay, with bid increments in place, bid shielding may require the use of three participants in the racket—or someone with access to three IDs.

Try this on. A bidder/scammer places a proxy bid of $500 on a silver tray with an opening bid of $15. The tray is worth $75. With proxy bidding, any other bidder's bid will be topped up to the unrealistic $500. A second scammer (possibly the same person with another ID) bids $450. That ratchets the price up to $450 and wards off any other bidders. Then, the second bidder backs out of the $450 bid, and the auction closes at the first bidder's low opening bid of $15. That opening bid becomes the final price.

How can you protect your auctions? Monitor bidders and check their feedback. If they have withdrawn bids before, beware. Quickly consider canceling their bids or even canceling the auction. If your actions are too late, be sure to report the irregularities to the auction site's security staff, such as eBay's Safe Harbor.

Canceling Bids—When and Why

In today's e-commerce era, some sellers have encountered undesirable bidders. Community spirit reigns but a rare few are no longer welcome. These undesirables likely brought on their own bad press. They may have poor feedback ratings, a poor record of paying for their merchandise, or they may have tampered with an auction.

At most sites (especially the big ones), it is possible to cancel bids. This can incite email and feedback flames, so make sure you have a good reason before embarking on this adventure. The best reason to cancel a bidder's bid is a prior negative experience. If your china dog has received a bid from the same character who failed to pay for the pottery cat, that's a reason to cancel the bid. Other reasons include a bidder who is unwilling or unable to complete the auction terms, or the seller is unable to identify or contact a bidder.

You may be asking, "Why not wait until the end of the auction, and then refuse to complete the sale?" If this undesirable character is still the high bidder at the end of the auction, the second in line has no obligation to buy from you. You can only reinstate the second bidder into the winning position if, during the auction, you cancel a higher bid.

It's also possible, and reasonable, for a seller to cancel an auction because he decides not to sell any more. To cancel an auction, you'll have to cancel each bid prior to canceling an auction. (Canceling an auction that doesn't have bids isn't likely to infuriate anyone).

I once canceled an auction when I discovered I could put together a more desirable combination of items. I had listed a group of Oshkosh baby shirts. Upon delving into the stash of outgrown baby clothes, I found a group of Oshkosh rompers that coordinated with the shirts. The shirts had not received any bids, and that made it easy to cancel. I didn't have to contact anyone or cancel any bids. After canceling the auction, I was able to post a new auction with more "value" for the bidders. It resulted in a nice funds transfer to me.

While a cancellation policy is not imperative, it's a good idea to include one in your auction ad. Typical cancellation policies include:

- Seller reserves the right to cancel bids from bidders with negative feedback ratings.

- Seller reserves the right to cancel bids from bidders who previously failed to complete auctions.

- Seller reserves the right to cancel bids from sellers with more than three negative feedbacks.

Know your site's policies for canceling bids or refusing to conduct transactions with specific bidders. The best place to check is the auction's site map or customer service links for their policy.

MONITORING THE COMPETITION

Keeping an eye on the competition helps you track your auction's likelihood of success. Auction monitoring is really just another type of research. You'll learn something from each auction that you can apply to the next one.

Note which auctions are getting bids. Do they have reserves? Have the reserves been met? Do their titles make better use of keywords? Do they have a better, faster-loading image?

Do they have "placeholder" bids? While you're not likely to find what the high proxy bid was, some bidders enter a low bid early in the game, just to take a chance on winning. They'll get the daily status; the auction will be included on their bidding activity page; and they'll be notified if outbid. They may win for a low bid or they may be encouraged to up the bidding when they encounter bidding competition. They may actually take mental ownership, the longer they hold the winning bid position. If outbid, they'll jump back in to keep the bidding going.

Compare the auctions. Learn what you can. Modify or revise your listing. Add another photo.

CLOSING AUCTIONS EARLY

Many bidders like to wait 'til the last hours or minutes of an auction to place their bids. They do this because they may be able to get a steal of a deal by not showing an interest earlier in the auction. Any decision to close auctions early will leave these bidders out of the running. Potentially, that action may reduce your take from the auction.

You may wish to close an auction early after an outage. When auction sites go down, the impact can be significant. Perhaps you feel that the bidders, who placed their bid before the outage, shouldn't be penalized by an extended auction. Oftentimes, bidders aren't aware of an outage, especially if they signed off minutes before an outage. I once had an auction close within minutes of an outage. I contacted the high bidder with my close-of-auction note. Imagine my surprise, the next day, when I saw that the auction had been reopened after the outage. At that time, I could have closed my auction to preserve the high bidder's status. I waited to see what would happen, and the high bid held.

Family emergencies happen. If you find that you will be out of town during the planned closing time, give thought to closing an auction early. By closing early, you can notify the high bidder of the win and make plans for shipping the goods.

If you choose to close an auction that hasn't received bids, no one's feelings will be hurt. At most auction sites, this won't be a black mark on your character. The rules for closing auctions are very similar across all sites—the basics hold true.

When you close an auction because you no longer wish to sell an item, you must cancel each bidder's bid before ending the auction.

Auction fees are still incurred on closed auctions. If there are no bidders, you are only out the listing fee. At Amazon, closing early is reflected on your feedback page.

WHEN CLOSING TIMES CHANGE

As much as we like to plan, there are going to be events that are out of our control. As Internet merchants, stock traders, and auction sites know, glitches happen. When a power outage closes a gift shop for the afternoon, it inconveniences a few people in town. When a major Internet site goes down, it aggravates tens of thousands of people around the globe.

Downtime is a particular concern for sellers, as scheduled and unscheduled outages prevent potential bidders from posting their bids. Strategic sellers choose specific times for their auctions to end, with the idea that an evening closing will attract bidders from both coasts and everywhere in between.

Get to know each site's policy for handling system glitches. Depending on the duration of the outage, auctions may be extended for 24 hours. On the other hand, an auction closing just a couple of hours after the site gets back up will close on its original schedule. (In our opinion, the policy places those sellers at a disadvantage.) When an outage is long enough, bidders find other things to do. There's nothing more tedious than waiting for an Internet site to come back up!

At eBay, hard outages are defined as outages during which no one can place a bid on an auction. eBay refunds all fees for auctions that meet the criteria for hard outages in excess of two hours. "All fees" includes Insertion Fees, Final Value Fees, and Optional Fees. eBay's Automatic Extension Policy defines hard outages, where no bidders can bid, as the type of outage that activates the extension policy. For any hard outage that lasts two or more hours, eBay extends auctions for 24 hours. This policy applies to any auction scheduled to end during the hard outage and to any auction scheduled to end in the hour after the hard outage.

Be aware of outages on eBay:

- Each Friday morning, eBay has a scheduled outage planned for 1 to 5 A.M. Pacific time. Based on this known scheduled outage, which has the possibility of being extended, savvy sellers do not schedule auctions to close during this time period.

- To find the announcement board, select the Communities link from the upper navigation bar. In the News area, select the Announcements link. This board provides the most accurate and reliable information.

Compare eBay's and Amazon's outage policies in Table 17.4.

When my *closed* auction reopened, I asked eBay for advice. The customer service rep advised that I was within my rights to close it early. Had another bidder won the reopened auction, I would have asked eBay to adjudicate. I had printed the auction screens and, if necessary, could have included them in letters or faxes to eBay.

Excite's outage policy is a bit more liberal in how it is applied. When Excite's servers go down (meaning no bids can be placed), a 24-hour extension is issued for any auction scheduled to end during the outage.

Auctions.com closing policy allows for flexible closing times, and protects bidders from problems caused by outages and slow connections. Auctions close at the scheduled closing time or—if the bidding continues—5 to 10 minutes after the last bid. As long as users are continuing to bid within five minutes of each other, the auction

TABLE 17.4

Outage Policies at Amazon and eBay

Event	Amazon's Extension Policy for Outages and Maintenance	eBay's Extension Policy for Hard Outages
Outage less than or equal to 30 minutes	No auctions are extended.	
Greater than 30 minutes but less than or equal to 2 hours	Affected auctions are extended by twice the outage.	
Greater than 2 hours	Affected auctions are extended by 24 hours.	Auctions scheduled to close during the auction or 1 hour after are extended by 24 hours.

does not end. This rule is intended to prevent buyers from being locked out (due to a slow connection), and to help sellers achieve the highest price a buyer is willing to pay.

Auctions.com has slated scheduled maintenance every Monday from 4 A.M. to 6 A.M. Eastern time. This may or may not cause system downtime.

Like Auctions.com, Amazon Auction's "Going, Going, Gone" feature ensures bidders have the opportunity to top last-second bids. Whenever a bid is cast in the last 10 minutes of an auction, the auction is extended for an additional 10 minutes. The auction closes when this time period has passed without the entrance of a new bid.

City Auction's policy mirrors the policies at Auctions.com and Amazon Auctions.

WHEN THE IMAGE HOST GOES DOWN

The service providers known as image hosts can incur havoc on auction sites and sellers when they, too, experience an outage. While most outages are of a short duration, I've seen agonizingly long outages lasting days.

When an image host fails, you'll first want to verify the outage with the site or other users. You may be able to access a status board at the site. Otherwise, visit a message board or chat area at any auction site associated with the image host to learn what you can about the anticipated duration of the outage.

Based on what you learn, decide whether cancellation or modification is appropriate. These are options worth considering. It's also worth considering whether to add a note through an auction revision that you are willing to send photos via email. Depending on the site, the revision option may also be used to link another image, stored on another image host's site.

Participants in auction-related email groups and newsgroups can also be a good source of assistance and ideas.

RESOURCES

Join an auction-related email group. When searching for the groups, use the name of the auction site or search by the type of merchandise (for example, Beanie Babies). Participants on these groups often ask site status questions.

- **www.egroups.com**
- **www.onelist.com**

Your Internet Service Provider (ISP) may provide access to newsgroups such as **alt.marketing.online.ebay**.

If not, you can access newsgroups through the web site Deja News (**www. dejanews.com**).

Check auction-related message boards at **www.auctionwatch.com**.

KEY POINTS

In this chapter, we took a look at actions that sellers can take during the auction. Once the auction is up and running, the seller maintains control and can make changes to his or her advantage:

- Consider listing changes.
- Change categories.
- Monitor bidders.
- Understand the impact of proxy bids.
- Reply to bidder email.
- Address bidder retractions.
- Cancel bids.
- Monitor competitive auctions.
- Close auctions early.
- Deal with auction site outages.
- Troubleshoot when image hosts go down.

18

CHAPTER

RELISTING WHEN IT DOESN'T SELL

MAKING THE DECISION TO RELIST

What do you do when your collection of international Coke cans doesn't sell? Consider relisting the auction. Should you relist at the same site, or move the well-traveled Classic Cokes to another site?

There's a financial incentive to relist with the same site. The second listing is almost always *free*. Most auctions allow you to relist unsold items within a certain time period, generally 30 days from the close of the unsuccessful auction. eBay refunds the second insertion fee if the collection sells on the second try. Yahoo! makes it possible for your auction to be relisted automatically. Make that selection when you first post the Yahoo! auction ad.

With a 30-day window for relisting, you'll need to give some thought about when the relisting should take place. Consider whether the Coke auction should close on a different day and whether the duration should be extended. If it was a three-day listing, give thought to a standard seven-day listing. During the busy summer months, a ten-day auction may be best to attract bidders and bids. If a holiday—or your vacation—falls within the 30-day period, take that into account before hitting the Relist link.

Don't rush to restart the auction. There can be calculable advantages to taking your time. Wait two or even three weeks before relisting, to allow time for a new group of bidders to form. (Thousands "discover" online auctions every day.)

Flea market sellers recommend raising auction prices a tad when relisting. Raising the price at a "fee" auction may not qualify it for the relisting credit. What is

TIP

Change the Title

It can be a good idea to make changes to the title when relisting. That way bidders won't recognize the same title as they research in the closed and open listings. Don't let your auction look like a loser.

the "fee" worth? It may be very worthwhile to pay a second 25-cent fee to recoup an extra $2. Consider changing:

- Opening bid
- Reserve
- Title
- Description
- Selling terms
- Shipping terms
- Duration of auction
- Closing day (of the week)

Search through "completed auction" listings and you'll quickly see that items priced at the very top or at the bottom of a category often don't sell. While it is easy to understand why some bidders don't wish to take part at a high price, it's a bit different at the other end of the scale. Toward the bottom of the price category, items need a "perceived value" to sell. When I auctioned my Motorola Cell Phone, I noticed this phenomenon. Phones priced at $5 didn't attract bids, but phones priced higher did.

Let's say that you auctioned a 35mm camera on eBay, without a reserve, and it didn't sell. eBay, like most other auction sites, lets you relist the item for free if you begin the second try auction within 30 days after the completion of the first. (eBay's reserve fee is not refundable.)

One of the requirements for relisting is that the new item must have the same or lower opening bid or reserve. If you listed the camera at $100 (without a reserve) on the first try, you can't open the second-try at $100 with a reserve of $125. Likewise, you can't open the relist bidding at $125. What you can do, though, is open the bidding at $75 with a reserve of $100. This allows you to adhere to eBay's rule that the reserve must be the same or less than the original opening bid for the item to be eligible for the relist credit if it sells during the second auction.

In Table 18.1, look at the pertinent details for relisting at major sites.

RELISTING WHEN THE BIDDER DOESN'T PAY

In the chapters ahead we'll cover deadbeat bidders. Let's jump ahead because an unfortunate deadbeat can be the cause of a relisting.

It's imperative to stay on top of bidders at the close of the auction. Sellers stay in charge by sending a prompt email with the total fee, including the shipping and pay-

TABLE 18.1

Auction Sites and Relisting Details

Site	How	Fee	Deadline	What Can Be Changed:
eBay	From the Closed Auction page, select the link to Relist.	Relisting is free if the item sells the second time.	Thirty days from close of initial auction.	Title, description, opening bid, and reserve can only be changed if the opening bid and reserve are the same or lower than initial auction.
Amazon	Select the Your Auctions link from the upper navigation bar, then choose the relisting link adjacent to the Closed Auction.	Basic relistings are free.	Thirty days from close of initial auction.	Title, description, opening bid, and reserves.
CityAuction	Go to My Account and choose Seller Info to relist an auction.	Free listings; final value fee paid on auctions with winning bids.		Title, description, opening bid, and reserves.
Yahoo!	Choose Auto Resubmit on the initial auction listing, or select My Auctions, Auction title, and Resubmit.	Free site.		No elements will be changed. Opening bid, quantity, reserve.
Excite		Free site.		Durations of open auctions can be extended.
Auctions .com	Access Auction Management with your email address and password; select Auction and Relist. Autorelist available.	No fee for relisting.		Title, description, opening bid, and reserves.

ment terms. The quality of communication—and the speed of the bidder's response—will be a good indication of the high bidder's reliability.

Keep in mind that time is of the essence, as auction sites have policies for dealing with deadbeats and for relisting. At most sites, you have a 30-day window in which to apply for final value credits and relist the auction.

There are two phases to a deadbeat relisting. The first phase is to notify the auction site of the deadbeat and request any applicable refunds. As part of this, your fellow sellers will appreciate your efforts when you add true feedback comments. The second phase is the actual relisting.

While insertion fees are generally not refundable, the situation changes with final value fees. On eBay, when the item sells after the second auction, the insertion fee for the relisted item will be credited at the end of the billing cycle. Of course, the final value fee is only paid when there's a winning bid.

When you apply for a refund or credit of the final value fee, the auction site will ask you to provide a reason for the request. Good sites track deadbeat bidders and remove them from the community. Don't absorb those final value fees when a deadbeat bidder leaves you holding the goods. Complete the form, request your refund, add feedback comments, and take your part in the community. Help yourself and other sellers by properly putting deadbeats where they belong—offline.

BABY BOTTLES: A BETTER SECOND TRY

I encountered my first deadbeat when selling a cute lot of baby bottles and bibs. The auction opened at $3.00 with a reserve of $6.00. One bidder offered the reserve level and won the auction. After a couple of emails, she dropped off the face of the Internet. Messages began bouncing. I reluctantly conducted a search on her other auction wins and sent emails to four other sellers. She failed to complete their auctions, and they neglected to post accurate feedback. After my prompting, the other sellers added their feedback and the deadbeat now has a negative feedback rating. I requested a refund of the final value fee, and eBay was notified.

After recovering from this disappointment, I relisted the auction. The relisting was for $3.00 and the reserve was lowered to $5.00. Of course, the bidders didn't know that I had lowered my reserve. I just wanted to cut my losses and get the bottles out of the house. The first auction opened and closed on a Tuesday at 9:37 A.M., PST, and the second opened and closed on a Wednesday, at 7:05 A.M., PST. The first attracted one bid and the second attracted nine bids from four bidders. It closed at $11.50. The high bidder was an American State Department employee living in Africa. She was enjoying the midafternoon when the auction closed.

Can we say, "thrilled"? That describes my emotions at the close of this auction. I'd gone through the agony of dealing with a deadbeat, relisted the auction, and come out far ahead. The timing of the auction was not significantly different. In the three weeks between the close of the two auctions, a new group of bidders formed. I got (strategically) lucky.

After encountering a deadbeat, you may offer the item to the second-highest bidder or runner-up. Neither is obligated to complete the auction, but the offer is worth the cost of the email. For any auction that charges final value fees, request a credit after an encounter with a deadbeat. When you've dealt with a deadbeat, eBay will refund your final value fee, and not take a commission if you are able to complete the transaction with another bidder.

How can you protect yourself from deadbeats? In all categories, sellers list auction terms with this caveat:

High bidder to prepay within 14 days or the item will be relisted.

Any seller who posts this means *business*. She's not going to let a transaction drag out for weeks. The Singer Sewing Machine will be sold—or else!

Another seller lists the communication and payment policy quoted below. Obviously this is a seller who is fearful of encountering deadbeats. If you were to look at the complete text of her ads, you'd see that more than 50 percent of her ad text is composed of an extensive list of payment, shipping, and handling terms.

Here is her policy:

Payment must be received within 10 days from auction close unless other arrangements are made.

Unfortunately I feel I have to clearly spell out these due to some situations. Most of my customers are FANTASTIC and I really appreciate their business!

PLEASE DO NOT BID IF YOU DO NOT INTEND TO HONOR IT. Winner of the auction is to reply back to the initial email within 3 days or bid will be cancelled and negative feedback will be left. I retain the right to reject bids from anyone with negative or hidden feedback.

Firm terms are important, but don't scare off good bidders.

In Chapter 20, "Getting Paid," we'll take another look at deadbeat bidders.

FAILED RESERVES AND SECOND CHANCES

Any auction with reserves can fail to sell. If the auction for the Royal Doulton Captain Ahab Mug ends without the reserve price being met, both the seller and the high bidder are released from any further obligation. After the auction closes, the seller may offer the mug item to the high bidder, but the high bidder is not obligated to complete the purchase. Consider making the offer to the high bidder before relisting.

One seller uses a form letter to contact the high bidder when the bids do not meet the reserve. You can draft one like this:

Thank you for bidding on the Royal Doulton Captain Ahab Mug. Unfortunately, the reserve was not met. The reserve was $25. I hope we meet again through eBay, and I wish you the best with all of your auction purchases. If you are interested in purchasing it for the reserve price, I would welcome your return email.

RESOURCES

Before relisting, review the research techniques presented in Chapter 10, and reread Chapter 17, "During the Auction," for tips on monitoring bidders.

Visit your favorite site's message boards (check the site map) to find out what techniques other sellers are using for relisting and dealing with deadbeats.

KEY POINTS

In this chapter, we covered details pertinent to the second time around. There's almost always a financial incentive for relisting at the same site. If your auction doesn't sell the first time, consider making these changes for the second listing:

- Opening bid
- Reserve
- Auction ad title and description
- Selling terms
- Shipping terms
- Duration of auction
- Day and time for auction close

19 CHAPTER

ORGANIZING TIPS
FOR BETTER SELLING

GETTING ORGANIZED

Anyone running more than one auction concurrently will tell you that it can get confusing. The details that need to be tracked for each auction grow exponentially for sellers involved in multiple auctions. Hang out awhile and you'll hear stories of disorganized sellers who've listed the same auction twice, with only one item to sell. In this section, we'll take a look at low-tech and high-tech organizing options.

PAPER METHODS

Paper tracking methods tend to rely on paper in one of two sizes—index cards or computer printouts. Use index cards and dividers, if that's your style, or use printouts of personal pages on the auction sites. Give thought to your work style and make the selection that works best for you.

Index Card Format

Early in my auction selling experience, I tracked auction details with index cards formatted like the one in Table 19.1. It didn't take up much space, allowed me to keep my office neater, and had enough room for all pertinent details. Index cards come in multiple sizes, 3×5 inches, 4×6 inches, and 5×8 inches. They're inexpensive. Three hundred will cost less than $4—and they come in multiple colors. To take

TIP

Auction Checklist

Refer back to Chapter
15, "Posting Your Ad,"
and take a look at the
auction checklist.

index cards to their full potential, color code. I use pink for baby things, yellow for household items, green for garden tools, and purple for collectibles. Use section dividers to organize:

- Open auctions
- Closed/waiting for payment
- Shipped/feedback verification
- Completed

Track auction details on the front of each card, and after-auction details on the back. The front of the card should feature the title, date posted, date and time for the auction's close, auction number, reserve, and shipping terms. Among the after-auction specifics, include winning bidder's email and mailing addresses, and note the date for each email contact along the way.

When an auction closes, move the card to the "Closed/Waiting for Payment" section. Hold it there until the payment clears. After the payment clears, ship the item, and move the card to "Shipped/Feedback Verification." Once you and the buyer have posted feedback, relocate it to "Completed."

One of my favorite methods takes this one step further. Just as above, create an index card with the primary auction details. Post the auction and use the auction link provided in the auction confirmation message. Print two copies of the auction listing. Attach one to the item in your storeroom. Keep the other at your desk. Set up tracking *folders,* just as described for sections in the index card file. As you track the auction details, add notes to the printed auction page. When the check arrives, staple the index card and even the envelope (it has the post office cancellation) to the auction page.

TABLE 19.1

Format for Index Cards

Auction Title and Number	Opening and Closing Dates	Site: eBay, Amazon, Yahoo!
Opening bid	Sold for	Image host
Shipping	Total	Counter
Sold to		
Check received	Shipped	
Feedback posted (by me)		
Feedback posted (by buyer)		

Use an Auction Search

On any auction site, run a seller search on your name. Note with "C" bidders who have contacted you; "P" for auctions for which you have been paid; "S" for items that you have shipped; and "F" when Feedback has been completed by both parties.

This technique may not be detailed enough to satisfy the most organized among us. Still, it's a good double-check on current or recent auctions.

QUICK TIP METHODS

- Print out "My eBay"—or the account tracker at another site. Use this to review the status of all current and recent auctions. Locate "My eBay" through the site map, or enter the URL, **pages.ebay.com/services/myebay/ myebay.html**.

- Request a statement of your account, and print it.

- Run a seller search on your user ID each week. Use that to review the status of each auction.

- Track in Excel. Set up a spreadsheet with a single line for each auction. For the columns use listing date, closing date, opening bid, final bid, shipping fee, date check received, payment method, date check cleared, date package shipped, date feedback posted (by you), date feedback posted by bidder, date bidder confirmed receipt of package. Use the sorting function to keep track of the post-auction checkpoints.

T I P

Prepare to Post

Print a blank auction posting form when creating your auction listing. Use a pencil to complete the details before committing electrons to the task.

Techie Methods

Use Your Email Client

Another good tip is to use your email client's folders to stay organized. Keep a folder for messages pertaining to open auctions (add more folders to track specific classes of auction items), another for bid confirmations and responses, and a folder for items that have shipped. Move the correspondence from paid to shipped, and you'll know who needs attention.

Consider this detailed filing system that works with AOL's Favorites folder or with any email program that allows you to create folders. It takes a bit of dedication and may be too complicated for anyone who leans away from perfectionism.

This system depends on multiple levels of folders. The top level includes folders for each item, late responses, and late pays, as seen in Figure 19.1

FIGURE 19.1

Outlook Express handles folders alphabetically. Play with the alphabet to
organize the folders as you need them.

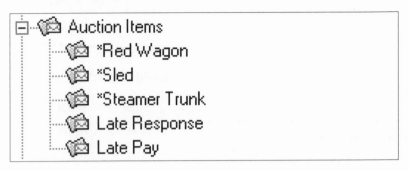

Let's follow the Sled auction to completion. The Sled folder contains an email
with the link to the item description. At the end of the auction, the letter from the auction site and a copy of the end of auction letter ("you won") are both filed in the
folder.

Each day, review the item folders. If bidders fail to respond to the end of auction notice within three days, send a "late response" letter. Be sure to send a blind
copy to yourself and add it to the Sled item folder.

At this point, move the entire Sled folder to the Late Response folder. After 10
days in this location, send a "late pay" letter, again blindcopying your own account.
Then move the Sled folder, in its entirety, to the "Late Pay" folder.

When a response arrives, the Sled folder is dropped back into the root folder:
Auction Items. To keep a tight eye on the bidder, don't move the folder while waiting for a late payment. Additional folders can be seen in Figure 19.2.

When payments are received, the item folder is moved to the Check or Money
Order folder. Send an email stating that the payment has been received and direct a
blind copy into the folder.

The Item folders for checks go into subfolders bearing the release date of the
item, 10 days out. When the item has been shipped, move the Sled folder to the
Shipped folder. That's a reminder to send an email notifying the winner that the item
has been shipped and asking to be notified when it has been received. This is a good
point to tell the winner that you have left (favorable) feedback and to include a link
to your feedback page.

Upon notification that the winner has received the sled, the Sled folder gets
moved to Shipped/Received. If I don't get confirmation of the sled's arrival, I'll forward the "shipped" message with a reminder.

The next three folders are used occasionally:

With creative spelling, I've set up these folders to track auction transactions.

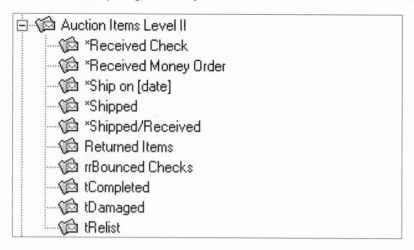

Auction Items Level II
  *Received Check
  *Received Money Order
  *Ship on [date]
  *Shipped
  *Shipped/Received
  Returned Items
  rrBounced Checks
  tCompleted
  tDamaged
  tRelist

- *Returned folder.* If allowed by your policy, track returned items in their own folder. After the item has been returned, move the item to the Relist folder.
- *Bounced checks folder.* This holds transactions that are waiting for second-try payments.
- *Damaged folder.* This holds details on transactions involving damaged merchandise and insurance claims.

Then, there's a Relist folder. When items fail to sell or the high bidder fails to pay, it gets moved to the Relist folder so I am reminded to do so. Review this folder to find items that can be combined or items that may be designated for another auction site.

Lastly, the Completed Auctions folder holds the electronic carcasses of all those great things you've sold. (This folder hierarchy can be duplicated for each auction site.)

Need more ideas? Other low-end high-tech methods include:

- Saving auction shortcuts (URLs) to the desktop
- Saving auction favorites or bookmarks within a folder

Organizing Images

- Select one image host for use with each auction site. For example, Picturebay hosts eBay images, and have AuctionWatch host Amazon images.
- Print out the image status page at each host to keep track of uploaded images and their expiration dates.

AUCTION SOFTWARE

At the high end of high tech, there are computer programs designed to help you design, post, track, and manage auctions. If you are in the market for a package, read descriptions carefully. There can be significant variations in the capabilities of these programs.

List and Load

The following collection of programs includes ad designers and listing programs.

Advertisement Wizard

Priced at $14.95, Advertisement Wizard helps expert and novice Internet users create attractive advertisements in minutes. Ads made with this wizard can be posted on auctions, as well as on "for sale" newsgroups and classified listings that allow HTML.

With a simple-to-use "fill in the blanks" interface, you can create great-looking ads for auctions, message boards, classifieds, and guest books. AdWiz includes spell-checking to clean up nasty typos.

You'll find a 15-day free trial download at **www.samcool.com**. Just follow the software link.

Auction Assistant

Some very busy collectibles sellers rely on Auction Assistant, which, due to the level of customization, works only for eBay users. Visit Blackthorne Software (**www. blackthornesw.com**) to download the demo.

Get the auctions ready when it is convenient for you. Create auction listings in the Ad Studio. Change a font, add a background, select a theme, and include standard details, such as your shipping policy and payment terms. Then, just list the auctions. You'll efficiently create auctions and list them in record time. Auction Assistant can also be used to track sales, payments, and shipping. Any time spent making selections among the many options will be repaid by the speed with which you'll post all future auctions.

This program provides specific instructions for AOL users, adding to its value. The time spent setting up "Options" will be repaid with hundreds of hours of ease of use. While many programs are designed for volume sellers, Auction Assistant seems to be a favorite of sellers who post a couple of auctions a day.

Auction Assistant's main window appears in Figure 19.3. The Options cards are featured in Figure 19.4. The open card shows selections for shipping and payment. Select your standard terms here and they'll be preset for all auctions.

Auction Assistant is $59.95. Blackthorne Software also publishes Auction Assistant Pro (in beta) and Auction Ticker Software ($19.95).

Auction Poster98

Auction Poster98 (**www.auctionposter.com**) aids eBay auction posting. After the easy download and installation, set preferences on the option cards. Auction Poster

FIGURE 19.3

List and manage auctions efficiently with Auction Assistant from Blackthorne Software.

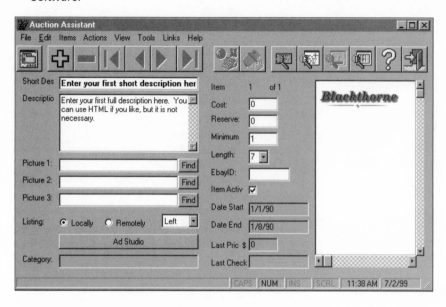

makes it simple to add pictures, and the program interacts directly with eBay. Add backgrounds, photos, and free counters at the touch of a button—without having design or programming knowledge. Create all auctions offline, and upload them when you're ready. With Auction Poster98 you can create up to 100 ads at a time. A future enhancement is planned to allow presetting the date and time for uploading. Auction Poster98 also supports eBay's bulk listing program, Mister Lister.

Auction Poster has a unique pricing policy. It's free for the first seven days, and during that time you may post a limited number of auctions with the 20 tokens. Based on your usage patterns, you can anticipate using Auction Poster98 on a sliding scale that ranges from $6.95 per month to $29.95 per year.

Auction Wizard

Auction Wizard, also eBay-specific, is more advanced and has more features than Auction Assistant. This program allows you to upload 100 items at once. Just preview each and hit the Submit button.

Priced at $16.95, Auction Wizard is an auction-posting tool that saves cutting and pasting. It's only necessary to enter your information once. After that, each listing is as easy as relisting. The Wizard also enters user ID, password, auction title,

FIGURE 19.4

Select shipping and payment defaults to take the tedious and repetitive work out of your auction listing process.

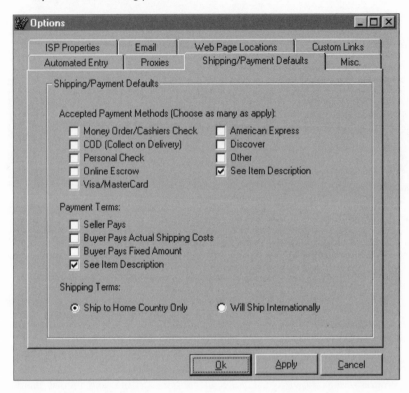

location, opening bid, category, and auction duration. Speedy sellers find that they can add 50 to 60 auctions in an hour's time. You'll find a download link at **www. mr-wizard.com/software/auction_wizard.htm**.

EZ-Ad-Pro

EZ-Ad-Pro is a *freebie* that's available with a quick download. It's a handy little program that helps you to make more attractive auction ads. Create your ad in the EZ-Ad-Pro window, and the HTML-coded ad will be copied to the clipboard. Open the eBay "Add Your Item" screen and copy the ad into the description window. An HTML ad will greet prospective bidders.

EZ-Ad-Pro is available free at **http://www.flash.net/~etx/turbo/products. htm**. Check this site for other demos and downloads, too.

Pre-Lister for Mac Users

Pre-Lister eases the lives of Mac-based sellers by allowing you to preload repetitive data such as username, location, and payment terms. This auction utility is also specifically designed for eBay sellers. Whether you list Lionel trains, helicopter parts, or blank videotapes, you can take advantage of HTML buttons for frequently used tags (bold, italic, colored text, and lists). Headers and footers can be used to add logos, auction terms, and shipping details.

Auction listings are created offline, when you have the time. Listings are saved as HTML forms. Upload them to eBay when you are ready to post the auctions. Visit **www.blackmagik.com/gavelware. html** to download a demo.

After-Auction Software

If you find auction posting fun, but fall apart at the detail tracking, take a look at this collection of after-auction software.

Easy Auction

For AOL users and everyone else, there's Easy Auction (**www.auctiontools.net/easyauction**), available from the noted site or through frequent Dutch auctions on eBay. PC-using buyers and sellers can track all auctions with Easy Auction. It's an auction tracker, database, accounting tool, and contact manager. Easy Auction includes a dual time zone clock for tracking auction closings, and can submit feedback automatically. The Pro version ($39.99) allows an unlimited number of auctions. The email function fully handles AOL, something not done by other programs. Easy Auction Pro automatically imports data from eBay and supports Dutch auctions, and eBay's Mister Lister.

Easy Auction Lite (priced at $10) tracks up to 30 auctions simultaneously, but does not feature the email functionality of the Pro version.

If you would like to make the purchase and add to your feedback, place a winning Dutch bid at eBay. Search for Easy Auction to locate the soft-

T I P

Software Sleuthing

To look at auctions that use popular auction software, search an auction site's inventory by searching for the name of the auction listing program. Search titles and descriptions.

T I P

Auction Home Software

Go to your favorite auction site and use keywords like *auction manager* or *auction organizer* to find software written specifically for that site's features.

TIP

**Finding Auction
Listing Software**

Due to the popularity
of eBay, most
auction management
programs have been
created for eBay
sellers. Programs
have been created
for other sites, too.
Search the sites
using keywords
like auction
software, auction
management, and
auction tools.

---

ware auction. You'll find links to the trial version within the eBay auction ad and through the Easy Auction Web site.

BidTrack

The post-auction tool BidTrack automatically reads the eBay "end of auction" email notices, and culls the names of winning bidders. Use BidTrack to print shipping labels, track payment and feedback dates, and compose payment reminder notices. It can also print sales reports. If you're looking for an organization system, BidTrack appears to be well worth the $29.95 fee.

BidTrack is from the makers of EZ-Ad-Pro. This source has also created a suite of programs including TurboBid and RoboFeedback. All are available at **www.flash.net/~etx/turbo/products.htm**. This same company produces a few other useful utilities, listed in this chapter's "Resources" section.

AUCTION SITE TOOLS

When you've made it to the big leagues (the bid leagues?), you'll want to consider bulk loading tools provided by the auction sites. eBay, Amazon, and Yahoo! feature customized bulk loading tools that help their volume sellers sell more efficiently. Each tool lets you prepare auctions offline, and load batches of auctions quickly and efficiently.

eBay's Mister Lister

Big-time sellers may want to take advantage of eBay's bulk upload feature, Mister Lister (**pages.ebay.com/services/buyandsell/mrlister.html**). Advanced sellers can upload many items at one time. Software programming is required. eBay recommends contracting a programmer to design and test a software interface that works with your computer and mail server system as a relatively small investment to improve your eBay business.

Amazon Bulk Loader

With Amazon's (**www.amazon.com/auctions**) bulk loading tool, you can load auctions into a spreadsheet program (like Microsoft Excel) and load a large group of auctions in minutes. To locate the bulk loader, choose Help from the banner. Next, choose Seller's Guide, and The Bulk Loader.

Yahoo!'s Bulk Loader

With Yahoo!'s Auctions Express Bulk Loader (**auctions.yahoo.com**) you'll soon be adding auctions by the dozens. From the Seller's Guide choose the link for listing multiple items. You'll then access the Auctions Express Bulk Loader.

The other auction sites may soon add bulk loading tools. Check the sellers' help pages, message boards, and chat rooms—and review the site map.

DR. JEKYLL AND MR. HYDE
Your favorite auction site may allow more than one registration. Some sellers have different names in different categories. BoPeep may do well in children's books, but that seems to be a silly name for someone promoting power tools. Will MrRugged do for the drill auctioneer?

Be sure to investigate whether your feedback will be tracked separately, as is generally the case. Multiple registrations may require multiple email accounts. A good reason to establish multiple accounts is to conduct sales for others. With separate IDs, you'll be in the best position to track fees and shipping expenses.

TIP

Who Made It?

If you see an auction format that you like, take a good look at the complete ad. You'll often find the logo belonging to an auction software program. Click on the logo for more information.

RESOURCES

Search your favorite auction site for templates and programs for sale that work specifically with that site.

Stop by **www.auctiontools.com** to examine the auction programs for searching and bidding. Check out the Free Stuff link for clock synchronization, ad templates, and a picture tutorial.

Handy Homepage Helpers has utilities for creative auctions and Web pages. Often found on eBay, it can also be found at **www.firstdesign.com**. Look in Auction Software and Free Stuff.

You'll find a collection of useful auction utilities at **www.flash.net/~etx/turbo/products.htm**. One, eBar, autotypes your name and password on any eBay screen. If you run the same searches over and over again, eBar holds up to 15 of your favorite complex searches. Press one button to search for one—or all—and bookmark the results.

KEY POINTS

This chapter highlights methods for staying organized. As you participate in more auctions, you'll want to choose a method that works for you. Among the organizational tips:

- Try all-purpose index cards.
- Keep a notebook with auction site printouts.
- Use the inbox sorting function of your email client.
- Employ auction software.
- Utilize after-auction software.
- Take advantage of auction site tools.

20
CHAPTER

GETTING PAID

COMMUNICATING AT THE CLOSE OF AUCTION

The most critical step in the payment process is to communicate promptly at the close of auction. Within an hour or two of the auction's close, it's my goal to get an email out to the high bidder. In the email, I remind the winner of the auction terms and request that he or she confirm receipt of the email. The auction hosts (Amazon, eBay, whoever . . .) will send out a confirmation letter, but I find that it's easy to beat them to the punch. We can assume their systems are overwhelmed when it takes a day or two for the close of auction letter to be generated.

Auction sites advise buyers and sellers to contact each other within three business days. Most buyers and sellers (particularly sellers!) are more comfortable when that communication takes place the very first day. Sellers, be proactive on this. Don't let the high bidder cool off. The deal isn't done until the cash is in your pocket and the gizmo is in the buyer's hands. Be friendly and stay on top of things.

When preparing the close-of-auction email notice, access the auction directly with the link found in the confirmation email received at the start of the auction. The same link can be found in the daily status email sent by most auction sites. One way or another, navigate to the auction page, and obtain the email address for the high bidder. Double-check the terms that you offered. In the close-of-auction email, confirm the auction number, high bid, payment terms, and shipping details. If you did not mention insurance in your offer, make it available in this note. Include the auction venue, auction number, and item name in the email subject line.

Refer to this checklist for the close-of-auction note:

- Include auction item number and name.
- Include buyer's auction ID name.
- Include seller's auction ID name.
- Confirm the price.
- Confirm the shipping terms.
- Confirm the funds policy.
- Offer insurance (or else!).

Below, I'll list two letters for your use. Your close-of-auction note can be simply written like this:

Subject: eBay Walkman #96751668

Dear Mary:

Thanks for being the high bidder on the Sony Walkman.

Please send a check or money order for $15.70 ($12.50 + $3.20 Priority Mail) to me at the following address:

Luanne O'Loughlin
100 Home Drive
Honestly, VA 22222

Please confirm receipt of this message and include your address so I can prepare the shipment. If you would like this shipment to be sent insured, please add $.85. Include a copy of this message with your payment.

Luanne
eBay name: LuanneO

Other sellers take a different approach by injecting humor in their close-of-auction letters. With a twist of humor, my letter could take on a new character:

Dear Bob:

Congratulations on being the high bidder on the Sony Walkman. Please send $15.70 ($12.50 + $3.20 Priority Mail) OR $16.55 ($12.50 + $3.20 Priority Mail + $.85 insurance) so that I receive it within 10 days to:

Luanne O'Loughlin
100 Home Drive
Honestly, VA 22222

Haggling at this late date gives me the willies, so please don't get me upset. When I get the willies, well . . . let's just not go there. One more time, and I'm going to need a medication refill, if ya get my drift.

Money orders or cashier's checks are best for both of us. I'm reassured that it is good, and you'll get your goods much faster. If you send a check, you'll have to wait a bit longer (up to 10 days!) for check clearance as my bank can't provide that info. I should be grateful for the occasional interest payment they tuck into my account. In the meantime, I have to check the mail each and every day after the deposit to make sure they don't tell me something unseemly about the insufficiency of your checking account.

My trusty Pinto and I hike over the river and through the woods to visit our friendly Postmaster every Tuesday and Friday loaded with deliveries. Take that into consideration in getting your check to me and when waiting for your package.

Please be sure to note the item number, description, and your full address with your payment. Better yet, print off this letter and send it to me with your name, address, and payment. While I have developed many talents, psychic clairvoyance is not one. As a mother, I have eyes on the back of my head, but alas need a hormone infusion to improve my memory.

Please send your pertinent details by return email within three days of the date of this email. I'll pack and repack your box while I wait. Failure to do so may result in a new auction (extra work for me) and feedback (most assuredly, unfavorable for you).

Thanks for bidding . . . I can't wait to hear from you ☺

Luanne
eBay name: LuanneO

Either of these letters achieves the same result. The high bidder knows that you are on top of things and that it's time to get the money to you. The sooner the money gets to you, the sooner he or she will receive the goods.

As long as the buyer remains actively involved in the transaction, it's unlikely that they'll get cold feet. The sale isn't closed until the check has cleared and the merchandise has been shipped and received.

To stay on top of the buyer, I like the 48-hour rule. If you don't hear from the buyer after your first message, wait 48 hours and send another message, entitled "Second Notice." If the auction site allows you to access personal information, use that for a third or fourth attempt to contact. The personal information may include an address or phone number. If you have difficulty reaching the bidder, you can also leave a message on their feedback page. After three attempts you can send a message that indicates that negative feedback will be posted and the auction will be relisted or offered to the next-highest bidder. Before leaving that negative, consider leaving a neutral feedback message. This may cause slight embarrassment and should get their attention. Don't link the neutral feedback comment to the auction number. Simply explain you are having difficulty and need a direct email. (By noting it as neutral and not linking it to an auction, you can later add a linked positive or negative.)

T I P

Customize Yahoo!
Select the Customize button from the banner to change notification preferences. One of the best features allows you to enter a text block to be used to customize winning emails. That one block can be completed so that Yahoo! includes your standard closing and shipping terms.

Ps AND Qs: GETTING THE FUNDS

After the auction our goal is to receive the buyer's funds and convert the instrument into cash. Only foolish buyers send cash through the mail; they most often send personal checks or money orders. Many sellers, for whom auctions are more than a hobby, set up a credit card merchant account.

Payment options include personal checks, money orders, cashier's checks, and credit cards. Other alternatives include escrow services and C.O.D. (Collect on Delivery) shipments. The pros and cons of the various payment methods appear in Table 20.1.

For many sellers, the size of the transaction dictates the level of security attached to collecting funds. An item worth hundreds of dollars will cause different terms to be specified—such as money orders only—or will extend the period that checks are held.

The method of shipment often dictates the method of payment. If an item is advertised with overnight shipping, then it behooves the seller to dictate a fast method of payment, such as credit cards or money orders.

Some sellers advertise that they ship only on Tuesdays and Fridays (or a similar pattern). This simplifies their lives and encourages the buyers to pay promptly—or to be prepared to wait until the next shipping day. Include this in the ad *and* in your close-of-auction note. If you've promised overnight shipping, you can't wait for the Tuesday-Friday deal.

When accepting personal checks, many sellers deposit the checks and wait up to 10 days before shipping the merchandise. This allows the bank time to notify the depositor when the high bidder's checking account has insufficient funds. While this is referred to as "holding" checks for 10 days, it is imperative that the check be deposited!

In my selling experience a buyer forgot to sign the check—and I didn't look closely at it before making the deposit. I'd even shipped the merchandise (without waiting for the advised 10 days) before receiving a notice from my bank. I quickly sent an email, and the buyer immediately sent a replacement check. She added a couple of dollars to the tally for my inconvenience!

Whether it makes sense or not, I am more concerned about getting the funds when the buyer is lax in communicating or delays sending the check. Like most sellers,

T A B L E 20.1

Positive and Negative Aspects of Various Payment Methods

Method of Payment	Pros	Cons
C.O.D.	Buyer generally pays fee. Seller is assured of payment.	Bidder or agent must be present to receive the item, and remit appropriate funds for the auction high bid and the C.O.D. fee. Seller must complete extra paperwork to send C.O.D.
Cashier's check	Stop payments are rare; seller is assured of funds and can ship merchandise promptly.	Requires a visit to the bank, and possibly fees.
Credit cards	Easy for bidder; seller is assured of payment.	Seller must establish a merchant account and pay associated transaction fees.
Money order	Stop payments are rare; seller is assured of funds and can ship merchandise promptly.	Requires buyer makes a visit to the Post Office or another agency that sells money orders. Fee incurred.
Personal check	Easy for bidder.	Both buyer and seller must wait so seller can be assured the check is good.
Third-party escrow	Fee is negotiable but generally paid by buyer. Fee is set by escrow company. Buyer can verify merchandise is as advertised.	Escrow adds one layer of communication and the transaction fee.

I'm most confident when the high bidder is conscientious in communicating and expeditious in delivering the funds.

Money Orders and Cashier's Checks

Money orders and cashier's checks are the most secure currencies for auction transactions. They add a level of payment security when dealing with faraway buyers. Money orders are available in hundreds of locations, with the Postal Service and major grocery chains leading the pack. The fees start at less than $1. Cashier's checks are bank instruments, and banks often make these available to good customers for free.

To obtain either, each bidder must go to one more place and stand in one more line. As a seller, you may not care if that's inconvenient for the bidder, but your demand for payment in this fashion may discourage bidders from bidding. Some sellers offer an incentive by reducing the final transaction price for sellers who pay by money order. It may be worth it to you to offer $1 off the purchase price to anyone who uses money orders rather than personal checks.

What can go wrong? There have been rare instances where money order purchasers reported the money orders as lost, in effect placing a "stop payment" on the check.

Personal Checks

Personal checks are the most common method of payment in consumer-to-consumer online auctions. With appropriate precautions, reasonable sellers accept personal checks.

It's easy to understand how personal checks cause concern. Even if you've never written a bad check, you know it wouldn't be hard to do. With the fun of online auctions it can be easy to extend purchases beyond the limits of one's checking account.

As I wrote this chapter, I was notified of a bidder's bounced check from an eBay transaction. To the bidder's credit, she notified me before my bank did. And, she stayed in touch until a replacement—in the form of a money order—arrived. I appreciated her diligence and her constant communication efforts. Because of that high level of communication, I stood by the positive feedback I'd left for her.

Credit Cards

If you're planning to make your auction sales a business, give thought to getting a credit card merchant account. With an account, you'll be able to accept credit cards from buyers—and you'll no longer have to wait for checks to clear.

An alternative is Billpoint (**www.billpoint.com**) or CCNow (**www.ccnow. com**), which facilitate person-to-person credit card transactions. These services enable buyers and sellers to use their credit cards to conduct online transactions. Sellers who use these can offer instant online acceptance of credit cards.

Billpoint's payment processing system offers many of the same protections as escrows (read ahead for information on escrows). Payment processing, shipment tracking, fraud protection, and customer service come together at this e-commerce site. There's no membership charge, and transaction fees begin at $1.99.

The fee for using CCNow's card services is a flat 9 percent of the transaction.

I'd consider using either of these services whenever an auction is expected to cross the $50 threshold. Your personal comfort point may be $25—or $100! Compare these sites to see which works better for you.

Escrow Services

Escrows add a layer of protection to online auction transactions. They also add a layer of details and communications. The involvement of the third party changes the transaction from the typical check-to-seller, box-to-buyer transfer.

The vast majority of auction transactions are trouble-free. An often-quoted figure is that fewer than 2 percent of all transactions are troubled.

With escrows both parties can appreciate the added security. For a fee, the escrow holder acts as a middleman, ensuring that buyers pay and that sellers deliver the goods as promised. Buyer's funds are held in an escrow account until buyers receive and inspect their purchases. Upon the buyer's approval, the escrow service releases the funds to the seller. Escrow fees are generally set as a percentage of the transaction, with 5 percent being typical. Either buyer or seller can pay the transaction fee.

Escrows add a twist to shipping and an extra level of communication throughout the end-of-auction transaction. Through the escrow setup, shipping criteria are determined. Often, the escrow service determines the shipping method, or buyers and sellers choose from a selected group of shipping options. Packages are sent via a method that is both traceable and insured.

Sellers are attracted to the step-by-step process, with continual status updates. Escrow services add assurances that the deal is done, both parties are satisfied, and that there will be no returns.

The leading escrow services are:

- i-Escrow (**www.iescrow.com**)
- Trade-Direct (**www.trade-direct.com**)
- TradeSafe (**www.tradesafe.com**)

Chapter 23, "Protecting Yourself," includes a complete escrow transaction.

C.O.D. Details

Would you like to be assured that you'll be paid when the bidder receives the goods? You can with C.O.D. Called both *Cash on Delivery* and *Collect on Delivery*, COD transactions take place at the bidder's front door. The postal carrier or shipper's courier acts as your agent in collecting the funds just before the delivery is complete. The delivery agent collects for you whatever funds you've specified.

How does a buyer pay for C.O.D.? Often, the larger carriers also don't want to handle cash. At Federal Express (**www.fedex.com**), C.O.D. means Collect on Delivery. They accept a cashier's check, money order, certified check, company check, or personal check. When specifying C.O.D., be sure to know the carrier's terms, and how the check's *payable to* line should be completed.

FedEx and UPS charge flat rates for C.O.D. services, while the U.S. Postal Service (**www.usps.gov**) fee increases with the value of the shipment. Table 20.2 compares C.O.D. rates.

TABLE 20.2

C.O.D. Rate Comparisons

Service	Base Fee for C.O.D.
U.S. Postal Service	$4.00
Federal Express	$7.50
UPS	$5.00

To protect your backside, be sure to read each shipper's guidelines carefully. UPS (**www.ups.com**) accepts up to $50,000 per package. They'll only accept cash for consignments up to $1,000. Conditioned upon instructions from the shipper, UPS accepts cash, cashier's checks, certified checks, or money orders. Checks and money orders are transmitted to the shipper. If the recipient pays in cash, the shipper receives a check from UPS.

You can even ship freight (Hey, how 'bout a piano?) with FedEx. The C.O.D. fee on freight is higher, at $50.

We'll take another look at C.O.D. in Chapter 21, "Shipping."

DEALING WITH DEADBEATS

If a high bidder fails to meet his or her obligation to complete a sale, that person becomes a deadbeat. The seller may contact the next-highest bidder. That underbidder is not obligated to purchase the item at any price, but may nevertheless appreciate the opportunity to do so.

Within each auction site's guidelines are the terms for contacting the buyer and seller. Typically, buyer and seller must contact each other within three business days of the close of the auction. When you send your first close-of-auction email, ask the bidder to confirm receipt of your email. I had a bidder who failed to acknowledge my email, and I was beginning to get worried. In five days, the buyer's check arrived with shipping instructions. My worry was for naught!

In the event you're not successful in making contact, most auctions allow you to request a credit within 30 days of the close of the auction.

Deadbeats may also be defined as potential buyers who:

- Did not respond after you attempted to contact them
- Submitted a check that bounced (or they placed a stop-payment)
- As high bidder, claimed that the sales terms were unacceptable

For another look at deadbeat bidders, review Chapter 18, "Relisting When It Doesn't Sell."

GOOD TERMS

Good shipping terms are closely related to fair policies. Just how long you should wait for a check to clear is up to you. Let me caution that this is a good question to pose to your banker. Yes, I know the ATM can't answer questions, but most banks still have personnel who can answer a few questions over the phone.

One seller I'm acquainted with holds personal checks if the buyer's feedback rating is less than 30 with no negatives on eBay. On Amazon auctions her policy is to hold checks when the buyer has completed fewer than 30 transactions and/or has a rating less than 4.5. She assumes that by the time a buyer has reached 30 transactions and has an Amazon rating above 4.5, the buyer has achieved a track record and a solid reputation. This is not fail-safe policy, but it seems to be a reasonable one.

Another seller has told me that she asks all first-time buyers (first time buying from her) to pay by money order. If a Postal Service money order is used, the buyer can deduct 40 cents from the total bill. The buyer and seller split the cost of the money order. After that first transaction, customers may pay by check or money order, with the checks being held for 10 days before the shipment is released.

RESOURCES

Close-of-Auction Postcards and Thank-You Notes

The now-familiar image host, Auction Watch (**www.auctionwatch.com**), makes it possible for you to create a customized close-of-auction or thank-you note. From the home page, select the epostcards link. Have fun with their greetings and make your note memorable. Your greetings can carry music, too.

Credit Card Merchant Accounts

Contact your local bank or start with your favorite search engine. Enter a search for "credit card merchant accounts" and you'll soon see a list of dozens of companies wanting to do business with you.

Consider other electronic transactions. Visit PayByWeb (**www.paybyweb.com**) for more information on using merchant accounts and electronics checks.

Consumer Protection

Zip over to Consumer Reports (**www.consumerreports.org**) and look for its Cyber-shopping Guide: **http://www.consumerreports.org/Special/Samples/Reports/9812shp0.htm**.

Read the Federal Trade Commission's (**www.ftc.gov**) Consumer Alert, *Going, Going, Gone!*: **http://www.ftc.gov/bcp/conline/pubs/alerts/gonealrt.htm**.

KEY POINTS

This chapter covers the all-important aspect, getting paid. Adhere to these details to ensure completion of the auction:

- Communicate promptly and include full details in email.

- When setting payment terms, consider the pros and cons of each payment method.

- Deal with deadbeats and request credit according to the auction site's guidelines.

21

CHAPTER

SHIPPING

If it weren't for my seven-year-old, Carly, I wouldn't know that Beanie Babies are supposed to keep their tags on. A movie fan may know, and I may not, whether it is okay to roll a movie poster into a tube for shipping. My shipping recommendations are based on shapes and sizes, and not on preserving collectible values.

ESTIMATING COSTS AND SHIPPING TERMS

It may seem late in the game to chat about shipping terms, but they are so important that it is a good idea to review them. With luck, you'll skim this chapter before posting your first auction.

The more you are involved in auctions, the better you'll be at estimating. If you don't have a scale, and don't want to make an extra run to the post office, you can make an educated guess. The "educated" part comes from research. Check similar auctions for shipping terms! Sellers with high feedback are likely to have correctly determined the shipping weights. Unless you use layers of heavy packing material, you can use this intelligence to set the shipping rate.

Like many sellers, I've used the Postal Service's Priority Mail for auction shipments. When I am not sure whether an item will fall in the "up to two pounds" rate of $3.20 or the "up to three pounds rate" of $4.30, I'll round it to a flat rate of $3.75 or $4.00, and I'll pay the difference out of my auction proceeds. In the auction description, be sure to note that "buyer pays a flat rate for shipping and handling."

The majority of my shipments fall into the first two Priority Mail price levels. When selling Katie's clothes, I put together bundles to maximize but not exceed the $4.30 price break. I find that name-brand children's lots seem to go well, so I gather up some Oshkosh rompers, add matching shirts, and a few pairs of socks, fit them in a Priority box, and list the auction.

If in doubt about the fees, you can list the auction with "Buyer pays" and negotiate the shipping method with your high bidder after the sale. This can be less appealing if it means extra steps for you. If you prefer to take packages to the post office, an extra stop at UPS may not suit you.

Home-Based Shipping Station

By now you think I have nothing left in my house, right? Katie is about to hit that magical "20 pounds and one year" rule, which in Virginia means that her car seat can face forward. Of course, I need to buy a new car seat (nope, not through an auction). So, what does this have to do with shipping? I've already been thinking about what I can ship in the box that I'll get with the new car seat.

It gets worse. Whenever we buy something that comes in a box, I save the box. Someday I'll sell the backpack or the toaster in the original box. I'll be able to add the coveted "in box" phrase to my auctions. (In the descriptions, they'll be noted as lightly used.) I caught myself this morning. It's trash pickup day in suburbia, and as I looked down the street, I began coveting my neighbors' discarded boxes.

No one likes to pay for boxes. The best way to keep those costs down is to get freebies wherever you can. First, don't forget to look around the workplace. There's a good chance your employer is paying to have that stuff hauled away; any boxes you take can only help. Ask your office manager or facilities manager if you can take packing material and boxes. Copier paper cartons are useful for shipping small appliances. They may also have shredded documents (financial statements!). Shredded paper makes great packing material. It's fairly light, easy to handle, and mostly free.

Set aside a place in your kitchen, closet, basement, or bedroom with everything you need for your auction sales. For each auction item, attach a copy of the auction ad. Keep shipping envelopes and boxes on hand. Don't forget strapping tape, shipping labels, and return address labels.

Rare but wonderful sellers make an extra effort with their packages. Those packages arrive gift-wrapped in tissue paper with ribbon around it. If that's your style, stock those items at your packing place. That's the best community spirit in the auction community.

Another nice touch is a thank-you note. It can be handwritten or preprinted. Use it to ask the buyer to notify you when the package arrives. With the auction number and your ID, it serves as a reminder to update your feedback, too.

If at any point in your life you started work in the mailroom, you'll have the skills needed for this job. Semi-neatly with shelves and a big table, you'll want to have these supplies on hand:

- Boxes
- Tyvek envelopes
- Padded envelopes
- Scissors
- Utility knife
- Clear shipping tape with a self-cutting dispenser
- Return address labels
- Shipping labels
- Filler (shredded paper, newspaper, Styrofoam popcorn, plastic grocery bags)
- Paper/cards for thank-you notes
- Wrapping paper and/or ribbon

Packing Techniques

Supplies and packing techniques must be suitable to the task at hand. If you're not selling refrigerators, you don't need to keep refrigerator boxes on hand. I tend to sell excess baby clothes and computer devices. These fit well in small and medium boxes.

Calendars, documents, photographs, and antique advertisements call for extra cardboard to make firm encasements so that these paper forms do not wrinkle. If the documents can be rolled, cardboard tubes are useful. Flat envelopes can travel well, especially when supported by sturdy cardboard.

Fragile ornaments and decorative items do well with a strong box and generous popcorn surrounding and encasing the item. The more fragile an item is, the more filler you need between it and the sides of the box. Double boxing works well for fragile items, as well. Pack the item in a small box surrounded by shredded paper or Styrofoam peanuts. Place that box in a larger box, and also pack the larger box with protective material.

A slightly more expensive but very innovative technique is to use insulating foam available at your favorite hardware store. If you've ever lived in a northern climate, you may be familiar with the stuff. It's a Fall/Winter tradition (performed once in each home). This spray foam expands to fill the gaps near electrical outlets in exterior walls, or any other hole you find.

To use insulating foam as a packing material, select a box and spray some to fill the bottom third of the box. Press a plastic bag onto it and make a depression to hold the fragile item. Place the fragile item in another plastic bag; place the bag and item in the box; and spray around the bag so that the foam gently encases the bag. Don't over-fill the foam! Place peanuts or other lightweight packing toward the top, and leave the bag top available for the buyer to grab. A can of this foam typically costs $3 to $4.

A most unusual auction item was also the easiest to ship. Check the auction sites, and you'll find folks selling batches (they call them "lots") of coupons—just like the ones that come in the Sunday newspaper supplements. For my coupon auction, payment and shipping terms involved the seller sending a self-addressed, stamped envelope (SASE) along with the check.

Need more? Shipping tape, shipping boxes, Styrofoam popcorn, and bubble wrap are all great search terms if you'd like to bid on and buy shipping supplies through your favorite auction site. If time is an issue, the best places to check are the warehouse/club stores and office supply superstores. Smaller shipping stores will be happy to sell you boxes, but the prices will be higher.

SAFE SHIPPING TIPS

Place an extra address label inside the package in the event the outside label becomes damaged.

Seal packages securely with 2-inch-wide plastic tape.

Wrap glass items individually, cushion them well, and separate them with cardboard.

Place sufficient cushioning material at the bottom of the box.

Center the item in the box and surround it with packing material.

Use Styrofoam or shredded filler so that spaces are firmly filled.

Closing the Box

Before you take that last step to seal the envelope or close the box, tuck in the thank-you note. Handwritten notes are far better than preprinted ones.

If there's a chance that you've overestimated the shipping charge, leave the box or envelope open until after the postal representative has weighed it for shipping. Be sure to bring a few loose dollar bills with you to tuck into the package in the event you've overcharged the high bidder. Your honesty and good customer service will be rewarded in positive feedback ratings and future auction sales.

HANDLING FEES AND OVERCHARGES

There's lots of negative potential in the area of excess charges. Some sellers justify handling fees as a charge for their time. Savvy sellers start auctions at slightly higher opening bids rather than tacking on handling fees.

When charged for easy-to-ship items, I find handling fees distasteful. Books, leather goods, clothing, software, and videos are simple to ship. Handling charges are fair and appropriate when the seller has to take special steps in preparing shipments. Fragile crystal, computer hardware, framed artwork, and antiques require special packaging and make take additional, valuable time to prepare.

With traditional mail-order, I squirm at shipping and handling charges. I'm not any more generous with my feelings toward auction overcharges. I recently paid $3.00 shipping and handling for a software CD that was shipped (without a box) in a padded envelope. The postage tape indicated that the seller paid $1.22 for postage. It's easy to assume that this high-volume seller paid a low price for the padded bag, leaving over $1 profit on the shipping and handling fee.

In the bidding transactions described in Part Two of this book, my coauthor took a good look at shipping terms and handling fees before she bid on any auction. Look at this topic from the bidder's side of the table by reviewing Chapter 6, "Bidding Tips and Tricks."

GUARANTEE FEES

Both C.O.D. and insurance assure that either the package gets there or the parties are compensated. These are covered in the prior chapter, "Getting Paid." They fit here, too, so a quick review is in order.

Insurance

To help resolve the question of whether the buyer or seller is responsible for getting a crystal vase to its destination intact, there's an easy answer called *insurance*. Sellers of high-value items may be well-positioned to absorb the cost of insurance, but most sellers advise high bidders to assume the cost. The best way to do this is to refer to insurance in the auction description *and* in the "terms and address" email sent by the seller at the close of auction.

Insurance is available from all shippers. Overnight couriers (including the Postal Service's Express Mail) include a base amount of insurance for all packages. United Parcel Service (UPS) starts with automatic protection against loss or damage up to $100 for every package.

Table 21.1 compares two- and three-day shipping options for a cross-country two-pound shipment with the U.S. Postal Service, UPS, and Federal Express. In each case, it is assumed that the seller does not have an account and the seller is transporting the packages to the shipper's customer counter.

T A B L E 21.1

Comparative Rates for Shipping a Two-Pound Package

Carrier	Packaging	Shipping Method	Shipping Rate	Rate for Insurance	Total for Shipment
U.S. Postal Service	Priority box	Priority (2–3 days)	$3.20	$1.80	$5.00
UPS	Seller's own box (same size as priority box)	2-day	11.50	included	11.50
UPS	Seller's own box (same size as priority box)	3-day	9.90	included	9.90
Federal Express	FedEx Box	2-day	11.00	included	11.00
Federal Express	FedEx Box	3-day	9.80	included	9.80

If the insured package arrives damaged—or fails to arrive—the buyer notifies the seller. Either can initiate the claim. It works best when the seller sends the shipping receipts (keeping copies) so that the recipient can present the damaged package and receipts with the claim.

A note about value: While you can insure for more than the value of the item, the carrier will only reimburse for the value as established by the auction transaction. Don't go crazy if a bidder asks you to insure a $5 item for $50. If the buyer wants to pay for insurance on $50, let them. In the event of a loss, your documentation will show the true value of the transaction.

C.O.D.

Whether the post office calls it *Collect on Delivery* or you call it *cash on delivery,* it means the same thing. The bidder pays upon arrival. You're guaranteed payment. The delivery agent collects for you in the funds that you've specified. The U.S. Postal Service's terms are similar to those used by FedEx and other overnight carriers.

When shipping merchandise through the Postal Service, C.O.D. can be used with First-Class Mail, Express Mail, and Priority Mail. For added security, C.O.D. may also be combined with registered mail. The fees include insurance; the maximum insured coverage is $600.

The Postal Service C.O.D. fees appear in Table 21.2. From the previous chapter, we know that C.O.D. fees range from $4 to $10, depending on the shipper and the value of the shipment.

TABLE 21.2

Postal Service C.O.D. Fees

Amount to Be Collected or Insurance Desired	Fee in Addition to Postage
$ 0.01 to $ 50.00	$ 4.00
50.01 to 100.00	5.00
100.01 to 200.00	6.00
200.01 to 300.00	7.00
300.01 to 400.00	8.00
400.01 to 500.00	9.00
500.01 to 600.00	10.00

SHIPPING SERVICES

The auction's done and the moose head needs transportation from the taxidermist in Missoula to the crown prince in Monaco. Most sites have a shipping calculator. The Internet shipping sites have shipping calculators with comparative pricing. Here are some ideas on where to turn.

U.S. Postal Service

Many auction sellers have found that the good ole snail mail Postal Service provides the best value. Whether shipping by Express Mail, Parcel Post, Book Rate, or Priority Mail, the U.S. Postal Service provides easy-to-understand options, value, and services at prices comparable to or better than those of the other services.

Auction sellers like Priority Mail because it's simple to pick the shipping price and start the auction. Sellers only need to know the weight of the package to list the shipping cost in the auction. There's no need to know the high bidder's zip code. A two-pound package is $3.20. A three-pound package is $4.30. Residential deliveries are made Monday through Saturday, and Express mail can be delivered on Sunday. In addition, the USPS is one of the few services to deliver to post office boxes.

Packages can be insured, sent C.O.D., Certified, Registered, or with Delivery Confirmation. Delivery Confirmation, at 35 cents, is planned as the first step toward full tracking. Delivery Confirmation is often paid by the seller to verify the receipt of the shipment.

U.S. Postal Service advantages include:

- Free packaging materials
- Easy-to-understand rates

- Two- to three-day delivery service
- Monday through Saturday residential deliveries
- Perceived as a valuable and trustworthy mail service
- Priced by weight, not zone
- Can deliver to post office boxes

Priority Packaging

The USPS makes free shipping supplies available through the Priority Mail service. Priority Mail boxes are stored flat, ready to be squeezed into their boxy shape. You can also use them flat, by taping the ends in the flat shape to ship magazines, autograph documents, record albums (remember them?), advertisements, books, and trays.

Priority Mail address labels, boxes, envelopes, stickers, and tape are all free. On the Web, order supplies at the Priority Mail page (**supplies.usps.gov**). Scroll down and click Order Supplies, and then Click Here to Continue, followed by another click on the Priority Mail logo to view a selectable list of supplies. While some of the quantities are fairly large, all items are free, and you might as well stock the shipping closet as long as you have the storage. It is a simple form to click your way through, and in just a few days you'll be well-stocked.

The Priority Mail supplies Web page is not reliable. If it's down, you'll see the toll-free number 800-221-1811 and the supplies list. Call and order the supplies you need to ship collectible Band-Aid boxes, Disney videos, baskets, and just about anything else. They'll be delivered within three to four days at no charge. You can also obtain some at your local post office, but it's rare to find the full range of sizes at one office.

USPS Rate Calculator

The USPS calculator (**postcalc.usps.gov**) provides a great way to estimate postage on domestic and international shipments. Savvy sellers bookmark this site to run their postal options. Enter the package type (envelope, box, oversized package), weight, special characteristics (Is it a rolled poster in a tube? Is it a tree?), and the origin and destination zip codes. You will be presented with a list of options based on price and delivery times. Choose one. Next, select the desired shipping features—insurance, C.O.D., registered mail, return receipt—and the package delivery costs will be clearly presented.

TIP

Priority Pickup

For $8.25 per pickup, the Postal Service will pick up Priority Mail packages. While not economical for a single package, this is a great deal when multiple packages are involved. Postage must be on the packages when picked up.

FedEx

No company has changed the face of shipping more than Federal Express (**www.fedex.com**). Its purple and orange logo is as well known as the red, white, and blue Postal logo or the brown of UPS. FedEx made its mark—and made the others compete—with the original launch of overnight delivery.

Federal Express now offers a range of shipping options, and is often recognized as the Cadillac shipper for consistent reliability (and premium pricing).

You can set up an account for free and will only be charged when FedEx makes a shipment. Through a professional association, you may be able to obtain an account with the benefit of a group discount. My account came through a group membership. My FedEx charges are billed to a credit card.

FedEx offers overnight, two-day, and three-day services. Use the chart at **iship.com** (more on this in a few pages), and you'll see where FedEx rates and services fall in comparison to USPS and UPS. This company's track record is impeccable.

For high-value auction items—or when time is of the essence—select FedEx for reliability and ease of use. I'd offer FedEx for sales of jewelry, watches, small pieces of art, cameras, and computer parts.

The overnight (afternoon), two-day, and three-day options for near and far are included in Table 21.3.

Like UPS, FedEx offers a maze of products and services. (There's nothing to compare with UPS's ground service, though.) FedEx pricing is based on weight and distance. To use FedEx shipping in auctions,

---

TIP

Need the Rules? Postal Service documentation is available online in Adobe's PDF format. Access the Postal Explorer (**pe.usps. gov/**) and you'll get any rules you might need. One of the most valuable—and often referenced—documents is the *Domestic Mail Manual.*

T A B L E 21.3

FedEx Rates on Overnight, Two-Day, and Three-Day Two-Pound Shipments

Time	Overnight	2-Day	3-Day
In state	$15.00	$ 7.50	$6.45
Cross-country	22.75	11.00	9.80

---

you may wish to note the maximum shipping price or include a link to the site's shipping calculator so potential bidders can assess their shipping options.

UPS

The ubiquitous brown van. There's nothing quite like the rumble of the UPS truck backing into the driveway. The brown truck, the uniform, and the ring-and-run are all part of the fun of working with UPS (**www.ups.com**).

If your online auctions are up and running with a substantial volume, consider an account with daily pickup service. For a weekly service charge of $6 to $14, depending on volume, one of the fine brown-wrapped representatives will swing by daily, Monday through Friday, to check for packages. Without daily service, on-call pickups are available for express and international shipments. On-call pickups add $3.00 to the shipping fees for a package.

No carrier offers more choices from more locations than UPS. In the United States, Canada, and Puerto Rico, there are over 50,000 UPS starting points. Drop-box letter centers, UPS Customer Service counters, and Authorized Shipping Outlets count in the total. Authorized shipping outlets are known to us as Mail Boxes Etc., Parcel Plus, Postal Annext, and similar outlets. UPS Customer Service can be reached at 1-800-PICK-UPS (1-800-742-5877).

UPS services are a bit more complex than the U.S. Postal Service options. UPS has seven zones across the county, and each package price is determined by shipment method, zone, and whether the delivery is to a residential or business address.

That's a lot of questions in the fast-paced world of online auctions. Before figuring shipping costs, sellers select a service (overnight, two-day, three-day, ground), and must know whether the destination is a business or residence. Depending on the distance between the origin and destination, *ground* can mean delivery will be as soon as tomorrow or as long as a week from today.

To get an idea of what it would cost to have a daily pickup account, I contacted my local representative. The fee, billed weekly, ranges from $6 to $14 based on the total value of shipments for the week, and can be viewed in Table 21.4. (With $50 in shipments, the weekly fee is $6.)

T A B L E 21.4

Daily UPS Pickup Account Fees

$ Value of UPS Shipments	Weekly Fee
Over $50 in shipping	$ 6
Less than $50 in shipping	10
No shipment during the week	14

Now that I have an idea of the fees, what will it cost to ship a package?

For this example, I assumed a cross-country shipment from Burke, Virginia 22015, to a residence in Monterey, California 93940. A two-pound package that would cost $3.20 with Priority Mail costs $5.22 to $13.00 with the UPS options in Table 21.5. Having a UPS account saves $3 per shipment over UPS without an account.

When shipping to the next town over, I could use UPS ground for $3.99, and they'd likely get it tomorrow. That's still more than $3.20 for Priority Mail. The main advantage is that with an account, the driver comes to the door for pickup. Don't forget—for a call and $8.25, the Postal Service will pick up as many Express and Priority Mail packages as you have ready to go.

There are so many shipping possibilities that comparisons are difficult. For sellers with a UPS account, it can be hard to justify the higher cost of UPS ground when compared to Priority Mail. While UPS includes insurance, the higher shipping rate outweighs the perceived value of the insurance.

The options here are available for Monday through Friday deliveries. Higher-priced overnight delivery can be made on Saturday for an even higher fee. USPS Priority Mail delivers on one more day of the week, for less money. That makes UPS a hard choice.

MAIL BOXES AND MORE

Shipping storefronts known by their tradenames, such as Mail Boxes Etc., Parcel Plus, and Postal Annex+, can provide the full range of shipping services. Need help? These services can handle all tasks, but this often involves a high price.

Despite the costs, it's smart to be aware of these resources, as you may someday need their services for difficult-to-ship items such as a grandfather clock. While buying packaging materials can quickly cut into your proceeds, these centers also have a large variety of shipping materials for sale. You do not have to ship through them to purchase their shipping cartons.

- Mail Boxes Etc. (**www.mbe.com**)
- Parcel Plus (**www.parcelplus.com**)
- Postal Annex+ (**www.postalannex.com**)

T A B L E 21.5

Example of a UPS Cross-Country Shipment

UPS Method	2nd Day	3-Day Select	Ground (7 Days)
With account	$10	$ 8.40	$5.22
Without account	13	11.40	8.22

Of course there are Internet shipping options, too. It would be great if shipping were as easy as email. It is getting easier. Internet shippers rely on the real world shippers we've just covered.

iShip.com

The Internet package shipper iShip.com (**www.iShip.com**) helps auction sellers by providing a one-stop integrated service for processing, shipping, and packing e-commerce packages (see Figure 21.1). From the home page, utilize the price comparison center for UPS, U.S. Postal Service, FedEx, and Airborne Express. Access the shipping and price comparison chart from the home page. Start with the origin and destination zip codes; choose the package weight; and you'll be presented with a chart featuring options arranged by price and delivery time. For efficient pricing, shipping, and tracking, start here.

The shipping services have caught on to the needs of auction sellers. eBay, iShip, and Mail Boxes Etc. have begun a cooperative deal. The complete plan is to

FIGURE 21.1

iShip's colorful chart makes it easy to compare services and rates.

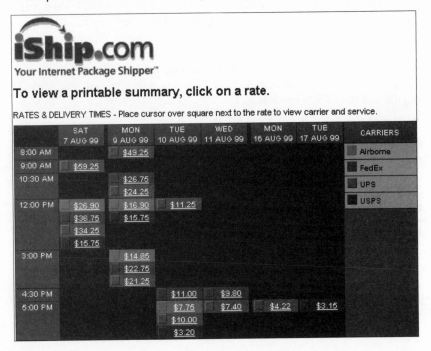

make it possible for sellers to give buyers a choice of carrier services with zip-to-zip pricing comparisons. You'll be able to print labels from your desktop printer, and let iShip automatically email bidders when shipments are on their way. Every shipment can be tracked and insurance can be added with a click. Package histories and costs are maintained in the comprehensive shipping log. A "hold for inspection" program is planned. As a variation on the escrow theme, MBE locations will serve as a place for the delivery and inspection of goods.

SmartShip

Arrange and pay for any U.S. shipment, completely online, with SmartShip (**www. smartship.com**). The payment is easy (courier account or credit card). All shipping information is saved, making it easy to ship to repeat customers. An extensive log of each shipment is kept so you'll always have a copy of your shipping history. Notification of shipping "milestones" and delivery confirmation will arrive in your email box. Forget about keeping track of tracking numbers—SmartShip does that for you.

Even if you didn't ship through SmartShip, you can take advantage of its tracking systems, on any package with a tracking number shipped through Airborne, FedEx, UPS, or USPS.

AuctionSHIP

Parcel Plus has put together a Web site specifically for auction users (**www.auctionship.com**). This handy site provides links to AuctionSHIP quotes, United Parcel Service (UPS), and the U.S. Postal Service (USPS). The quote link allows you to make a further selection from shipping only, packaging only, and shipping and handling.

Kinko's

Kinko's (**www.kinkos.com**) and eBay have announced plans to work together to provide services to eBay users. Kinko's has a full range of services that related to auctions. Auction sellers can scan images and documents for use in listings, and can use Kinko's' computers to upload and participate in auctions. And, Kinko's is well suited to ship packages with Federal Express and UPS from their thousands of 24-hour locations.

INTERNET POSTAGE OPTIONS

Internet postage options have arrived. They're making it possible to download postage, print "stamped" envelopes and labels, and ship from home with the blessings of the U.S. Postal Service.

The services charge monthly or annual convenience fees. Depending on the service selected, fees may include a postage scale or separate label printer.

For more information refer, to the following sites:

- Stamps.com Internet Postage (**www.stamps.com**)
- Simply Postage (**www.simplypostage.com**)
- E-Stamp Internet Postage (**www.estamp.com**)

Simply Postage

The do-it-yourself postage store is Simply Postage (**www.simplypostage.com**). Once you've become a Simply Postage member, printing postage is easy. Connect the Simply Postage stamp dispenser to your PC, log on, and download postage. With the press of a button you can print a self-adhesive stamp to affix to a letter or package. Skip the licks. When assessing Simply Postage for your needs, compare the $17.95 monthly fee with your time for standing in line at the post office. With this option, you only have to drop the packages at the PO or arrange for pickup.

Stamps.com Internet Postage

Stamps.com (**www.stamps.com**) Internet Postage allows users to print postage delivered over the Internet directly onto envelopes, labels, or business documents without any additional PC hardware.

Customers download a small software program, install the software, and apply for a U.S. Postal Service (USPS) postage meter license. When the account is activated, you can purchase postage as a debit from your checking account, through a bank-to-bank funds transfer. Office and home-based mailers can then print postage directly onto envelopes and labels using nothing more than an ordinary laser or inkjet printer with a 300-dpi (or greater) resolution.

E-Stamp Internet Postage

E-stamp.com (**www.estamp.com**) provides many of the same features as Stamps.com. Once installed, it is integrated in Microsoft Word. Draft a letter, click on a menu, and print a stamped and addressed envelope—complete with address correction.

RESOURCES

Consult Chapter 22, "Pros and Cons of International," for tips on international sales and shipping.

For additional overnight and internation shipping options, check out the DHL Worldwide Express (**www.dhl.com**) and Airborne Express (**www.airborne.com**) sites.

The Shipping Dock is the clever name for a message board accessible through Honesty Communications (**www.honesty.com**) and through the Online Traders Web Alliance (**www.otwa.com**). Ask for shipping tips and advice.

Like iship.com, mentioned earlier in this chapter, the Internet Shipping Center (**www.intershipper.net**) is worth a visit for pricing, shipping, and tracking.

A terrific shipping resource page has been put together at About.com. From the home page (**www.about.com**), select these links in succession: Business/Careers, Publishing, and More Links. Finally, select Packaging Supplies.

Need large boxes and other shipping supplies? Call your local U-Haul with the dimensions and get a box from them.

KEY POINTS

This chapter reveals the plain facts about shipping. Shipping terms can make or break a good auction deal. For your shipping concerns, include these ideas:

- Create a home-based shipping station.
- Pack appropriately based on the size and fragility of the item.
- Select the shipper based on fees and features.
- Consider the impact of handling fees and overcharges.

22

PROS AND CONS
OF INTERNATIONAL

INTERNATIONAL SALES AND SHIPPING

It's a big world out there. The Internet is a global village, and if you participate in international sales, you'll have to deal with the hard realities of geography and currency.

The number one reason to participate in international auctions is to make more money. There are uniquely American items that are very attractive to overseas bidders. Some, like popular collectibles, and American denim jeans and logo'ed athletic wear, may not be available in other countries. The bidders may be willing to pay far more than domestic bidders. Items for sale to the largest possible audience have the best bidding potential.

On the downside, there may be concerns that the transaction will consume disproportionate amounts of time. There may be valid concerns regarding tracking problem bidders. You can get around this by verifying feedback and exchanging personal information (such as addresses and phone numbers). Higher shipping costs are more likely to intimidate sellers than buyers. International bidders are far more accustomed to the related costs, documentation, customs fees, and currency transfers.

It's fair to make your "international" decision on an item-by-item basis. But, once you've conducted your first international sale, you'll have no qualms about future transactions.

Ad Notations

In the beginning, there's the ad. If you'd like to conduct an international sale, indicate your willingness in the ad form by making the appropriate selection in the checkboxes. Make a note in the text description, too. A simple notation "International bidders welcome" bespeaks your intentions. More specific comments about shipping and payment policies should also be added.

International Funds

If you are willing to sell internationally, add a note to your auctions that you will only accept U.S. funds. The best financial instrument is an international money order payable in U.S. funds. Sellers who accept international checks often encounter fees and assessments when they attempt to deposit or cash an international check. An international postal money order sidesteps these issues.

Another good choice is the use of credit cards. Even if you don't have a merchant account, you can take advantage of services such as Billpoint (**www.billpoint.com**) on individual transactions. For an international sale to work with Billpoint, cards must be issued by a U.S.-based issuer. Conducting the transaction through an escrow service can also facilitate international sales. You'll find more about i-Escrow, Billpoint, and other services in Chapter 20, "Getting Paid." With credit card transactions, buyers can take advantage of the current exchange rate, and the issuing bank may assess low percentage fees for converting the currency.

Your main goal is not to lose money on international transactions. This also means not incurring bank transaction fees. (A deposit of funds other than U.S. dollars will almost certainly incur fees.) The bulk of any transaction and currency exchange fees should be borne by the bidder.

INTERNATIONAL SHIPPING

Shipping a soap dish from Seattle to Savannah can get to be routine. Peoria to Paris adds a few new twists to shipping transactions.

All sellers have international shipping tales. In one learning experience, I lost $3 on the shipment of a book to Canada. My first error: I failed to note "U.S. sales only" in the descriptive text. Next, after the auction closed, I read the shipping chart wrong. I assumed that the small Global Priority Mail envelope was the same size as the standard U.S. Priority Mail envelope. At the post office, I was prepared to ship the $4.25 book in a $3.75 package, but the international mail fee was $6.95. After paying the extra $3.20, my net profit was $1.05. Eeeck!

A wise seller investigates international shipping options before initiating the auction. Once you investigate the shipping fees, you may decide to list your auction for sale only within your home country. On the other hand, the best market for your auction item may be international.

International shipments often involve extra paperwork such as customs documentation. Shipments to Canada, not always recognized as international, incur their own obstacles. UPS shipments to Canada seem to involve delays at the border. (Canadian authors tell horror stories of being assessed phenomenal fees to receive promotional copies of their own books.) As you prepare the shipping documentation, it can be wise to follow the guidance of the high bidder. That person may be more familiar with import requirements than you are with export requirements.

Who Pays?

With any international auction transaction, it's a good idea to note your shipping policy in the text of the description. A lightweight document, such as an autographed JFK, Jr., photograph may cost relatively little to ship in the United States. For an international shipment, the rates are significantly higher—$19.00 vs $11.75 for an 8-ounce Express Mail letter package sent by the Postal Service. Protect your transaction with a statement, in the descriptive text, that international buyers pay the actual cost.

Timing is everything. American auctioneers and bidders are accustomed to two- to three-day shipments with Priority Mail. Such short travel times are prohibitively expensive on international shipments. The good news is that your bidders are anticipating the longer delivery time.

Paris-Bound

Let's use the U.S. Postal Service and FedEx to estimate shipping costs for a queen-size Amish quilt, weighing six pounds. For the Postal Service, the selection includes airmail (four to seven days), return receipt, and insured for $500. With those specifications, the shipment will cost $47.02. Hand delivery to the post office is also assumed. Postal service personnel can guide you through completing

TIP

Get the Address ASAP

You'll need the delivery address ASAP after the close of the auction to accurately estimate the shipping cost.

any customs forms. The Postal Service's international rate calculator (**ircalc.usps.gov**) can be used to calculate this or other shipments.

To use FedEx International Economy service, the same package would arrive in four to five business days for a charge of $73.70. This includes FedEx tracking, and $500 declared value for insurance. This fee is the rate for packages carried into FedEx offices.

The home page for the International Economy service is located at: **fedex.com/us/services/international/economy.html**.

A link to FedEx's helpful international document assistance can be found on the same page. Use this site to compare prices with the Postal Service.

TIP

Know the Law

If you have any doubt about whether your merchandise can be sold internationally, perform some research before initiating the shipment. For example, shipping ivory to Africa would be prohibited. Among eBay's message boards, there's one for International Trading. Check the site map to locate the bulletin board.

HOME AND AWAY

I was shocked when I learned that my U.S.-only sale of baby bottles was won by someone in Pretoria, South Africa. But when I looked more closely at the shipping address, it became apparent that the high bidder was attached to the U.S. Embassy in Pretoria. I only had to ship the package to the U.S. Department of State in Washington, D.C. The State Department handled delivery to the embassy in Pretoria.

The personal check drawn on a U.S. bank took an extra week to arrive. The package made it to Pretoria two to three weeks after it was shipped. The high bidder sent her thanks by email.

Expats, U.S. citizens employed by U.S. corporations overseas, are others who will be able to conduct transactions like our embassy friend. Their checks will be familiar and their employers often handle the mail.

This leads us to APO and FPO addresses. Those are assigned to American deployable military units or ships, as well as to overseas bases. (A ship in San Diego has an FPO address.) Standard U.S. postal charges are the norm, although the shipping time may be long depending on the location of the military unit. APO and FPO shipments must be sent through the U.S. Postal Service.

Customs Concerns

Just like our government, foreign governments like to collect the taxes they think they're owed. International auction purchases incur extra fees for our customers, the auction buyers. These fees are not tacked onto our shipping fees, but may be tacked onto the transaction during the delivery process.

When you deliver the hand-painted coffee mugs, postal representatives will help you complete the minimal customs documents. They do this all the time! No matter what carrier you choose, their personnel can help you to quickly prepare the documents. Visit the FedEx Web site, and you'll find online forms for this purpose. Use the International Economy link in the Paris-Bound section of this chapter.

All international carriers have their own methods for getting through foreign customs. UPS shipments into Canada seem to fall into a separate category of discontent. They seem to incur more interruptions and they tend to arrive with more tacked-on fees than shipments through other carriers.

Problem Resolution

Due to the distances and borders, you'll want to be extra vigilant in protecting yourself on international shipments. With these distances, problem resolution has the potential to be more difficult. In reviewing the following list, please note that some of these criteria points may depend on the value of the transaction:

- Check feedback.
- Collect U.S. funds.
- Exchange full addresses, phone numbers, and fax numbers. You should have a contact method other than email.
- Test and verify the alternate contact method.
- Ship by a reliable courier.
- Ship by a traceable method.
- Insure the shipment.
- Verify delivery/receipt.

TIP

Let the Customer Decide

As long as the bidders are footing the bill, let them have a say in selecting a shipper. Ask their advice on shippers and any special addressing or documentation the package requires. In all likelihood, the buyer you are dealing with has made other international purchases and is well versed in selecting the best shipper for the transaction.

RESOURCES

For an exchange rate calculator, check the Universal Currency Converter at **www.xe.net/ucc/**.

The World Currency Exchange is at: **www.rubicon.com/passport/currency/currency.html**.

KEY POINTS

International sales can open new avenues for your goods. In this chapter we looked at the factors to be considered for "going international." Proceed wisely and:

- Access the largest possible market.
- Note international willingness in the auction ad.
- Specify acceptable funds and financial instruments in the auction ad.
- Know the international shipping options.
- Address customs concerns.
- Communicate fully to avoid problems.

23 CHAPTER

PROTECTING YOURSELF

AVOIDING PROBLEMS

It's much easier to avoid problems than to try to repair them later. It's best to check feedback to validate the buyer, utilize escrows for high-value items, and have a firm return policy in place.

EVALUATING BIDDERS' FEEDBACK

Each of the worth-their-salt auction sites has a feedback system whereby auction participants can leave opinions of auction bidders and sellers. It's an honor system, and like anything Internet-related, must be looked at with a critical eye.

Chapter 24, "The Importance of Ratings," takes a full look at feedback systems. Since feedback is one of the more important ways to evaluate a prospective buyer, please look there for a discussion of feedback and how to evaluate it.

Each site has policies and procedures for eliminating bad auction citizens. Do your part by reporting deadbeats and requesting credit when relisting auctions. Sites that provide refunds or credits track the problem-causing deadbeats. In Chapter 18, "Relisting When It Doesn't Sell," and Chapter 20, "Getting Paid," you'll find more on relisting policies and deadbeat bidders.

NEED MORE INFORMATION?
From eBay's site map, select the link for Search for Members, followed by Contact Info. Complete the form by adding your User ID, password, and the User ID of the other party,

and an email will be generated. You will receive the registered information on the other person, including email address, user ID, name, company (if included), city, state, country, zip code, phone number, and date and time of registration. You may then use this information to contact the other party by phone. The complete mailing address is not included, but you may be able to complete that from other sources.

TIP

Enhance Your Feedback

To gain the trust of buyers, sellers can do some "buying." All feedback points are equal and it may be worth it to buy a few small things. Selling with a star and 10+ comments boosts your credibility status.

Warning: Both parties receive copies of the same message. The other party will know you were looking for information on him or her. In my case, I'm assured that that person will never find out, since her email has been bouncing from her ISP's server.

WARNING SIGNS

Some sellers are skeptical of AOL users. That's because AOL users have been accustomed to their own style and have not been netiquette-aware on newsgroups. Here's the rub—there are more of *them* than anyone else. AOL's 20 million members (and I'm one too) do stand out in Internet dealings. Just because there are more of them, a poorly representative AOL-er may make you think poorly of them as a group. On the other hand, I find myself wary of those using free email accounts (What, they can't afford an ISP?). And those with WebTV often stick out like AOLers. Remember that old statement about first impressions? It works here, too.

I'm also skeptical of users who change their User IDs. It makes me wonder what they're hiding! A changed User ID, feedback of zero, and certain email hosts make me wonder about the stability of a user. Will the check bounce?

ESCROW SERVICES: EVALUATING THE MERCHANDISE

In Chapter 20, "Getting Paid," we took a look at escrow services, third parties that help a buyer and seller complete a fair sale. In a typical escrow transaction, the bidder pays the escrow company, while the seller ships the merchandise directly to the high bidder. Upon the high bidder's receipt and acceptance of the auctioned item, the escrow company releases funds to the seller.

Escrow services prevent unfortunate experiences, allowing transactions to proceed smoothly. The leading Internet auction escrow firms are i-Escrow (**iescrow. com**), TradeSafe (**tradesafe.com**), and Trade-Direct (**trade-direct.com**).

The auction sites have links to specific escrow programs. Auctions.com has its own Bid$afe escrow program. Excite links to Billpoint for combined credit card processing and escrowlike services. (You'll find more on Billpoint in Chapter 20, "Getting Paid.") eBay links to i-Escrow, while Amazon links to both TradeSafe and i-Escrow. Auctions sites and their escrow partners appear in Table 23.1.

Testing Escrows: Baby Gap

At the close of a Baby Gap dress auction, I offered to run the two dresses through escrow services. Additionally, I told the buyers I would pay all escrow fees. The first bidder took me up on the offer, and we ran the transaction through i-Escrow. The other auction's winner agreed to try TradeSafe.

Setting up an i-Escrow transaction from eBay is easy and direct. From the site map choose the link to the "SafeHarbor" page, and then select the link to i-Escrow. The eBay transaction information is carried over. Simply add eBay's auction number. Confirm the selling price and shipping information. Next, i-Escrow sends an email to the high bidder to conduct the next step of the transaction.

TIP

Take Control

Review Chapter 17, "During the Auction," for information on canceling bids and closing auctions early.

Using email and i-Escrow's Web site, buyers and sellers take turns progressing through the postauction steps. The process at i-Escrow is typical of the system at each escrow site.

- Seller visits escrow Web site and enters auction information.
- Escrow site sends email to high bidder.
- Bidder visits escrow site to indicate acceptance of terms (or to proposed counterterms).

T A B L E 23.1

Auction Sites and Their Escrow Partners

Auction Site	Preferred Escrow	URL
Amazon	i-Escrow	iescrow.com
	TradeSafe	tradesafe.com
Auctions.com	Bid$afe	auctionuniverse.com
CityAuction	i-Escrow	iescrow.com
eBay	i-Escrow	iescrow.com
Excite	Billpoint	billpoint.com
Yahoo!	None	Use any of the above.

- Bidder pays escrow.
- Escrow sends seller specific instructions for shipping.
- Seller ships.
- Seller visits escrow site and enters shipping information.
- Bidder receives merchandise and notifies escrow of acceptance.
- Escrow releases funds to seller.

In our transaction, there were two minor delays. The first was when I returned from shipping the package and forgot to update to the escrow site with the shipping and tracking information. The second delay occurred when the bidder needed a reminder to notify i-Escrow that she had accepted the merchandise. (If she hadn't notified them within the specified three days, the payment would default to me at the end of the same time period.) i-Escrow's new transaction screen appears in Figure 23.1.

The second transaction was initiated with TradeSafe. Without a direct link from eBay, I began by entering the URL to start at TradeSafe's home page. Trade-Safe's on-screen directions are not as clearly formatted as those on i-Escrow, and the

F I G U R E 23.1

The escrow for the Baby Gap dress test began with this clean screen.

bidder asked to complete the transaction without benefit of the escrow protection. Still, TradeSafe offers useful options that can work to the buyer and seller's advantage. A TradeSafe window appears in Figure 23.2.

Each escrow site has slight but important differences in assessing transaction fees. TradeSafe features a calculator to determine the total fees including deposit and escrow. TradeSafe's escrow options include:

- Buyer pays escrow fee; seller pays shipping.
- Buyer pays escrow fee *and* shipping.
- Seller pays escrow fee; buyer pays shipping.
- Seller pays escrow fee *and* shipping.
- Buyer and seller split escrow fee *and* shipping.

RETURNED MERCHANDISE

Just what do you owe your bidders? I think you owe them accurately described merchandise and clear terms. Some sellers dedicate themselves to customer service,

F I G U R E 23.2

Here's the beginning of the TradeSafe transaction.

while others clearly spell out "no returns" in the text of their auction ads. Your choice to accept returns may depend on the type of merchandise, its condition, and your ability to resell it at the same or better price.

It's best to specify the return policy in the auction ad and in the close-of-auction email. One seller's packing slips state that she is happy to accept returns as long as the buyer contacts the seller within three days of the receipt of the package. Consider this as a possible addition to your shipping note. Getting down to the details, the option is yours. It is better to be specific than to go without.

Here's what happened to a used-book seller. She posted an auction, and the bidding soared beyond her wildest dreams. After the money and book had changed hands, she received the book in the mail, with a note asking for a full refund. (The bidder skipped the expected step of sending an email!) He complained that it was not a first edition—it was a book club edition. The seller returned the book (not the money) with a very polite note and a copy of the auction ad, which clearly stated the tome was a book club edition. Remember that it's not your fault if the bidder doesn't read the description!

"Busytown" Returns

As children grow, their interests change. Our master plan has been to sell Carly's software as she outgrows it, in order to buy new programs of interest. Also, as technology advances, it's not worth saving the programs for her little sister Katie.

The first program to sell was *Busytown*, and it sold through a Yahoo! auction. The buyer, who I trusted to be honest, sent an email a few days after receiving the program. They were having an installation problem. I had no reason to think that there was a problem before I sold the software, and I offered a few ideas to try to fix the problem. I responded promptly, to the best of my ability and recall, and suggested that when they felt they had exhausted all options (like checking the manufacturer's Web site) I would refund their money.

In a second email, I provided links to other software auctions I was running. I offered to apply the money they had already paid to either of the other auctions if they won either of the auctions. (Hey, I might as well maximize my current auctions!)

> **TIP**
>
> **Marked Returns**
>
> China and pottery sellers have been known to mark their pieces with ink that appears only under ultraviolet light. If their bidder returns a piece, they check to see if it has the mark they placed before shipping. With the marking, you'll know whether someone is trying to pull a fast switch.

In the message, I advised them of the reserve levels for each. I also offered a full refund or equal credit on other kids' software I had up for auction.

In the end, they requested a full refund, and I sent a check refunding their purchase price and the shipping cost. Additionally, I asked that they not send the software back to me. My primary interest was to end the auction on a good note. So, what happened? They asked for a refund, and I complied.

"Busytown's" Feedback Impact

Just after I took *Busytown* to the post office for its Priority Mail journey, I posted positive feedback. After the conclusion of the return, I had no reason to change or modify the feedback. While I would have appreciated a feedback note that indicated I was a fair seller who refunded promptly, they did not leave feedback. The transaction may have scared them away from online auctions because they have participated in no other Yahoo! auctions.

THE MISSING PACKAGE

Package tracing provides security to sellers. With a tracking number or shipment confirmation you'll be able to verify a bidder's queries about a missing package. You'll also learn whether the recipient is truthful about a missing package.

The mystery of a missing package can be avoided with forethought. Each shipping service provides at least one option for tracing packages and verifying delivery. The Postal Service has added inexpensive delivery confirmation to the popular Priority Mail line, and it's long had "return receipts" that can be added to most shipments. Federal Express and UPS also feature package-tracking services.

> **TIP**
>
> **Check Your Feedback** Truly diligent sellers don't consider the deal done until they have received confirmation of the high bidder's satisfaction with the merchandise. One way to do this is to check your feedback ratings to see if the bidder has posted feedback.

A return receipt or delivery confirmation verifies that the recipient received the package you shipped. It doesn't prove that Cinderella's mirror arrived in good shape. For that, you need insurance.

INSURANCE

If insured merchandise arrives damaged, or never arrives, the buyer or seller can initiate the claim for damage or loss. In many cases the process begins with the seller because that party holds the shipping receipts. Take a look at Chapter 21, "Shipping," for more information on insurance.

When *auction sites* provide insurance, it is to protect against fraudulent transactions. Auction site insurance protects bidders when sellers collect and run. It also protects bidders when auction merchandise differs significantly from how it was described in the auction listing.

AUCTION SITE SAFETY RESOURCES

Each auction site provides a selection of safety resources. These may include insurance, authentication, tracking and removal of fraudulent bidders, and Internet fraud links.

At Auctions.com, buyers or sellers can take advantage of fee and free protections. Pay $19.95 to join the Bid$afe Gold program, where bidders can use credit cards to speed transactions. The Bid$afe Gold program also provides insurance against loss or theft. Bid$afe Buyer allows users to participate as a buyer only. They can also take advantage of this transaction security.

eBay's SafeHarbor area include links to the Verified User program, escrow services, authentication and grading services, and insurance. Most eBay transactions are covered for up to $200 after a $25 deductible.

Similar guarantees are available at eBay, Amazon, and Auctions.com. For transactions above the limit of the auction site's guarantee, participants should consider escrow services.

The eBay Verified User program involves a small fee ($5), and Equifax provides online verification of user information. It's a voluntary program that allows users to submit personal information (Social Security number, driver's license information, and date of birth) in order to establish proof of identity. Those who participate receive a Verified User logo that appears adjacent to their user ID in all auctions. (In the next section, we'll take a look at eBay's authentication services.)

On Amazon, each auction participant's identity is verified with a valid credit card. They also provide the Amazon Auctions Guarantee. Most auctions carry the guarantee (it depends on the merchandise category), and those closing under $250 are eligible for the guarantee. The guarantee protects bidders from fraudulent sellers. For more information on this guarantee program, see Chapter 6, "Bidding Tips and Tricks."

Excite, Yahoo!, and City Auction do not provide the extensive services found at eBay, Amazon, and Auctions.com. They do provide links to fraud services and guidance on filing postal fraud complaints.

AUTHENTICATION SERVICES

From the sites we've looked at, eBay is the leader in providing authentication services. eBay offers authentication and grading services in various categories such as autographs, trading cards, rare coins, and beanies.

Through SafeHarbor, you'll find links to the International Society for Appraisers (ISA), as well as Professional Sports Authenticators (PSA), PSA/DNA for autograph authentication, Professional Coin Grading Service (PCGS), and Real Beans for Beanie Baby identification.

While these services may seem to owe their existence to bidders verifying their merchandise, they also provide security to sellers in closing the deal and reducing the possibility of after-auction problems.

Sellers send items for grading and authentication. Service fees depend on the turnaround time needed (one to thirty days). Sellers can include a logo in the eBay item description that identifies the item as *authenticated*. Additionally, the seller's eBay ad can carry links to information about the item's specific grade and authenticity.

FRAUD RESOURCES

Whether buyer or seller are wronged, auction participants should be aware of and report incidents to the appropriate agencies. Always start with an auction site's fraud links. The following sites are also good sources of information:

- *Federal Bureau of Investigation.* The FBI's Infrastructure Protection and Computer Intrusion site (**www.fbi.gov/programs/ipcis/index.htm**) is the best of the federal government's sites. The FBI's pages include forms for reporting suspected credit card fraud, the latest press releases related to scams, and advice pertaining to electronic-commerce security.

- *National Fraud Information Center.* The Center (**www.fraud.org**) maintains an Internet Fraud Watch and Online Incident Report Form.

- *Federal Trade Commission.* You can access the Federal Trade Commission's pages on E-commerce and the Internet (**www.ftc. gov/bcp/menu-internet.htm**). These pages are consumer-oriented and offer valuable tips for fraud prevention. You'll also find updates on FTC antifraud activities.

- *U.S. Secret Service.* If a fraud incident has to do with money, it falls under the jurisdiction of the division of the Treasury Department known as the U.S. Secret Service (**www.ustreas.gov/fincen**). You thought they only protected the president? The Secret Service is very interested in online credit card scams. Visit this site to find information about the various types of online fraud. It also includes contact information for reporting crimes.

- *FraudDetector.* Although FraudDetector (**www.munica.com/ frauddetector**) is not a federal site, there's lots of good information here. Look carefully and you'll find a search tool for determining whether a credit card has previously been involved in fraud. This is also a good place check out suspicious email addresses and track IP addresses. Register for free membership.

- *Internet Scambusters.* Scambusters (**www.scambusters.org**) is one of the top anti-credit-card-fraud sites. Smaller merchants, who may not have access to the elaborate verification systems, can find the information they need. It's also useful for acquiring tips on the latest fraud schemes. Track thieves' operating methods and the IP and e-mail addresses they are using. Internet scams, spamming, and phony domain registration are attacked here.

- *National Check Fraud Center.* This site (**www.ckfraud.org**) has good sources for alerts to criminal activities centered around scams and credit cards. It lists bank accounts, aliases, and methods utilized by criminals.

RESOURCES

You'll also find Internet fraud links at the Web page called 411 for eBay Users. The links can be used by auctioneers of any "brand": **www.geocities.com/MotorCity/2625/baddealhelps.html**.

KEY POINTS

In this chapter we reviewed the basics of protecting sellers in auction transactions. The best form of protection is to avoid problems. During and after the auction, follow these points:

- Evaluate bidders' feedback.
- Utilize an escrow service to facilitate a fair deal.
- Establish a return policy.
- Trace missing packages.
- Utilize auction site safety resources.
- Be aware of Internet fraud resources.

24

THE IMPORTANCE OF RATINGS

THE VALUE OF FEEDBACK RATINGS

Back in Mayberry, North Carolina, Sheriff Andy and Aunt Bea knew everyone—and everybody's business. On the dynamic, ever-growing Internet community, it's more difficult to know who's who. To combat the anonymity factor, each of the auction sites has developed a citizenship rating system, most often called *feedback*. At the conclusion of a transaction, buyers comment on sellers. And, sellers can add their comments about buyers. Feedback ratings are auction traders' report cards.

Before making a bid, a savvy bidder checks the seller's feedback. Ideally your bidders will encounter glowing feedback about you. You can be relied upon to communicate promptly, have fair payment and shipping terms, and deliver the merchandise that you painstakingly described.

Treat your high bidders well, and they will bestow flattering feedback. Garner these points to validate your status as an excellent seller. Stellar ratings pay dividends in future transactions.

Do your part to be a good auction citizen. Leave accurate feedback on bidders so that other sellers will know whether to trust them. It's your community responsibility.

SEEING STARS

eBay's feedback system rewards colored stars to buyers and sellers when they achieve certain levels. With each feedback achievement, a new star is awarded. Auction participants take these stars seriously and work hard to achieve each level.

- A yellow star depicts a Feedback Profile of 10 to 99.
- A turquoise star depicts a Feedback Profile of 100 to 499.
- A purple star depicts a Feedback Profile of 500 to 999.
- A red star depicts a Feedback Profile of 1,000 to 9,999.
- A shooting star depicts a Feedback Profile of 10,000 or higher.

The Types of Feedback

Feedback ratings are cumulative net scores at eBay, Auctions.com, Excite, and Yahoo!. Each positive, negative, or neutral rating is tallied into your total score. A positive adds a point (+1), while a negative deducts a point (−1). Neutrals are neither positive nor negative (0).

- Positive feedback includes praise for someone who has complied with, or exceeded, the auction's terms.

- Neutral feedbacks reflect auction experiences that were neither positive nor negative.

- Negative feedback reflects criticism and serves as a warning or caution flag to users regarding this party in future transactions.

CityAuction's feedback system is unique among the auction sites we've visited. Following a CityAuction username is a code like this (20: 8+ / 0 / 1−). That means the user has participated in 20 auctions. Eight positive comments have been recorded, along with zero neutrals and one negative. For a more detailed look, you can click on the ratings to see specific comments.

TIP

Add Your Comments

At CityAuction, a seller can leave a comment pertaining to any bidder (i.e., not just the high bidder).

Amazon's feedback system incorporates two components. The first component, based on stars, is the rating. For each transaction, you can rate your counterpart on a 1 to 5 star scale. (The star ratings are transaction-based). The number of stars awarded from each transaction are compiled into a running average. If one person grants three stars, and another grants five, the graphic will display as four stars.

The descriptive feedback comments are the second component. Comments do not contribute to the star-based rating system, although they may be posted at the same time. Feedback comments may also be posted by any user and do not have to be transaction-linked. Adjacent to the participant's auction ID is the star rating earned and, in parentheses, the number of transactions included in the calculation.

Amazon's feedback system has two components: descriptive feedback and ratings. Those ratings are on a scale of 1 to 5, with five being the best. For some busy people, this rating system asks too much. Early in the history of Amazon Auctions, I completed a transaction with an attorney who hurriedly checked "1" and then wrote glowing feedback. Once she realized her rating error, she was quick to apologize. Amazon now refers to the rating system in terms of stars, and emphasizes that 5 is better than 1. In cases like this, it is unfortunate that feedback is cast in stone. Read carefully and rate correctly.

At eBay, feedback comments can be left for any reason or can be transaction-related. Negative feedback must be transaction-related. That means that the auction number must be included. This allows anyone reviewing the feedback to access the related transaction. Transaction-related feedback makes the process more valuable, as it more accurately reflects the parties to and details of the transaction. Here's why transaction-related feedback is important: It allows bidders to see that you can be counted on to deliver the rocking horse, just as you fairly sold the hammock, chaise lounge, and antique canning jars.

In view of the community experience, anyone can leave a message that says "great seller, great buyer, exactly as promised." It means more when a buyer or seller is willing to identify the auction, merchandise, terms, and bidding history. Hence, the value of transaction-linked feedback. Transaction-related feedback can be left for 60 days after the close of auction.

TIP

Positively eBay

At eBay, positive feedback can be left for anyone in the community.

Only sellers and successful bidders can leave transaction-related feedback. Those same folks can also inadvertently leave non-transaction-related feedback. This happens when they are a bit lazy and fail to include the auction number. The best way to leave feedback is to visit the auction page, and then choose the option to leave feedback. This action automatically carries the auction number into the feedback form.

Go Beyond the Numbers

It's tempting to assume that the number beside a buyer or seller's name represents the total number of positive feedbacks. But that may not be true. The urn-bidder's 25 rating points may reflect 35 feedbacks—including 10 negatives and a couple of neutrals.

When you visit a buyer or seller's feedback page, you'll often encounter a chart showing the total number of positives, negatives, and neutrals received since they registered at the site.

Conduct a background investigation on your auction counterpart.

- Look at the auctions she has won.
- Look at the auctions she has participated in.
- Look at her current auction activity.
- Run a seller search to see if she is also a seller.
- Assess the total number of auction transactions. Compare the total number of transactions to the number of feedback comments. Be skeptical if she has sold 60 items but only has 15 feedbacks.

Cast in Stone

Your feedback ratings are cast in stone. Be honest, be truthful, and above all choose your words carefully. Before you hit the "post" button, take a deep breath, reread what you've written, and contemplate the impact of what you are saying.

Most sites do not allow anyone, ever, to retract feedback. Except in rare instances, your comments will forever be tied to your username and that of your bidding counterpart. Some sites allow additional comments to clarify or neutralize prior entries, as seen in Table 24.1. Responses to negative feedback are allowed at eBay, Auctions.com, and CityAuction. Auctions.com allows anyone who has posted feedback to submit a retraction.

When an auction site allows a response, the new comments are listed adjacent to the original comment. Feedback responses don't affect numerical tallies. They simply allow the user to explain more about the transaction, and why a negative comment may have been posted. If you are the recipient of an undeserved negative comment, take a break before choosing your words for a response. There's no sense in escalating a war. Simply post a constructive comment or invite concerned potential bidders to contact you directly. I've even seen sellers include a URL to direct interested readers to another site with a more complete explanation. Use what resources you can to protect your good name.

T A B L E 24.1

User Options Following Negative Feedback

Auction Site	Originating Party May	Recipient May
AuctionUniverse	retract	post response
CityAuction	edit feedback	post response
eBay	post a neutral comment	post response

Like pennies from heaven, it's possible to be the beneficiary of feedback intended for someone else. The point of misdirection is a typo. Misspell your username and it's likely you'll encounter someone with a similar name. One seller found that a dozen of her feedbacks had been misattributed to another seller. The first seller had over 900 feedbacks and the "recipient" had only 25. Surely the recipient knew she was benefitting at the expense of another. Had that party been a good eBay citizen, she would have notified those who left the feedback and eBay customer service in an effort to get the feedback to the right person.

Hidden Feedback

In your auction journeys you may encounter hidden feedback. It's feedback that's no longer available for viewing. This is a serious warning sign! Hidden feedback is quite rare—certainly less than 1 percent of auction participants choose to hide their feedback.

Hiding feedback is an "all or nothing" proposition. You can't selectively choose which feedback comment should be hidden, as that would undermine the integrity of the feedback system.

Go ahead and email bidders with hidden feedback. They may be able to provide plausible explanations. One possible reason for hiding feedback is that the auction participant has become a target of an Internet auction stalker.

Participants can hide feedback at:

- eBay
- CityAuction

At Auctions.com a buyer or seller can elect to be not rated. That's indicated by "NR" beside a name. Proceed with caution when a participant has elected not to be rated or has hidden formerly viewable feedback.

TIP

Read between the Lines

When you look at feedback, read between the lines to check more than the numerical chart. It's fairly common to find "positive" feedback worded with neutral terminology.

Why Ratings Go Neutral

When positives or negatives are converted to neutral, the most common reason is that the feedback poster is no longer a registered user at the auction site. As you review another user's feedback ratings you may notice neutrals carrying the notation that their "owner" is no longer registered. Formerly positive neutrals are a sore spot with some sellers. No one wants to lose hard-earned positive points, and the conversion to neutral incurs a negative impact among those who care most about feedback.

Individuals may elect to unregister, or they may be unceremoniously booted. Whatever the reason, they lose their feedback "voice." Neutralized comments weight feedback ratings toward active auction participants and silence those who post-and-run.

WHEN TO LOOK AT FEEDBACK

During an auction, sellers should check in daily to assess bidders and feedback. Back in Chapter 17, "During the Auction," we took a look at reviewing bidder's feedback and canceling bids from undesirable bidders.

There's no sense in letting a bidder with poor feedback drive your auction. That's not the winner you want. Just like in the real world, a bidder is only as good as his reputation. Remember, a high bid from a deadbeat means you'll be relisting the auction.

BURNED BY TONER

In the process of preparing this book, I've run reams and reams of paper through my trusty HP. Needing more toner, I found a cartridge at auction on eBay. I won the auction and paid by electronic check. Two weeks after the auction closed, I'd not yet received the toner. An email to the seller failed to generate a response. The seller's feedback was all positive, but there were only 15 feedbacks for 100 recent auctions. By this time, the seller was listed as "no longer registered." The system would not let me leave feedback for someone no longer registered. My bank confirmed the check had cleared. Other burned bidders began to band together, ready to prosecute. (My bank encouraged me to close the account used for the electronic check.) This was a bad deal getting worse. It took a very long time, but I finally received the cartridge.

My error was in not studying the seller's feedback well enough before placing a bid. I should have noticed glaring patterns or omissions in the feedback. It would also be beneficial if the site would allow buyers and sellers to leave feedback up to 60 days after the transaction—whether the seller is still registered or not.

WHEN TO LEAVE FEEDBACK

When should you leave feedback? There are two schools of thought on the best time to leave feedback. The first group leaves feedback after they are assured they have the funds in hand. They wait for the check to clear, mail the package, and then post feedback. (I participate in this group.)

Their counterparts post feedback after the winning bidder assures them that the sci-fi videos were received in good order. I think of this as the pessimists' group, but they may well be the pragmatists' club.

Leave feedback *when you think* the seller's responsibilities have come to an end. If you are confident that you accurately described your goods, then leave feedback after the check has cleared. On the other hand, if you anticipate problems with the transaction, wait, and leave feedback comments after the bidder has confirmed satisfaction.

When assessing the transaction experience, rate the *overall* experience. Ask yourself these questions before composing each feedback:

- Did the bidder respond promptly at the close of auction?
- Did the bidder follow your instructions for providing the shipping address?
- Did the correct payment arrive in a timely manner?
- Was it a pleasant experience?
- Would you conduct a transaction with this person again?

If you can answer yes to these, then give positive feedback. Bad checks, angry emails, "disappearing bidders," and poor communications are caution signs that should be flagged appropriately, often as negatives, in the feedback system.

MY COUPON BIDDER: BAD CHECK, LONG STORY

When a coupon auction closed, my high bidder communicated promptly. She included a link to her excellent feedback at another auction site and expedited her check. I didn't wait for her check to clear before sending the coupons. After all, we were only talking about $8.50. I posted glowing feedback.

Out of the blue, she notified me that her check had bounced. I gave her credit for notifying me before my bank did. My next step was to send a semi-firm message requesting a cashier's check for $18.50 to include my bank's returned check charges. She agreed within minutes. Then, her grandmother got sick, and I began to get messages from her sister. Instead of a cashier's check, the sister would send a postal money order. It's been deposited in my account—and for reasons unknown, my bank didn't assess returned-check charges.

I've sent her an email with thanks for "seeing it through." You may be wondering whether I posted additional feedback on this eBay bidder. I didn't. I'd originally posted positive feedback and still had a good feeling when deal was finally done. I'd be happy to sell to her again.

HOW TO LEAVE FEEDBACK

Many sellers will tell you that the hardest part of leaving feedback is finding the right page at the site. (I agree.) At some sites, locating the feedback page is a simple activity. At others, it is a bit more of an exercise.

Across the sites, you can access feedback pages:

- From site maps
- Through your account summary page, such as "My eBay"
- Through links found in close of auction notices

- Through links from the auction page
- From the feedback number next to another participant's user name
- Using the auction number on the auction search page

It's easiest to link from the auction pages or from the close-of-auction notice. When you approach feedback pages through these avenues, you'll be reminded of the transaction details. The auction number will also be automatically carried into the feedback form.

Let's take a look at posting feedback at Amazon and eBay. They represent the two dominant feedback systems.

At Amazon you can leave transaction-based feedback with star ratings by selecting "Your Auctions" from the auction site's home page. From there, follow the "Leave Feedback" link associated with each auction.

Keep your close-of-auction email. It contains a link to the feedback for the auction. (You can also link to the feedback from the auction page.) Transaction-based feedback can be left within 30 days after the auction's close.

As a seller, you'll first make the one- to five-star selection to rate the high bidder and then add your comments in the field below. Evaluate the transaction for the acoustic guitar. Eighty character spaces are allocated for your melodious comments. You can also post feedback on other bidders and sellers, but your comments won't be linked to the transaction.

As with Amazon, eBay users can go to the feedback page (as seen in Figure 24.1) from a link in the close-of-auction email. With your user ID, password, and auction number, you'll be posting transaction-based feedback. When an auction number is included on the form, eBay verifies that you are a party to that auction.

Make your selection: positive, negative, or neutral. Then, craft a comment, up to 80 characters describing the merits or deficiencies of the transaction for the tennis ball machine.

TIP

Be Forewarned

Users who post excessive negative ratings can be banned from participation at the auction sites.

REQUESTING FEEDBACK

In my book, it's okay to request feedback. The system has made feedback valuable, and auction participants can only benefit from increased feedback compliance. Keep the requests simple and friendly. Don't overwork the request. I was turned off when a counterpart requested *positive* feedback. Just request feedback. For the system to work as designed, the feedback must be accurate and truthful.

Request feedback at any of several points along the transaction timeline. Just don't ask at every point. Select one or two from these points in the transaction:

With the link from eBay's email, the auction number is added for you.

Leave Feedback about an eBay User

Your registered User ID	**You are responsible for your own words.**
Your password	Your comments will be attributed with your name and the date. eBay cannot take responsibility for the comments you post here, and you should be careful about making comments that could be libelous or slanderous. To be safe, make only factual, emotionless comments. Contact your attorney if you have any doubts. Once left, Feedback **cannot be retracted or edited** by you or by eBay.
User ID of person who you are commenting on	
119566147	
Item number (include if you want to relate the comment to a transaction)	Please try to resolve any disputes with the other party before publically declaring a complaint.

Is your comment positive, negative, or neutral?

○ positive   ○ negative   ○ neutral

Your comment (max. 80 characters)

- In the thank-you note that's included in the shipment
- In an email sent when the package is shipped
- After the winning bidder confirms receipt of the package
- A few days after the bidder should have received the merchandise

Here's an example of a request sent by email:

Hi Judy—I shipped the steam iron today by Priority Mail. According to the Post Office, you should have it on Tuesday or Wednesday. I'd appreciate it if you'd let me know when it gets there. I've added to your feedback. After receipt, please add to mine at [include feedback or auction link].

To include your feedback link, locate your feedback page and copy the URL into the email. Then, Judy (or whoever) can just click on the link in the email, access the feedback page, and add the comments.

RESOURCES

Volume sellers find posting feedback to be a tedious task. RoboFeedback, available at **www.flash.net/~etx/turbo/products.htm**, aids high-volume buyers and sellers by posting feedback for them. Enter or paste a list of registered users. With the press of a button, RoboFeedback enters a single positive feedback to all users on the list. You may be asking, "Why only positives?" Consider it a safety mechanism. Would you want someone to be able to post hundreds of negatives? RoboFeedback processes up to 150 positive feedback postings in a single session.

KEY POINTS

This chapter takes a look at rating systems, the report cards assigned to buyers and sellers. Savvy sellers work to enhance their own ratings and should be wary of transactions with bidders with poor ratings. Take these items into consideration:

- Understand each site's rating system.
- Look beyond the bidder's rating numbers.
- Understand the permanence of ratings.
- Be wary of hidden feedback.
- Weigh neutral feedback.
- Review feedback during auctions.
- Decide when to leave feedback.
- Know when to ask for feedback.

INDEX

ABOUT THE AUTHORS

Luanne O'Loughlin (Fairfax Station, Virginia) and **Mary Millhollon** (Phoenix, Arizona) are authors, editors, consultants, Internet experts, and certified professionals with extensive experience writing about the Internet and other cutting-edge computer technologies. Some of Luanne's publications include *Free $tuff from America Online* and with Mary, *Microsoft Internet Explorer 4 Front Runner.* Mary's other recent titles include *Internet Explorer 5 Step by Step* and *Word 2000 Cheat Sheet.*

Jaclyn Easton (Sherman Oaks, California) is the author of *StrikingItRich.com: Profiles of 23 Incredibly Successful Websites That You've Probably Never Heard Of,* the best-selling entrepreneur book of 1999. She is also a columnist for the *Los Angeles Times* and has won an Emmy award for her on-camera work for CBS News in Los Angeles. She can be reached ateaston@easton.com.